SEARCHING FOR SITALA MATA

Eradicating Smallpox in India

Cornelia E. Davis

ISBN-13: 9780999303405
ISBN-10: 0999303406
Library of Congress Control Number: 2014921500
KonjitPublications Laredo, TX
BISAC: Biography / Memoir

TESTIMONIALS

"The arrival of your book was highly disruptive to my schedule... I would rate it as one of the very best accounts of "life in the field", told with humor, compassion, understanding, frustration, elation, and satisfaction... It is too interesting, too motivating to be consigned to just a few book shelves!"
D.A. Henderson, MD, MPH Director WHO Global Smallpox Program

"This is the remarkable story of a young epidemiologist, African-American and female, overcoming obstacle after obstacle to make important contributions to the eradication of one of humanity's most vicious scourges. As the leader of a team influenced by local cultural prejudices she had to find creative ways to inspire, to motivate, to galvanize and, most of all, to succeed. She did all. *Searching for Sitala Mata* tells an important story with humor, tenderness, and honesty. It is an important book, one that should be on everyone's reading list."
Ronald Waldman MD, Smallpox Eradication Volunteer 1975-1976

"Dr. Connie Davis had amazing experiences traveling to remote parts of India as a doctor trying to eradicate smallpox. She captivated the members of our large book club with tales from her book, *Searching for Sitala Mata, Eradicating Smallpox*

in India. The reader is taken along on the journey with her to places most of us will never experience. It is a great read and we were all inspired by her work and adventures. We hope she keeps sharing her work as a global public health doctor."
Robin Ahmann for The Woman's Book Club, Everett, WA

ACKNOWLEDGMENTS

First and foremost, I would like to thank D. A. Henderson, who took a chance on a junior doctor from California to go out to India and help eradicate a disease that caused untold suffering. He was my North Star; he introduced me to international public health, guided my path to an MPH at Johns Hopkins School of Public Health, and insisted I join the Centers for Disease Control and Prevention's Epidemic Intelligence Service (EIS), which prepared me for my subsequent life tackling infectious diseases overseas.

I owe much to my smallpox field teams in West Bengal and Rajasthan, India. I would particularly like to thank my Rajasthani team—Ramesh Chandra, Mandel Dutta, and Abdul Hakim—who endured long, hot days working with me to investigate rash-and-fever cases scattered throughout the state.

I really wrote this book for my fellow WHO epidemiologists, who worked not only in India but also in Bangladesh and far-flung African countries. We all had similar yet different experiences in the field, so I know that they have the best understanding of my adventures. Thank you for the memories of those long-ago days—David Heymann, Steve Jones, Mary Lou Clements, Stan Foster, Jane Brown, Don Francis, Paul Rotmil, Pierre Claquin, and Helen Tom, to mention just a few.

This Second Edition of the book would not have been published without the strong, capable assistance of my publishing team. Judith Briles in Denver CO produced the Back-Cover copy and provided key publishing tips. Rebecca Finkel designed the superb Front-Cover composition. Ashlee Bratton took the photos for the author biography and my website. Thank you all for your support. And finally, to my daughter, Romene Alaana, who helped me get my author website up and running!

Front Book Cover Photo: Rajasthani amulet portraying Sitala Mata (the smallpox goddess) as one of seven sisters with one brother.

CONTENTS

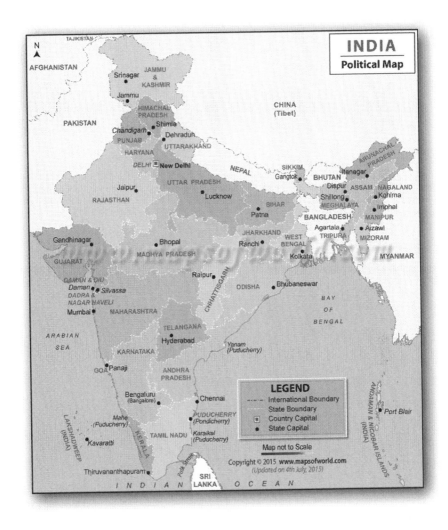

1

A JEEP AT THE FOOT
OF KANCHENJUNGA

I once had a jeep at the foot of Mount Kanchenjunga in Jalpaiguri, West Bengal. I would wake up early during the monsoon season, hoping to catch a shimmering, evanescent glimpse of the snowcapped mountain, which was ordinarily shrouded in cloud cover. On good days, I could detect a fleeting breath of cool air before daybreak signaled the start of another sultry day. I had a Muslim driver and a Hindu paramedic, and we were part of a vast army of foot soldiers tasked with confronting a goddess and eventually eradicating a disease.

But I'm getting ahead of my story.

I remember distinctly when I got the call. It was 3:12 p.m. in the pediatric outpatient department (OPD) of the Los Angeles County–USC Medical Center in East Los Angeles. It was an unnaturally slow day. All that meant was that I was not resuscitating a child or slipping in an IV (intravenous catheter) to rehydrate an infant with moderate diarrhea. I had just sat down to write a note on a chart. The phone rang—never a good sign—and I picked it up on the third ring. "Dr. Davis, OPD."

"Connie, they said I could find you here!"

I was surprised when I recognized the voice of Dr. Paul Wherle, the chief of pediatrics.

"Connie, just got a call from D. A. Henderson from WHO in Geneva."

My heart stopped. *Oh my God,* I thought. *He's talking about the Dr. D. A. Henderson from the World Health Organization.*

"He wanted to know if you are interested in working on smallpox eradication in India. Seems they need some young, energetic doctors to place in difficult, isolated areas, but he says the team is concerned about sending a woman alone to those rural areas. It's tough, and there's nothing there—no services, no hotels, no running water, no electricity."

I was momentarily silent. "And what did you tell him?"

"I told him no problem!"

I was frantic; my mind was racing. I think my brain stopped inputting correctly when Wherle said, "WHO in Geneva." I was finding it hard to form coherent thoughts.

"So, Dr. Wherle, I'm not worried about the no hotel bit." As a former Girl Scout with the highest honor, the Curved Bar, pinned to my sash, I had spent my summer vacations from university as a Girl Scout camp counselor leading backpacking trips in the Colorado Mountains. Roughing it on the trail was a no-brainer for me. "But I don't know anything about smallpox," I added.

He replied, "Oh, don't worry; WHO will orient you. Henderson said you need to be in Delhi by June sixth. They will contact you. You know, Connie, you really are lucky. What a great opportunity!"

Then the line went silent, and I hung up the phone before I realized that I had a stranglehold on the edge of the desk. *Thank God I'm not on call tonight—I need to look up everything I can find about smallpox.*

I was in my last year of pediatric residency and looking for that perfect first job. Before settling down in a position in a hospital or private practice, I wanted to work just for one year overseas, doing humanitarian work as a way to pay back all the opportunities I had been given. During my sophomore year in college, I had studied in Florence, Italy, where I learned Italian and was enticed by European culture. That experience led me to do a three-month medical school summer research project in Kuala Lumpur, Malaysia. I traveled solo from Kuala Lumpur to sightsee in Bangkok and Chiang Mai in Thailand before going back home to continue my medical studies. Solo travel in Asia for a woman in 1970 was not for the fainthearted. But I had been stung by the travel bug, and I was terminally infected. I asked Dr. Wherle to write some references for me. I sent applications to the Peace Corps and the USS *Hope*, the hospital ship, but I don't think I sent anything to WHO. I thought WHO was for experienced physicians. I didn't quite fall into that category.

In 1975, I couldn't just "Google it." This was decades before the cell phone, before the Internet, before the laptop. So I needed to delve deeply into a stack of textbooks on infectious diseases to find out why my training in pediatrics made me a perfect fit for the WHO smallpox eradication program.

My mind kept whirling back to the exciting (and frightening) thought of India. This fluke opportunity was going to take me out of my comfort zone. Who would have imagined that a black child born in Chicago and transplanted to Northern California before completing her first decade would become a doctor and head for India?

2

IT'S 3:00 A.M.; WELCOME TO DELHI!

I had been flying for over twenty-eight hours. Good-byes were hasty as I headed out from San Francisco for India via Hong Kong. My parents left the same day on a short trip to Britain for Dad's orthopedic surgery residency class reunion. Mom was more worried about me than I'd anticipated. Television news coverage coming out of India reported that Indira Gandhi was calling a state of emergency and assuming increased powers.

"Mom," I told her, "I'm sure if there were any danger, WHO would call me and tell me not to come." I had been working feverishly to close out my residency duties and get to Delhi to join the next orientation and training for the junior doctors scheduled to work on smallpox. I departed under strict orders from my parents to send a telex to their hotel in Britain as soon as I arrived.

In fact, the Indian Emergency lasted twenty-one months, from June 1975 to March 1977. Prime Minister Indira Gandhi declared a state of emergency under Article 352 of the constitution of India, effectively bestowing upon herself the power to rule by decree and to suspend elections and civil liberties. It would become one of the most controversial times in the history of independent India.

My theory on long-haul flights was that the only way to get through them is to fall asleep. I was in steerage and in a window seat. By leaning my pillow against the window, I could doze off and not be disturbed by fellow passengers. I always claimed that I never dream. The truth was that I normally could never recall any of my dreams. However, on that flight to India, I dreamed of Florence, Italy, and my great college adventures there. I awoke wondering if India would be the same.

My year in Florence was pivotal in my life. I still think of my life in terms of "life before Florence" and "life after Florence." I was a premed student at Gonzaga University (GU) in Spokane, Washington, and I knew exactly what the next four years would entail. Premed curriculum in any university meant science and biology courses and afternoon laboratory work. Everyone knew it was basically a grind. If students wanted to acquire a foreign language and discover another culture overseas, then they had to work at escaping.

Gonzaga University had started a yearlong program in Florence, Italy, in 1963. That put Colbert, my older brother, in the inaugural class as a sophomore. His tantalizing but markedly meager set of letters home spoke of hitchhiking through Europe, quaint trattorias in the Florentine countryside, palazzos full of Renaissance art, and wine. I would have wanted to go to Florence whether or not Colbert had participated, but my desire was intensified by our sibling rivalry. He went to Florence, so I was going to Florence. Truth be told, it was as economical to send me to Florence in those days as to pay for my tuition and dorm in Spokane. Thankfully, my parents felt that travel was educational.

My brother was barely back from Florence in time to join the family to drive me to New York to connect with the other eighty-eight members of the Gonzaga-in-Florence Class of 1964–65. We were booked on the MS *Aurelia*. The Italian student ship would take us to Bremerhaven, Germany, for the start of a two-week orientation tour of Germany, Austria, and Italy before our arrival in Florence. Colbert had come in handy in helping to persuade my parents to write an approval letter for me to hitchhike in Europe. The school demanded this letter, as it would effectively let them off the hook if something unforeseen happened.

"This is an acceptable way for students to travel, Mom, like taking the train," said Col. And in the 1960s, it really was safe, dependable, and economical. It also offered me a chance to meet interesting people who just might invite me to stay in their homes.

Who takes a ship nowadays to Europe? Who has ten days to cross the Atlantic? But what a voyage that was. Half the passengers were European students returning home from their American adventures, and the rest were Americans heading for European schools. The MS *Aurelia* had only one class: student. I am forever grateful that Gonzaga bequeathed us this slow, luxurious entry into European life and culture. This was no eight-hour flight from New York to Rome with an unceremonious deposit in some nondescript airport terminal with immigration and customs agents suddenly speaking Italian. As we sailed out of New York harbor, I silently said good-bye to the Statue of Liberty. It would be more than 365 days before I returned on this exact same vessel to New York. I didn't realize it then, but the next time I saw the great lady of the harbor, I would be irrevocably changed.

I woke up from my dreams of Florence both tired and restless. Pan Am Airways was on time; it was just a long way to India. We arrived at 3:00 a.m., and when I stepped off the plane, I was shocked by the tidal wave of heat that immediately hit me. My throat ached from inhaling the scalding air. I thought, *if it's this hot at three in the morning, what is it like at nine?*

In 1975, Indian customs went through all bags of arriving passengers. They acted as if I were an Indian national pretending not to know the local language. I had an Olympus OM2 camera that they tried to charge me duty for. Even when they finally let me go, they were still not totally convinced I was American. There was supposed to be a car from WHO waiting to whisk me to Claridges Hotel. As I was spit out of customs into the arrivals hall, I was assaulted by total chaos. How was I to find the WHO car and driver? Lots of people certainly wanted to "help" me. So I just stood my ground and shouted "WHO!" until the WHO chauffeur jumped out of the background. All I could think was how much I wanted a room and a bed. It was a clever plan to arrive on Saturday so I could recuperate from the journey all weekend before showing up for training on Monday.

Frankly, I don't remember much of the first drive into New Delhi. I'm sure there were beggars in the street and holy cows obstructing the right of way, but it was all a blur. I do remember Claridges Hotel, which seemed like a moment out of time—colonial time. I didn't have a suite—I was paying for the room—but still, the accommodation was *grand*. It just radiated charm and placed me back in a time perfectly elucidated in Paul Scott's *The Raj Quartet* novels, about the final days of the British Raj in India during World War II. Claridges just seemed to embody graceful architecture, elegant decor, and a seamless blend of old-world charm and contemporary facilities. I remembered to send the telex to my parents from the front desk, and then I was out cold.

Clearly, I was not in California. And in the ensuing days, India would prove to be totally different from what I had experienced in Florence.

3

NINE MEN AND ONE WOMAN

I woke up to light streaming in the window. I didn't know if it was morning or afternoon. I did feel so much better than when I arrived, but I was still drowsy. *Where am I?* I thought. *Right, I'm in Delhi.* I groped for the phone and pushed the button for the front desk.

"Can you tell me what time it is?"

"Eight o'clock in the morning," said the receptionist.

"Which morning?"

"It's Sunday, Dr. Davis," he replied.

Oh my God, how could I have slept this long? I got to the hotel on Saturday around six in the morning. I've lost a whole day. Still, I had a whole day to explore Delhi. I jumped into the shower, threw on a cotton pantsuit with long sleeves, and slipped into my Birkenstock sandals. I glanced into the mirror. *I guess I look decent.*

The breakfast lounge had a very English atmosphere, with big chairs, white linens on the tables, and waiters in white wearing cummerbunds and turbans.

"Memsahib, may I bring you some tea?" said the waiter.

"Actually, I'm a coffee drinker," I said. "And I would like a full English breakfast—I'm starving!"

He served me a beautifully cubed mango as a starter. Forty minutes later, I had finished a substantial breakfast and was ready to explore. I stopped to consult with the concierge.

"I just want to explore, like maybe go to a typical Indian market and take in the sights," I said.

"Madam, if you are new to Delhi, I think it would be best if you took a hotel taxi so the driver can help you," the concierge advised.

As I discovered, it was sage advice. When the doorman opened the hotel doors for me to walk down to the car, I was hit by blindingly bright light and searing heat and humidity! On the way to the market, the taxi was surrounded by a symphony of blaring horns, and vehicles were playing a sort of chicken game to decide who was going to be the first to take off after the stoplight turned green. The market was jammed, swarming with people and vehicles and animals. People crowded into what I, as an American, considered my personal space, until walking felt more like pushing through an obstacle course. In the midst of overwhelming heat, surging crowds, and exploding noise, I was accosted by the odors of Indian spices—cinnamon, chilies, and cardamom—that were emanating from a side alleyway leading to the fruit and vegetable section. My eyes started to tear up. I decided to stay on the main street, which had an assortment of fabric shops, boutiques with ready-made clothes, and jewelry stores with gold and silver bangles.

Even there it was unbelievably noisy! The touts, the young men hawking merchandise, were trying to entice me to enter their stores by yelling at me at every step. Their eagerness had the exact opposite effect on me; I couldn't wait to get away from them. And in the small patches of open space between buildings, there was garbage piled high. My sandal slid on some loose gravel, and I noted how important it was to look down at the ground. Not only was the sidewalk uneven, it was studded with surprises such as cow patties and dog shit. The taxi-*wallah* ("*wallah*" is an Indian word indicating a person in a particular occupation) was two steps behind me and acted as my chaperone, making sure no one got too close. I could only stand this massive assault on all the senses—on top of my healthy case of jet lag—for a short time before asking to return to the hotel.

What a relief it was to enter the cool, quiet shelter of Claridges. My encounter with the "real Delhi" that I was so anxious to explore lasted for only two hours. Exhausted, I headed to my room to take a nap. I set the alarm for dinner.

Early Monday morning I was scheduled to present myself to the South-East Asia Regional Office (WHO/SEARO) in Delhi. The group, as it turned out, included nine men, all European except for the one American male, and me, the only woman. We were all physicians; some had worked a few years, and the rest of us were straight out of residency. None of us had previous experience with smallpox. Following our one-week technical orientation in Delhi, the higher-ups would determine where to assign us, although it was already clear that most of us would go to Bangladesh. The smallpox (SPX) staff indicated that they were down to the last cases of SPX in India. I was appalled. I remember thinking, *I've come all this way, and now I learn that there's no more smallpox in India?* The focus was moving to the next endemic country, Bangladesh.

Our seminar started with the basics. The first in our series of lecturers was Dr. Basu, an epidemiologist who worked in the Delhi office. He started with the information I'd brushed up on before I started the journey. Smallpox was a viral disease; the human species was the only natural host. For the virus to live, it must pass from person to person in a continuing chain of infection. Smallpox was spread by the inhalation of air droplets, or aerosols. Some twelve to fourteen days after infection, the new patient typically developed a fever and severe aches and eventually collapsed outright with extreme exhaustion. Some two to three days later, a papular rash (small, raised, swollen bumps) developed on the face and spread to the extremities. Next the slide presentation moved from just text to graphic photos. Our group was pretty quiet. As doctors we had seen some gruesome sights during our medical training. However, the photos of people lying on the ground outside their huts with faces racked by misery were images that would stay with us.

The photos showed how the rash went through a series of phases and became vesicular (containing liquid inside each lesion, somewhat like a blister). Lesions on each area of the body were at the same stage of development and deeply embedded in the skin. Dr. Basu made a point of stressing that all the lesions were at the same stage of development. This turned out to be an important clue in the diagnosis of smallpox. The rash was denser on the face and extremities. Later, the lesions turned pustular (sticky, gooey, and with pus inside). The patients remained feverish throughout the evolution of the rash. They were also in considerable pain as the pustules grew and expanded.

Some of these pustules burst, and others merged and consolidated. The skin became a mass of open sores and scabs trying to form.

I wondered how it was possible to keep the lesions clean. Eventually these pustules formed scabs, which would then separate from the skin, leaving deep-pitted scars. Dr. Basu's photos were worth more than a thousand words. Certainly girls who were pretty before they contracted the disease wouldn't be attractive after it ended. The deep-pitted scars forever marked patients as smallpox survivors. Those scars also attested to the fact that they were forever immune to the disease. They could never get it again. This whole process of the illness lasted around twenty-one days. Death usually occurred during the second week for roughly one-third of patients who contracted the malady. The death rate was higher in children under five and higher yet for infants less than one year old.

I wasn't the only member of the group with little appetite during the short tea break after Dr. Basu's lecture. I was pleased to have a few minutes to start learning more about my fellow students. I hoped some of them could give me a lead on less expensive housing. Claridges was expensive, and I needed to make my per diem go as far as possible. After barely enough time to get tea and some snacks, we headed back to the lecture room.

The next speaker began by saying that the disease most commonly confused with smallpox was chickenpox. Well, I certainly knew about chickenpox. At least, I thought I knew what chickenpox looked like. I learned that day that during the first two to three days of rash, it could be difficult, and at times almost impossible, to distinguish between the two diseases.

Thankfully, there were some important clues to distinguish between them:

- All smallpox lesions develop at the same pace and appear identical, regardless of which part of the body they are on.
- In chickenpox, the lesions are superficial and develop in "crops." Examining any one part of the body, for example the trunk, you can simultaneously see papules, vesicles, pustules, and scabs.
- The rash in chickenpox is dense over the trunk of the body; the rash in smallpox is denser on the face, the arms, and the legs.
- A defining characteristic of smallpox is the rash on the palms of the hands and the soles of the feet.

Chickenpox almost never causes a rash on the hands and feet. In fact, few other diseases cause a rash in these areas, with the exception of tertiary syphilis. I had certainly not seen adult advanced syphilis in pediatrics. The instructor continued with a series of photos and then tested our growing knowledge by juxtaposing pictures of chickenpox and smallpox side by side.

By 4:00 p.m., I was more than ready to head back to the hotel. I needed to arrange to move the following day to join some of my colleagues at a four-star hotel. By moving to the hotel with the other doctors I would have instant company. I would no longer be a solo woman traveler constricted to stay in the hotel at night due to safety concerns. Together with my fellow doctors, we would be able to try the great little Indian restaurants in the neighborhood.

4

THE ORIENTATION CONTINUES

The next day our group was back to hear the continuing saga of the clinical aspects of smallpox. Dr. Basu then discussed a rapidly progressive, malignant form of the disease that affected some 5 to 10 percent of smallpox cases and that was almost always fatal within five to seven days. In hemorrhagic smallpox, patients would bleed into the skin and intestinal tract. He told us that the skin of a hemorrhagic smallpox patient looked like the skin of a person who suffered from third-degree burns. There was bleeding from the mouth, nose, intestinal tract, and urinary tract. It was invariably fatal.

Of course, the presenters showed us photos of this form of the disease. We had questions about the transmission of the virus and how contagious it was. Smallpox spread most readily during the cool, dry winter months in India, but it could be transmitted at any time, in any climate, and in any part of the world. It was frightening but true that the patient could be infectious in the nebulous stage two to four days before the fever started. In that stage, there were sores in the mouth, but the papular rash hadn't yet begun to appear. Unfortunately, before anyone noticed the rash, the person could have already infected others. This facet of the disease showed the importance of surveillance and the need to immediately start containment activities. We hadn't yet learned what containment entailed.

The mortality rate of the two predominant variants of smallpox, *Variola major* and *Variola minor*, differed greatly. *Variola major* had a death rate of 30 percent, whereas the less dangerous form caused death in about 1 percent of cases. At the time of my arrival in India, *Variola major* was the predominant endemic strain throughout the world, including in India. If a patient recovered from the disease, blindness was a common complication, and disfiguring scars on the face were nearly universal. In fact, the facial scars clearly marked those who were immune because they'd had the disease; we could tell instantly that they didn't need vaccination. In June of 1975, the last endemic countries remaining in the world were India, Bangladesh, and Somalia.

Appropriate emphasis was placed by the facilitators on identifying the clinical findings and providing treatment with supportive care. There was no cure. Our group was indoctrinated in program management, in particular the aspects of the national plan that the global program felt was impeding control in India.

Next we heard from another epidemiologist. This one gave us the history of the smallpox eradication effort, which started in earnest in 1967 when the World Health Assembly set a goal of ten years for the elimination of the disease.

The eradication of smallpox was vital. In the previous century, smallpox was believed to have killed at least half a billion people. All the wars on the earth during that same century killed perhaps 150 million people. For those with the disease, the pain of the smallpox pustular rash was almost unbearable. Patients imparted a sickly sweet stench. If one person in a family was infected, the whole family usually became ill, leaving no one to care for the sick. The simplest tasks, such as cooking, hauling water from the well, and gathering vegetables from the fields, became major challenges.

There were varying opinions in the scientific community on the feasibility of eradicating smallpox. The scientific community was not always of one mind, which sometimes created conflict. Opposing sides would cite their expert's opinion. The definitive story of this effort is found in *Smallpox: The Death of a Disease,* written by D. A. Henderson, MD, chief of the WHO Global Smallpox Eradication Programme. He provides the inside story on how smallpox was eradicated step by step, country by country, citing those who helped and those who hindered the process.

We learned the key elements that were crucial for eradication. Vaccines, preferably cheap, stable, and effective, needed to be available. At the time of our orientation, a potent, freeze-dried, stable vaccine was available. Once the vial was opened and reconstituted, the smallpox worker had thirty days to use the vaccine, and it did not need to be refrigerated. This was a major plus!

Another major advance was the invention of the bifurcated needle, which was a piece of sharpened steel wire about three inches long that had a double point on one end resembling a tiny olive fork; it held one small droplet of the vaccine between its points. The worker dipped the needle in the vaccine and lightly jabbed it into the skin of the upper arm, making ten to fifteen light punctures. The bifurcated needle was a vast improvement over the previous rotary blade. At the end of a day of vaccination, the bifurcated needles were placed in a plastic screw-top container with twenty small holes in the cap. The smallpox worker dunked the entire container into boiling water for fifteen to twenty minutes to sterilize the needles and get them ready for the next day of vaccination.

Another crucial program advance was to wean governments away from mindless mass vaccination. Instead of trying to vaccinate every person in a country or region, we would be using a powerful new approach, ring vaccination, which was born out of necessity from smallpox fieldwork conducted in Africa by program managers with limited access to vaccines. The key term we were given was "containment." We were taught to identify an outbreak and then to vaccinate every person within that community or ring of houses. Our instructions were specific: vaccinate everyone within a one-kilometer radius of the case and search for additional rash-and-fever cases within ten kilometers. This method surrounded each outbreak of smallpox with a wall of humans who were immune to the virus. The virus would burn itself out inside the ring vaccination and vanish. I thought back to the opening lecture of orientation: *For the virus to live, it must pass from person to person in a continuing chain of infection.* Success in eradicating smallpox would depend on a relentless, meticulous search for new cases.

And lastly, a global organizational structure was needed that could work with and in parallel with the national health bureaucracy. The country's commitment was crucial. And commitment was necessary at every level, from every state, divisional, and district officer. This was the task of the national smallpox program, yet there were states and districts that frankly could not be relied on to do the job. Glowing reports were received at the state and federal levels, but the work was not always done. By 1975 the national program knew which states and districts were weak and needed additional assistance. This made the foreign epidemiologists extremely valuable.

Politically, the Indian prime minister had declared a state of emergency and had suspended elections and civil liberties. Opposition politicians in certain states were being thrown into prison. Officials were afraid, and few dared to take any initiative or appear to not follow government rules exactly. There was a fixed rigidity in the way the Indian government bureaucracy sanctioned expenditures. There could be no deviation from the rules, even when faced with an epidemic. For example, many central and state government officers were not eligible for air travel. District staff could not get travel advances for visiting or staying in a problem area. The per diem allowance to put public health staff in difficult areas was grossly inadequate. As I would find on arrival to my area, health staff had not been paid for three to six months. It was hard to ask staff to work when they hadn't been paid.

The idea behind the use of foreign field epidemiologists was to make them mobile, place them in a team with a driver and paramedical assistant, and provide them with authorized funding. A field epidemiologist could act as a sort of catalytic agent by providing the right inputs (resources to pay for temporary staff and supplies) at the right time and in the required area. A foreign epidemiologist in a select district could ensure that the work was done. Each WHO epidemiologist was to report what was encountered in the area. If the work was not done, the WHO field epidemiologist would report it and then effect change to get it done. Because of the state of emergency, no state or district staff wanted to be reported for noncompliance. Another advantage was that it was difficult to corrupt the foreign field epidemiologists with bribes.

Henderson's task on the global stage was to find bright, enthusiastic, self-motivated junior doctors and give them enough authority to carry out continuous surveillance. Once orientation was completed, our group would be scattered to the four winds. Remember, there were no laptops, no mobile phones, and, in most rural places, no direct means of communication with the WHO office in the state. The field epidemiologist kept in contact with the local smallpox authorities by actually driving to the offices of the involved officials. Once we were sent out into the field, we were basically on our own.

5

PLEASE DON'T SEND ME
TO CALCUTTA!

With so many orientation sessions and training exercises, we were sprinting toward Friday's finish line and closing remarks. On Wednesday we were to meet individually with Dr. Nicole Grasset to discuss postings. Dr. Grasset was a Swiss-French medical virologist and epidemiologist and the senior smallpox advisor in the regional office in Delhi. Dr. Grasset was charged with the collection and collation of all information about smallpox from the Indian states, and she was known for both her determined leadership and her feisty personality. She was the only woman aside from nursing staff in the health unit in the entire regional office.

A rumor was swiftly spreading through our little group that smallpox case reporting was down to one-digit numbers, and the national smallpox team felt very confident that they were near the end of new smallpox cases in India. This meant that instead of staying in India, our group would all be sent to Bangladesh, which was the next endemic country. However, I wondered if they would send a woman to a conservative Muslim country. I needed to think really carefully. What should I ask for? My initial thought was that if I stayed in India, I would probably never see any smallpox cases! What a bummer. I didn't know how to approach Dr. Grasset.

In the end, I thought the best approach was probably the direct approach. I'd let Dr. Grasset open the discussion, and then I would take it from there. I thought, *I can probably appeal to her as a woman.*

When I went into her office for the meeting, her first words were, "Glad to see another woman. WHO needs more women in the program." Then she added, "You are presenting us with quite a quandary. There is a difference of opinion about where to send you. What do you want to do?"

It was perfect; the ball was thrown back into my court. I replied candidly, "I have been studying up on India, and I'm looking forward to working in any of the Indian states. Still, if I stay in India, I will probably never see a smallpox case, because it seems the national program is down to the end. I didn't come all this way not to see smallpox."

Thinking quickly, I added, "I mean, I'll do a million searches and investigate outbreaks, but they will probably all be chickenpox. So, you know, as far as I'm concerned, let me go to Bangladesh."

Nicole reminded me that Bangladesh is a Muslim country, and it would be even more difficult for a woman to work independently in a Muslim country than in India. The Bangladeshi program had lobbied for an increase in the number of epidemiologists. She confirmed that all the male junior doctors were definitely going to be sent to Bangladesh.

Dr. Grasset said, "Bangladesh has a lot of rivers and isolated communities along these rivers. The Bangladeshi program is planning to place the new epidemiologists on riverboats. Each boat will have a captain with a crew of three to five men. Basically, the smallpox program will hire these boats, and the captain will be taking directives from the epidemiologist. The epidemiologists will operate directly out of the boat. They'll live on the boat, cook on the boat, sleep on the boat, jump in the river to take a bath, and basically pee and shit off the boat. So, it is next to impossible to place a woman on the boat." Then she appealed to my sense of propriety. "How could you survive living on a riverboat?"

I reluctantly agreed that it might be difficult for a woman, especially one like me who didn't like water over six feet deep. "I understand the problem," I said, pleading, "but isn't there any other place in Bangladesh you could send me?"

"Connie, it's a nonstarter to even try and get the Bangladeshi program to accept you."

OK, Davis, I thought, *best to go to Plan B.* "OK, Nicole, I'll stay in India, but please don't send me to Calcutta. I came all this way to see rural India. In the big city I would have more conveniences, but I really wouldn't have a sense of how the majority of people actually live in India. So please, I'm not saying where, but at least send me to a rural area."

Dr. Grasset said she heard me and promised to see what she could work out. Then she made me another promise to seal the deal. "If at the end of your six-month tour you still haven't come across smallpox, I'll facilitate your travel to Bangladesh to at least see a few smallpox cases before you leave to go home."

That helped. It was a reasonable compromise. Still, I wondered where they would send me.

When I left Dr. Grasset's office, the rest of my group was clustered outside, waiting to hear where each person would be sent. My male colleagues were distraught when I reported that I would be left behind in India.

"Yes, but what to do?" I said dejectedly.

"How about we go get a drink?" said Paul.

That evening in my hotel room, I pulled out my map of India and pondered my situation. The southern states in India, such as Tamil Nadu and Kerala, were considered to have "good" smallpox programs and had, early on, reduced smallpox cases down to zero. By May 1975, the remaining major endemic states were Bihar, Uttar Pradesh, West Bengal, and Madhya Pradesh. In the west, Rajasthan and Gujarat had had many outbreaks in 1974, but they seemed to be getting things under control now. I surmised that if Bangladesh was the next endemic country to tackle, then clearly the border area between West Bengal and Bangladesh would be essential to hold the line and prevent cases from coming back into India. *Yes, I will be sent to West Bengal and most likely to Calcutta! Shit, I'm going to Calcutta.*

6

UNDER NO CIRCUMSTANCES ARE YOU TO GO TO SIKKIM

Friday finally arrived. It was the big day when all would be revealed, and I would know where fate had cast me for the next six months. Dr. Grasset returned to break the news individually to each of us.

As soon as I entered the office, she said, "You are going to Darjeeling!"

"What? I'm going to the mountains?"

"Yes, and it took some doing. You are assigned to three districts: Darjeeling, Jalpaiguri, and Cooch Behar. They are in the northern part of West Bengal, and Cooch Behar is probably the most worrisome. They have had importations of smallpox cases from Bangladesh in the recent past. As far as the Indian government is concerned, this area is extremely sensitive because it borders three countries: Nepal to the west, Sikkim to the north, and Bhutan to the east."

Normally, tourists were only given a one-week inner line permit to visit Darjeeling, and in 1975, foreigners also needed a protected area permit.

"They didn't want to give you a six-month visa, as you will be traveling around and going where you please," she said. "To them, you are an American, probably a CIA spy, and it doesn't help that with your long hair and complexion you look Indian and can blend right in. So here are the rules of engagement."

Dr. Grasset proceeded with the list of edicts. "When you finally arrive in Jalpaiguri, you need to check in at the police station and register. Every time you leave one district and enter another one, you *must* report to the police station. It doesn't matter what time it is, day or night. The national government is sending out a circular on you to inform the three districts." She then lowered her voice and used a more secretive tone. "In addition, Connie, I want to share with you some sensitive information from WHO. We have been trying for some time now to persuade the federal government to allow a thorough search for smallpox in Sikkim."

I was unaware that India had just seized the independent Buddhist country and added it as an Indian state in May 1975. The area was still recoiling from this incident. Nicole stressed, "We don't want anything to jeopardize WHO getting epidemiologists into the city-state to do this search. Under no circumstances are you to go to Sikkim! Your group will get instructions about what supplies to take to the field. Good luck!"

I practically skipped out of the office. Now the shoe was on the other foot. The other doctors were dying with jealousy that I was going to Darjeeling, even though I would more likely spend my time in Cooch Behar and the lowlands than in Darjeeling.

One thing was the same for us all. Whether the doctors were staying in India or going to Bangladesh, Delhi was our last, best hope for stocking up on essential items. We were told to expect that we would not be able to get anything outside the capital. I knew I needed additional clothes, and I needed to get them in Delhi.

The male epidemiologist in the regional office hadn't a clue as to what women should wear in the field. He had all sorts of advice for the men. For me he suggested, "Maybe a sari?"

Are you kidding? I thought. *Fat chance.* I was to have ten- to twelve-hour workdays, and he thought I could do it in a sari? It takes a good deal of finesse to just wear a sari, much less to walk in one without looking like a giraffe.

For the men he advised, "Pick up cotton *kurta pajamas.*" These involved a kurta, a tunic that reached the middle of the calf, and baggy, pajama-like pants.

That reminded me that I'd seen Muslim women wearing a kind of twin to the male kurta pajama. The *shalwar kameez* is a long tunic that hits at the hip or calf, worn with baggy pants that close at the waist with a drawstring. Completing the outfit is the *dupatta*, a scarf that can be worn over the head as a sign of modesty or draped around the neck. I wondered if everyone would think I was Muslim if I wore the shalwar kameez. I wasn't keen about that idea.

The best plan to find ready-made pajama sets was to head for the big market area called Connaught Circus and go to the state-run emporiums, where the best *khadi* clothes were available. *Khadi* is hand-spun and handwoven cloth from India, primarily made out of hemp. The raw materials also sometimes include silk or wool, both of which are spun into yarn on a spinning wheel called a *charkha*. This fabric is versatile—cool in summer and warm in winter. In order to improve the look, it is often starched to give it a stiffer feel and smoother finish.

Next, I needed to stock up on my checklist of medical supplies. Drugs in the rural areas were next to impossible to find and were often counterfeit. We were given the name of the only reliable pharmacy in Connaught Circus where we could procure genuine drugs for diarrhea control as well as antibacterials, chloroquine for malaria, and iodine tablets to purify water. Finding clean water, potable water, plain old drinking water, would be the bane of our existence. In 1975 there was no such thing as bottled water in India. We relied on our four-star hotel to boil water for fifteen to twenty minutes and place it in a thermos in our room. Soft drinks such as Coca-Cola were not available outside the capital and were three times as expensive as beer, and served warm to boot! Fresh-squeezed juices were available; however, we could not certify that the juices were hygienically squeezed, or if the ice that was plunked down in the glass was made with boiled water. We were strongly encouraged to drink tea.

Today, the health benefits of tea are extolled to the heavens. The laundry list of benefits is as long as my arm. But back then, the two reasons given to me to drink tea were that drinking hot tea was *hydrating* and *cooling* to the body. Talk about a hard sell. I wasn't convinced. When I got in from walking in New Delhi's searing summer days of 105 degrees Fahrenheit and above, I was perspiring profusely, and my clothes were sticking to me from the humidity. My first thought was of a cool drink—better yet, a cold drink. But the reality was that it was impossible to find a cold drink outside of a luxury hotel. The only thing readily available was hot tea. British black tea. I didn't see any green tea outside of Chinese restaurants. I eventually learned through trial and error that hot tea is indeed cooling and hydrating. And I would discover that up-country in the rural area, the chai-wallahs (teashop owners) would always have a pot of boiling water on the wood or charcoal stove.

Next on the list was toilet paper. I was told to pretty well count on TP not being available in any lodging. It would be difficult to find it in a rural marketplace, even with money to burn. What they didn't tell me was how to calculate the amount of TP to haul up-country. This question was not something the concierge in a Delhi hotel was normally asked. Of course, knowing that I'd have at least one episode of diarrhea, I wondered how to factor that into the equation. I don't remember how many rolls I tossed in my duffel bag. To save space, I first took out the cardboard center and then flattened the roll. I hated the cheap TP, the kind that disintegrates on the first hint of liquid. I would hand roll about ten sheets to put in my pants pocket. And I had another custom-rolled lot to throw in my shoulder bag. A Girl Scout was always prepared.

Then I realized that I would be six months in West Bengal, and even rarer than TP were tampons. This was something my male colleagues did not have to worry about. At least I'd thought about this dilemma back in the States and came prepared. Davis was not going to roll up rags or dried leaves and stuff it...where? No thank you.

I preferred to shop by myself, so I took off alone for Connaught Place (another term for Connaught Circus). Even today Connaught Place (CP) is instantly recognizable on a map of Delhi. It's the two big concentric circles with seven radial spokes (roads) shooting out from the middle. It is still a thriving commercial and business center for Delhi. In colonial times it was the headquarters for the British Raj. It was the showcase of Edwin Lutyens, the leading British architect from the mid-1800s who was responsible for the architectural design of Delhi when India was still part of the British Empire. All the state emporiums for handicrafts had their shops somewhere in CP.

I hired a taxi from the hotel so I could leave anything I bought in the boot (trunk) of the car and have some assurance that both taxi and the items would still be there when I finished shopping. In the end, I invested in several shalwar kameez sets and about four kurtas that could go over the cotton American trousers I had brought from the States. Once I got the British terminology down, things went faster. I was looking for a flashlight, and finally my taxi-wallah told me I needed to ask for a torch. Some nice soul told me about the secondhand bookstores close by, so I bought twenty paperbacks. They would last two weeks.

And because it was doubtful that there'd be a continuous source of electricity where I was heading, I bought a cute little red Chinese kerosene lantern about ten inches tall. It proved to be a crucial element in my kit. When the sun vanished at exactly 6:00 p.m. in the rural areas, it was pitch black. Batteries were too costly to waste reading by flashlight. So it was my Chinese lantern, stationed by my mattress, and the secondhand books that kept me sane while I was in the field. There were no iPods or iPads or the power to recharge them. In the rural areas, there were no bars, nightclubs, or any other sort of entertainment. Don't cry for me; after ten- to twelve-hour days, I was exhausted. Usually, I could only read a couple of pages before I was out like a light.

7

HEADING TO UTTAR PRADESH FOR FIELD ORIENTATION

The national smallpox program thought it best for me to gain something more than theoretical knowledge. The national smallpox program decided to send me to the Indian states of Uttar Pradesh (UP) and Bihar. The smallpox programs in these states were, respectively, the best and worst in India. I would spend about three days in each location and would get hands-on experience on how to manage the practical side of smallpox surveillance. I was thrilled. Finally, I would see more than Delhi. Off I flew to Uttar Pradesh.

I headed to UP with all my stuff, as I would not be returning to Delhi. Once I was settled in a small hotel, the smallpox program jeep deposited me at the bustling state office of the smallpox program unit. Dr. Don Francis, the epidemiologist posted in Lucknow, was an American and had been working there for some time. When I arrived, he looked up from his desk and said, "Welcome to Lucknow. We might as well get going. These are the types of documents that the program uses in UP." Then he proceeded to show me the form that the smallpox worker filled out weekly and indicated how the forms were sent up to the district for collation and then sent on to the state. He explained that the process would be more or less the same where I was heading.

He then outlined how he spent his day and explained that my schedule would depend on the work I felt I needed to do. "For starters, there is no such thing as a set day," he said. Sometimes I might need to analyze state or district reports to determine which areas were underreporting. Maybe I would need to make a surprise supervisory visit. At any time, I could get a message about a rash-and-fever case in some far-flung village. Then, a smallpox worker would go out and investigate, or the epidemiologist would jump in his jeep and investigate. There was no rulebook. In the previous year, the state had had numerous outbreaks, but within the last four months, the number of outbreaks had reduced drastically.

"Connie, you will need to investigate each and every rash-and-fever case to determine if it is smallpox. The key is really to supervise, to be in the field, to see what the workers are doing, and not just rely on reports."

This advice would stand the test of time. Not only would it guide me in my smallpox work, but it would form the bedrock for all my future international postings, no matter the country or the disease. We spent that day in the office looking at the state maps and the reports from districts. Don pointed out why certain numbers did not seem right, why certain areas were questionable, and which districts were doing good work. He decided where we would go the next day for a field trip.

I headed back to the hotel to eat and turn in early and get a good night's sleep. Before turning out the light, I picked up my guidebook to India and looked up Uttar Pradesh, which means "northern province." Lucknow is the capital of UP. Rajasthan is to the west, Haryana and Delhi are to the northwest, the country of Nepal is to the north, Bihar is to the east, and Madhya Pradesh is to the southwest. The state covers almost 7 percent of the total area of India, and at the time it was the fifth-largest Indian state by area. It was and still is the most populous state in India. Hindi is the official and most widely spoken language in its seventy-five districts. The state was home to some of the most powerful empires in ancient and medieval India.

Uttar Pradesh was packed with an abundance of historical, natural, and religious tourist destinations, such as the Taj Mahal, Benares (now known as Varanasi), Lucknow, and Allahabad. In the 1970s, Lucknow was the largest and most developed city in northern India after Delhi. The city has always been known as a cultural and artistic capital and the seat of power of the *Nawabs*. *Nawab* was an honorific title bestowed centuries ago by the reigning Mughal emperor to semiautonomous Muslim rulers of princely states in India. The term "Nawab" usually referred to males; the female equivalent was *"begum."* The primary duty of a Nawab was to uphold the sovereignty of the Mughal emperor and administer the concerned province. Lucknow was also known as the "city of splendors," and it had a certain graceful charm.

The smallpox jeep picked me up at 7:00 a.m., and we headed for the office to check in before taking off for the field. Don wanted to show me the rural area and what it was like on the roads—or lack thereof. Just as we started to leave,

Don received a message about a rash-and-fever case. The plan changed. I was excited; we were going to go track down this case.

We headed down the steps to find the vehicle, which was one of those famous Willys jeeps. The Mahindra Willys jeep was made for tackling India's terrain and its *kaacha* (bad) roads. The Willys used in the smallpox program were pretty basic. Don had a driver, and because in India vehicles drive on the left side of the road, British style, Don was sitting up front on the left. I was in the backseat and alone, so I could stretch out my legs.

I marveled as we drove, satisfied that finally I was in rural India: the kaacha roads, the heavily overloaded bullock carts headed for market, the bicycle rickshaws vigorously moving in and out of the congested traffic, and the ubiquitous sacred cow just wandering down the middle of the road. With the pervasive crush of people and animals, this type of congestion was seen only in Indian towns.

"So, Don, who owns these cows?" I asked.

"You never know," he responded. "Better not hit one, or all hell will break loose."

"Do you ever get a hankering for hamburger?"

"Yeah, you get those cravings periodically. But you won't find any hamburger, not even in Delhi."

When we got closer to the concerned district, the driver started asking directions to find the office of the chief medical officer (CMO). There was a certain protocol that we needed to observe. It was important to inform the district authorities of our presence. Also, the CMO would often join epidemiologists in the field, and would take a smallpox worker along to help find the affected village. Now with the jeep crammed with additional staff, we searched for the village with the rash-and-fever case. We eventually found it. It took some time because the road—well, actually the track—that we followed was full of massive ruts. I was convinced that I could walk the distance faster than the jeep, it was that slow.

The case was a five- or six-year-old boy with a rash that seemed denser on the trunk than on the face and extremities. He had dark skin, and the rash was practically invisible in the afternoon light in the hut. We brought him out into the daylight, as it could be difficult to see rashes on dark skin. He clearly didn't have any rash on the palms and soles of his feet. Don was very generous and didn't put me on the spot by asking my diagnosis.

Instead he started to explain what he saw and how he arrived at his conclusion. "So the rash is dense on the trunk, and in any one location there are all types of lesions: papules, vesicles, and some scabs forming. This is chickenpox, but let's check to see if there are other cases in the village and where the child has recently been."

Don talked to the village chief and villagers to find out if there were other rash-and-fever cases. There were no other cases, but the child and the mother had traveled to visit relatives in another village. The smallpox worker took the name of the village so he could investigate it later.

"So, Connie, now that we're really down to what seems like the last cases of smallpox, we epidemiologists need to investigate all these cases. It's very important that we don't miss any rash-and-fever cases. I would think that West Bengal, with its long border with Bangladesh, is really at high risk for smallpox importation. Your work will be cut out for you."

We had started out in the early morning, and it was now approaching 3:30 p.m. We started to retrace our steps and stopped to drop off the smallpox worker and the CMO in their district town. We then continued on to the madness of Lucknow traffic.

We'd been gone all day. I'd eaten nothing since breakfast at 6:00 a.m. We did stop at a chai-wallah and had some tea. Tea in the rural area was very different from the tea in the hotels in Delhi. A pot of water was boiling continuously, and the guy would throw in the tea, pour in some milk, and then throw in a handful of sugar. Depending on the region of India, other spices, such as cinnamon and cardamom, were also tossed in. When the chai looked sufficiently done, he poured it into small tea glasses. Chai was the only drink readily available in the rural areas in northern India. I almost forgot that I was a coffee drinker. As we came into town, Don said that he would drop me off at my hotel; he needed to stop by the office. He invited me to come round and have dinner with him in his house later that evening. He said he would send a rickshaw-wallah for me.

"How will I know which one it is?"

"I'll just tell the guard at the door of your hotel that a rickshaw-wallah is coming at about five thirty this afternoon to pick you up. The hotel will alert you."

As I gingerly extricated my arms and legs from the back-seat of the jeep, I breathed a sigh of relief that I could finally straighten out my cramped body. I felt like a Mack truck had run over me. A layer of dust had accumulated on my hair and clothes. My clothes were quite damp—OK, they were sopping wet from perspiration. All I could think of was how much I wanted a hot shower.

I guess it might sound strange that I wanted a hot shower and not a cool one, but hot water always relaxed me and took away my aches and pains. I didn't have too much time before that rickshaw would be there, but it was heaven to just stand in the shower and let the water flow over me. I did not know it then, but I would not have the luxury of hot showers in West Bengal. That night, though, I was looking forward to dinner, and Don seemed like a nice guy. Plus, dinner would be an opportunity to find out everything I forgot to ask in Delhi.

The front desk sent up a boy to tell me the rickshaw had arrived. The bicycle rickshaw was a common means of transport. A bicycle was welded to an armchair-like buggy with big wheels behind the driver's seat. Typically, the scrawny little guy wearing a *dhoti* (a linear piece of cotton about four feet wide) wrapped around his waist wasn't wearing anything else, not even shoes. There was an accordion-like canvas roof that came up over the rickshaw to protect the passenger from the sun or rain. The rickshaw-wallah who arrived was shorter than I was, and really skinny. I was dismayed when I realized that I must have weighed twice as much as he, and I wasn't fat. It was strange to get into a rickshaw and not really know where I was going. I just had to trust that I was in the right rickshaw and that this guy knew where Don lived.

The afternoon light was starting to recede. The rickshaw was actually going at a nice clip. We rounded a bend by the river, and I saw a temple up ahead. There was a small crowd of women doing *puja* (offering prayers), but I didn't have a clear view of which god they were worshipping. I motioned the rickshaw-wallah to pull closer to the temple. Then, oh my God, I saw a towering marble statue of a man-sized, upright monkey god: Hanuman. His face was remarkably expressive and so much more human than monkey. Years later when I saw *Planet of the Apes*, I thought of this Hanuman, with his kind-hearted gaze looking out and a serene smile on his face. He was dressed like a king, and he was striking. I didn't have my camera with me, and it was getting late, so I couldn't jump out to investigate. But this replica of Hanumanji (the "ji" added to a name is a sign of respect) was so extraordinary that I can still remember it vividly, some thirty-eight years later. Later I learned more about Hanuman and found out that he was one of the most popular in the entire Hindu pantheon. Hanuman was worshiped as a symbol of physical strength, perseverance, and devotion.

In the ancient Indian epic *The Ramayana*, Hanuman's role was as the invaluable sidekick of the hero, Lord Rama. His most famous feat was leading a monkey army to defeat the evil demon-king Ravana, who had abducted the wife of Lord Rama. The tale of Hanuman was instructive, for it taught that each of us has an unlimited power that lies unused within us. We just need to harness it. Hanuman was able to move mountains and fly across the ocean; he outwitted a sea monster and searched the world for a life-restoring herb to save Lord Rama's wounded brother. He perfectly exemplified devotion. His greatness lay in his undying friendship and total loyalty, which made him a beloved figure across India.

As much as I admired Hanuman, I could never get into Hinduism. There were just too many gods, avatars of the gods, and different manifestations of the gods. It was all overwhelming. Still, I had two favorite Hindu deities: one was Hanuman, and the other was Ganesh, the elephant-headed god.

It took about twenty minutes to get to Don's house. He greeted me at the door with a cold, cold beer. "Oh, thank you, thank you," I said. There is nothing like a cold Kingfisher beer at the end of a long, hot day. It hit the spot. It really was nice of Don to prepare dinner, as he also had been out all day tracking down this rash-and-fever case. I don't remember what we ate. It will not go down in the annals of gourmet cooking, but it was nice to relax in a real house with a delightful ambience and feel I could let my hair down. I was so comfortable that I asked all the questions I had failed to ask in Delhi because I thought I might look dumb. And Don seemed delighted to play the perfect host with all the answers.

He had been in UP for going on a year, but I sensed he was tired and looking forward to heading back to the United States. He was going back to the Centers for Disease Control in Atlanta. I didn't admit that I didn't know about the Centers for Disease Control. I hadn't heard of it before then, but I would definitely learn about it in due course.

We talked about other subjects until we realized it was late and time to get moving.

"Oh, Connie," Don said. "I had a message in the office. Change of plans. It said you were to proceed directly to Calcutta, and skip Bihar. Seems they need you right away." I thought, *This is OK by me; the quicker I get to Darjeeling, the better it is for me.*

Don drove me back to the hotel. I was fading fast. The last thing Don said was, "The office is working on your plane ticket. They will get a message to the hotel."

In my room, as I undressed, I thought, *What a fast trip. Just when I meet someone interesting, I have to move on.* As it turned out, that would be one of the many truisms of my smallpox days in India. I worked alone. I was never in any one place long enough to build up friendships with fellow epidemiologists.

Long distances separated us, so contact was difficult. There were national or state meetings where I could finally put a face to a name, but they were rare. I needed to be self-sufficient.

I didn't find out how brilliant some of these guys were until long past the eradication days. And I say "guys" because during the time I worked in the smallpox program in India, I met only one other woman in the field.

I was too tired to think about that then. Just as I drifted off to sleep, I realized I was not sad about missing the state of Bihar, and I was excited about moving on to West Bengal.

8

HOW MANY SUITCASES DO I NEED TO CARRY $5000 U.S. IN RUPEES?

I was finally on my way to Darjeeling via Calcutta, where I would have a short layover in the airport before continuing on to Bagdogra Airport in Siliguri, the city nearest to Darjeeling. I was flying Indian Airlines, the domestic wing of Air India. It wasn't known for its punctuality, although to be fair, it was the monsoon season, and schedules could be disrupted due to heavy rainfall and fog. I would have no orientation in Calcutta because of the airplane schedules. With only one flight per week to Siliguri, the office deemed it best for me to go directly there and overlap with the outgoing epidemiologist, who I suppose really was the best person to orient me anyway.

I had been trying to glean more information about my three districts from whatever sources I could find. I had heard only of Darjeeling. Who hasn't? Darjeeling tea was one of my mom's favorites. The name means Land of the Dorje, or thunderbolt. The hill station was also known as the Queen of the

Hills. During the time of the British Raj, the entire civil government moved up to the hill stations in the summer to escape the intense heat of the lowlands, called the *terai*. The district was bounded on the north by Sikkim, so I wouldn't be going north. To the west was Nepal, and I wouldn't be crossing that border either. To the east was Jalpaiguri district. I had a feeling that Darjeeling would not be the problem; I expected few smallpox cases there. My work would be in the terai.

The pilot announced that we were approaching Calcutta. I wished I knew a few more hard facts about Siliguri, like who was going to meet me at the airport and where I would stay. I assumed I would have a Willy's jeep for work. Once in the airport in Calcutta, I needed to find my connecting gate. The departure board was not enlightening. *Well*, I thought, *I'll just ask one of these friendly male assistants sitting behind the flight counter in the departure lounge.*

"Yes, hello, I am going to Siliguri. How long is the layover here in Calcutta? Is it three hours?" I asked. The male assistant looked up and smiled and did this thing with his head. It looked like a cross between a nod and a shake. Did it mean yes, or did it mean no? Or even maybe? My confusion was made even worse because the wobble was silent. Without speech to provide any sort of clue as to the message the wobble was supposed to convey, I felt bewildered and then frustrated and then just a little irritated. I learned later that this gesture was called the "Indian head wobble."

The wobble is the nonverbal equivalent of the multipurpose and omnipresent Hindi word "*aacha*." *Aacha* can mean anything from "good" to "I understand." When one has been in India for some time, it is possible to ascertain what that head wobble means in each circumstance. Actually, it was surprising how infectious this gesture is; even foreigners start to unconsciously use it. Probably the most common use of the head wobble was to respond in the affirmative. For example, if I asked someone, "Is this train going to my destination?" and they wobbled their head to reply, it meant yes. The head wobble could also be used as a sign that the person understands what is being said. If I told someone, "I'm going to meet you under the clock at five o'clock," and the person wobbled his or her head, it meant yes, OK. But when I saw it for the first time in the departure lounge, I was thinking, *Are you mute? Can't you just say yes or no?* I returned to my seat in the waiting room, hoping I could eventually decipher the garble that was emanating from the overhead speakers.

I started to search for my paperback book when a guy walked up to me.

"Hi, are you Dr. Connie Davis?" he asked.

I wanted to say, "Well, it all depends on why you want to know," but I just said, "Yes!"

"I'm David Heymann, with the smallpox program in Calcutta. I've got some things for you. As you know, the plane only goes up once a week to Siliguri, and the current epidemiologist who is posted in the three districts is leaving in one week. He only has one week to introduce you to district authorities and orient you. Since you are heading straight up to Siliguri and bypassing the office, I came here to bring you some cash."

He was carrying a dark brown, soft leather suitcase about the size of a small messenger bag, about fourteen inches square and eight inches deep. He unlatched the top and then flicked it open and shut rapidly. *Oh my God!* I thought. There were thousands of small bills crammed in the suitcase!

David said, "Let's go to the back of the room, behind those large pillars there. I don't have much time, and I need to give you these funds, but first I have to count it in front of you; then you will need to count to make sure it's the correct amount."

I said, "Are you crazy? We're in an airport waiting room. There are hundreds of people here. We're going to count money behind a pillar?"

"Connie, we don't have much choice here. The program has no way of getting funds to you in Jalpaiguri. There are no banks. You need to carry cash. The bills need to be small, because no one will be able to change big bills in Jalpaiguri," said David.

"How much money are you giving me?"

"This suitcase has five thousand dollars in ten-rupee notes."

I was incredulous. "I'm just supposed to walk on the plane carrying a suitcase with five thousand dollars in it?"

"Connie, we really don't have much time. I'm going to start counting."

David squatted with his back to the pillar and started to count while I stood in front of him, acting as lookout and trying to keep stray eyes from seeing what was in the suitcase! It took some time for him to count all those ten-rupee notes. Then, it was my turn to squat before the pillar (thank goodness I had on a long kurta and pants that covered me appropriately), and I started to count. Soon, my knees and back started to hurt. I mean, what American over five years old can squat for longer than five minutes? *I guess this is good practice for going to the toilet,* I thought. After a while I just wanted the pain to be over.

"So fine, it's all there," I said. "For heaven's sake, let's sit down on a chair." I signed a chit that said I received 41,950 rupees (at 8.39 rupees to one dollar in 1975) from David Heymann, dated it, and handed it to David.

"So you know how to make receipts," he said with a grin.

I did that little Indian head wobble gesture. Seems it did come in handy.

David said, "It's important to keep track of all funds. When you come in from the field in a few months, bring the receipts for the WHO administrative officer in Calcutta. Giorgio, the epidemiologist in Jalpaiguri, will go over all this, but the funds are to be used to put petrol in the jeeps, pay temporary workers that you may need to hire, and pay your per diem in the field so you can eat and get lodgings. The program thinks this should be enough until we call all the epidemiologists to Calcutta for the WHO meeting. Then you can get more funds, once you turn in your receipts."

"So, David, how am I to safeguard these funds?" I asked.

"Keep the suitcase in the jeep with you. Stash it under your feet in the car. At night, you can put it under your pillow for sweet dreams."

I looked up to see him smirking. "Shit, I'm going to be killed for this," I mumbled.

"Well, not right away," he said. "Do you have any more questions?"

"How am I getting on the plane with this money?"

"Just walk on," he said. "Sometimes they don't even check your carry-on. Just say you are WHO and on mission."

Right! So why is it that I feel like some criminal with all this cash on me?

"And at the airport in Siliguri? What does this Giorgio look like?"

David replied, "No problem. He will be at the airport and will recognize you. Everything is taken care of."

He was sincere, but I had a sinking feeling that things just weren't right.

"OK," I said, "but just in case we miss each other when I come off the plane, what do I do?"

David thought a hot second and said, "You know what the smallpox vehicles look like, right? Find the jeep and tell the driver you are Dr. Davis. No problem."

Well, I was slightly comforted to think that I knew what the smallpox vehicles in Uttar Pradesh looked like. The words Smallpox Eradication Programme were etched in a semicircle on the front doors of the jeeps. But why wasn't I convinced?

And he was off! Maybe he said good luck, or see you soon. I'd heard about Heymann in Delhi. He was a sharp epidemiologist, knew a lot about smallpox, knew how to get things done. They failed to mention that he was quite handsome, and boy, did he look young. He had to be older than me, but he looked like he was still in college. And how in the world was he able to enter the airport departure lounge while carting a suitcase full of rupees and find me in the waiting room? But then, airport security was different in those days.

And then I heard an announcement over the loudspeaker, something about how the plane to Siliguri was departing from gate three. Finally, I was leaving.

9

NO, YOU ARE NOT DR. DAVIS

In the end, they didn't check my carry-on bag with those thousands of rupees. They did look at my boarding card. I stashed the suitcase under my seat on the Indian Airline Fokker F27 Friendship turboprop, ready for takeoff. Finally! The last leg of the journey. I would eventually have a close relationship with Fokker planes in Asia and, in due course, Africa. Those early Fokkers were still hauling people and transport in the most unlikely places in the world. I would end up affectionately calling it my little F--ker plane.

I sure hoped the epidemiologist working in Jalpaiguri would be at the airport. Communication was difficult. The phone was unreliable. That left only the telegram. I tugged my guidebook out of my shoulder bag and boned up on the area. The name Jalpaiguri came from the Bengali word "*jal-pai*," meaning "olive," because of the olive trees that grew in the town in the 1900s. I never saw one olive tree during my entire stay, but then again, I wasn't really looking for trees. It was Mount Kanchenjunga I wanted to see. Everyone said that

I could see it from the town's center on a clear day. However, it was monsoon season, and Delhi folk said I would never see the peak during monsoon season.

Jalpaiguri district had international borders with Bhutan and Bangladesh to the north and south, respectively. The district bordered the Indian state of Assam in the east and Darjeeling to the west and northwest. I couldn't find out much about Bhutan. It was supposed to be another Buddhist kingdom in the Himalayas. Apparently, it was harder to get into Bhutan than into Sikkim!

The pilot announced, "We are on the final descent to Bagdogra Airport." Bagdogra was a military airport open to civilian flights. The airport received tons of tourists destined for the hill stations of Darjeeling and Kalimpong. No one in their right mind attempted to drive up from Calcutta, and since there were limited flights, I was lucky to even get a seat on the plane.

The airport was tiny; it was just one building with an open veranda that wrapped around it. The plane parked close to the terminal. It was a short hop down the Fokker's steps and then twenty feet to the three steps leading onto the veranda and then inside the building. Back then, people could directly access the tarmac to pick up travelers. People were greeting friends right on the veranda. I slowly walked the twenty feet or so while looking intently at the porch.

Most of those waiting for the visitors looked like tourist guides, but I noticed a European man and an Indian man standing together. I looked at them expectantly; evidently they were clearly looking for someone else. No one was shouting out my name or holding a card that said Dr. Davis. Before I knew it, I was up the steps and in the empty waiting room.

Everyone was out on the veranda. *Damn it,* I thought. *I knew this would happen.*

OK, on to plan B. I quickly moved to the front of the airport and looked out at the parking lot. There were lots of jeeps crammed in the area. I looked intently for the familiar semicircular logo on the doors. I realized that it might be etched in several languages. There, I saw the word. Smallpox! *That's my jeep.*

The driver was dozing, and his window was half rolled up. I trooped over to the jeep and tapped on the window. The driver woke with a start. He looked surprised and anxious. I guessed he wasn't expecting a woman to be tapping on his window. Then he started with a flood of Bengali and began to rapidly close the window.

"Hey, wait, I'm Dr. Davis," I said, as I pounded on the window.

He shook his head and said, "No, no, Dr. Davis," and pointed toward the airport.

I motioned for him to lower the window. I calmly said, "I am Dr. Davis!" with my index finger tapping my chest.

"No, you are not Dr. Davis," the driver replied emphatically. He looked at me again, with a quizzical look on his face. "You, Dr. Davis?"

Now I was getting slightly annoyed. The driver, shaking his head, slowly maneuvered out of the vehicle like he was hoping to avoid a confrontation with a mad, barking dog. He yanked the keys from the ignition, slammed the door, and beckoned for me to walk behind him. Clutching my bag of rupees, I thought it best to follow at a discreet distance.

As I stepped back into the airport, I finally heard my name blaring over the loudspeakers: "Dr. Davis, please report to the airline counter." And then, up ahead, I saw the driver talking to the European and Indian guys whom I had spotted earlier on the veranda. The driver then turned and pointed at me. I could see right away from the expressions on their faces that I was not who they were expecting.

"You are Dr. Davis?" the European asked incredulously.

I felt like I was in *The Twilight Zone*. All I could say was, "Yes."

They recovered quickly. "We need to get your gear and head off to a meeting." Evidently, the district authorities had convened a meeting of all the smallpox workers to meet me. They had gathered at 9:00 a.m., and it was now close to noon. Great! This was going to be fun.

Knowing I had a long travel day from Lucknow to Calcutta and then on to Siliguri, I thought I should wear comfortable clothes on the flight that were also appropriate for the field. So my travel outfit was just a long kurta over American-style cotton trousers and my Birkenstock sandals. Now, some seven hours later, the kurta was wrinkled, I felt disheveled, and I was without the dupatta, the ever-present scarf that Indian women wear to show modesty. There was no time to freshen up, wash my face, or brush my now-tangled hair, which was pulled into a chignon at the back of my head.

Next thing I knew, I was walking onto the stage where all the dignitaries were sitting. I felt like I had just crawled out of some hole and was thrust into the bright sunlight. The money bag was slung over my shoulder.

I was tired, hungry, and desperately trying to think up some ad-lib words to say. So I put on a brave face and pretended I was back in the theater in college, acting in a role. Really, I didn't have to play enthusiastic; I was excited to finally be there.

I managed to say, "We are really close to zero cases of smallpox in the country. Now it will be up to each and every one of us to do our bit to find and investigate all rash-and-fever cases. Our major difficulty will be making sure no smallpox importations slip in from Bangladesh."

I don't know what the smallpox workers thought about this American doctor. I knew from others' comments that they thought I looked Indian, yet my accent didn't fit, and that threw them off. They were used to a proper British accent. I was also wearing clothes certainly never before seen on any proper Bengali woman doctor. In the end, I guess this meeting was a good idea. Everyone got to see me, so when I eventually materialized at the remote health clinics, they would at least know who I was.

After the smallpox meeting, I sensed that the urgent agenda on the table was where they could put Dr. Davis. The current smallpox team was lodging at some place by the bus station. *The bus station?* I thought. *What about the traffic?* I imagined the noise of all those Indian buses constantly blowing their horns, not to mention the heat and dust in the center of town. Finding a hotel (I'm using the term loosely) that possessed a tranquil environment was well-nigh impossible in that location. The smallpox team sheepishly showed me the lodgings. There were six "rooms" side by side. I am being polite by calling them rooms. They were really more like flimsy shacks, each outfitted with an Indian string cot without a mattress. A minuscule window was located in the back of each room. The temperature in there was oppressive.

When the door was shut, I could still see into the room because there was a gap of about a half inch between the door and the doorframe. It would not take much to kick down the door with one foot, even for me. All I could think was, *This is not a secure room in which to leave my money bag! And where are the showers and toilets?* There was no other woman in sight. Probably during the night, there would be a lot of women gathered around, but I doubted that any of them would become my best friend. We unanimously agreed that maybe this particular rest lodge was not quite the perfect place for me.

Part of the problem, of course, was that unlike smallpox workers in the urban areas, I would not have a permanent home. I would be moving around most of the time. When we heard a rumor, my team would search it down. We would be traveling constantly to evaluate the work conducted by the smallpox workers and their supervisors. However, I couldn't help thinking that it would be nice to have a secure place where I could leave most of my things. I needed something like a forward operating base. Or, at the very least, I needed a place to hang out and chill on my one day off, Sunday.

I have to admit that the smallpox team tried hard to find me a place. They did a reconnaissance of the town and made an inventory of possible lodging facilities, including the compound of "the good nuns" on the outskirts of Jalpaiguri. Of course, a male epidemiologist could never stay with them, but as I turned out to be female, it just might fit the bill. The good sisters were sympathetic to my plight, and they were willing to put me up in their compound, which was fenced, gated, and had a guard. And it was clean and quiet. There were four nuns in the house: two nursing missionaries and two teachers. I was welcome to share in their life and take meals with them if I was around for breakfast or dinner. I wondered if I also would be expected to pray with them.

They strongly recommended that I should try and get in at a reasonable time. I was not sure what "reasonable" meant to them.

"Besides," one of the nuns said, "the roads are dangerous after dark."

Actually, the roads were also dangerous during the day. I saw innumerable road accidents, mostly involving heavily overloaded trucks. When night fell at 6:00 p.m. sharp, I needed to be where I planned to sleep. Life became a juggling act to figure out lodging details by 4:00 p.m. to allow enough travel time to arrive before sunset.

Once I had found lodgings, the all-male smallpox team made a hasty exit. "See you tomorrow," they said. I desperately wanted to take a shower and eat. The male cook at the convent (women in the rural area did not work outside the home) hauled up a big aluminum bucket half full of steaming-hot water for my bucket bath. First, I diluted the hot water with cool water from the tap to find the perfect temperature. Next, I removed all my clothes and left them in the adjoining bedroom. The bathroom, which included a squat toilet, was so tiny that anything in there would be drenched.

With difficulty, I squatted down on my haunches to reach the bucket. Then I poured a few cups of water over my head, face, and back, using the large plastic cup. I used soap sparingly because it took a lot of water to rinse off the suds. Bengalis could take a bath squatting down the entire time. After a few minutes, I had to stand and stretch my leg muscles. Then I picked up the bucket and poured the remaining water over my body, hoping all the soap rinsed off. If I discovered I'd missed some soap, I would need to douse cold water over myself. I dried off with a bath towel. There was a hint of a breeze, and it almost felt like air conditioning.

Then I was ready for dinner. Interestingly, this house did have electricity in the dining room, thanks to the nuns' small generator. The electricity was only turned on for an hour each evening. After that it was pitch black. That first night I hadn't had time to buy kerosene for my little red Chinese lantern. It was just as well, as I could hardly keep my eyes open. I knew this would be my haven as long as I was working in Jalpaiguri. I would need to find something similar in Cooch Behar and Darjeeling. But first things first: I needed to find the police station and look for a bank!

10

A WHIRLWIND ORIENTATION

The next morning, Dr. Giorgio, an Italian epidemiologist, arrived bright and early to collect me at my lodgings. He had only four working days to explain the details of the smallpox program and hand it over to me. His plan was to introduce me in all three districts and visit some subdivisions to see how the smallpox workers were handling the job. I insisted that we needed to first go to the police station so I could register. Apparently, Dr. Giorgio did not have to perform this onerous duty. But then, his posting was only for three months.

We had a bet that the police would not even know who I was and, in addition, that no circular had reached the area. We were wrong. To our surprise, the superintendent said, "Yes, I got something from the federal government."

He called a subordinate and asked to see the file. What was the likelihood that, given the lumbering bureaucracy of the Indian government, a circular was prepared and expedited to the districts before my arrival? Incredible as it seemed, the chief pulled out the circular in Hindi, where I could see my name, Dr. Cornelia E. Davis, in the official record. He smiled. I assumed he recognized that I certainly didn't look the type to do nefarious activities. And then we left. The whole effort—from getting to see the head of police to searching for and locating the file—took over one hour. I could see this was not going to be an efficient process.

Next we tracked down a recently opened bank. The bank manager was really excited to have me as one of the very first depositors. I opened an account for the WHO epidemiologist with my signature. I had the manager note also that a WHO epidemiologist from Calcutta could also access the account in the case of an emergency. I couldn't think of what kind of emergency right off, but one never knows. I deposited the 41,950 rupees so I could show Calcutta that the funds had arrived safely. Then I immediately withdrew half of the funds. I couldn't predict how rapidly I would deplete the funds, so I thought it best to take half with me. That meant I still had a significant amount of money, and if the locals knew, I might be a target. I would keep the money under the seat in the jeep during the day.

As I expected, Giorgio informed me that Jalpaiguri and Cooch Behar, located to the south and southeast of Darjeeling, would likely cause me grief. The Jalpaiguri division, which encompassed all three districts, had a long border with Bangladesh. He pointed out the Jalpaiguri district headquarters, and then we proceeded to the district hospital. In the early 1970s, smallpox cases were transferred to the infectious disease ward of the hospital. It appeared that all that accomplished was to transmit smallpox to other patients in the hospital. By 1973, the program had learned to leave smallpox cases in their villages, perform ring vaccinations around them, and maybe hire a temporary guard from the village to ensure that the patient did not leave his or her house. The guards were instructed to keep people from entering the quarantined house and to keep the ill individual and his or her family from leaving until the patient recovered (or died). Some funds were provided for food for the family.

I was not impressed by my tour of the district hospital. The level of hygiene—or lack thereof—did not meet the minimum standard of any US hospital. And mind you, I had worked in a county hospital that had few resources. The Jalpaiguri hospital consisted of wards that held twenty to thirty patients segregated by sex. I don't know what they used as disinfectant, but there was this horrendous odor that would make me gag every time I entered a ward. I didn't see one waste bin in the entire structure. Outside, in the back of each of the wards, was a shallow pit. All the biological waste, syringes, and needles were thrown there for eventual burning. All I could think was, *Please, God, under no circumstances let them bring me here after a car accident. Just let me die immediately on the road.* I didn't realize how close I would come to having that wish granted!

There was one road in the district that was paved. That meant it was macadam. Macadam road construction was pioneered by Scottish engineer John Loudon McAdam around 1820. Aggregate layers of small stones were mixed in an open-structured roadway with a coating of binder as a cementing agent. The majority of roads in the district were just packed dirt. A macadam road was considered a *pukka* (good) road. Dirt roads with ruts were called kaacha (bad) roads. These Hindi words would form a major part of my vocabulary. All manner of things were classified kaacha or pukka. For example, a string cot bed was kaacha, whereas a bed with a mattress was pukka. This was a pukka rest hotel, and that was a kaacha restaurant.

For my orientation we agreed to simplify life, and we returned each day to Jalpaiguri so I could use the lodging of the good nuns. We would not try to stay at the *dak* bungalows, the government rest houses, at this juncture. I would experience them later, on my own.

Giorgio felt compelled to explain Cooch Behar in some detail as we headed to the district. He felt it would be my most formidable district. During the time of the British Raj, Cooch Behar was the seat of a princely state. The name was derived from the name of the Koch tribe, which was indigenous to the area. "*Behar*" is a Sanskrit word meaning "to travel." This was the land in which the Koch traveled. Cooch Behar has gone through a series of reincarnations, so to speak, from a kingdom to a state and from a state to a district. I guess you could say it lost status over the centuries.

The date August 28, 1949, was pivotal in Cooch Behar, because on that date, its maharaja (king), Jagaddipendra Narayan, ceded full and extensive authority and power to the government of India. Cooch Behar, in the northeastern part of West Bengal, is surrounded by the district of Jalpaiguri to the north, the Indian state of Assam to the east, and Bangladesh to the west and to the south. Even today there exists a sort of no-man's-land between Bangladesh and Cooch Behar, consisting of 92 Bangladeshi exclaves in Cooch Behar and 106 Indian enclaves inside Bangladesh. I came to use the words "enclave" and "exclave" interchangeably. After all, one country's enclave (foreign territory within one's own) quite literally is another country's exclave (own territory surrounded by another country).

The folklore I heard was that these enclaves/exclaves were the result of chess games centuries ago between two regional kings, the raja of Cooch Behar and the maharaja of Rangpur. History buffs might indicate that these enclaves were the result of peace treaties in 1711 and 1713 between the kingdom of Cooch Behar and the Mughal Empire, ending a long series of wars in which the Mughals finally wrested several districts from Cooch Behar.

There was no way to avoid the ramifications of the partition of India. India and Pakistan won independence from Britain in August 1947, following a nationalist struggle lasting nearly three decades. Colonial British India was divided into two separate states: Pakistan, with a Muslim majority, and India, with a Hindu majority. The ensuring chaos was accompanied by the largest mass migration in human history of some ten million people. As many as one million civilians died in the accompanying riots and local-level fighting. Unfortunately, Pakistan was created in two halves, one in the east (formerly East Pakistan, now Bangladesh), and the other 1,700 kilometers away on the western side of the subcontinent (formerly West Pakistan, now just Pakistan).

When the Cooch Behar maharaja finally ceded his territory to India in 1949, it was one of the last of the more than six hundred princely states to do so. In 1971, East Pakistan gained its independence as Bangladesh. Incredibly, the enclaves survived all these changes of sovereignty on both sides of the border. Attempts were made in 1958 and 1974 to exchange enclaves across international borders. The exchange remained elusive, even though the international aspect of these enclaves made administering them extremely difficult at best.

The border situation made it impossible for people living in the enclaves to legally go to school, to the hospital, or to the market. Complicated agreements for policing and supplying the enclaves had to be drawn up and enforced. In a classic example of a vicious circle, residents of enclaves needed visas to cross the other country's territory toward the mainland. As there weren't any consulates in the enclaves, they were required to go to one in the mainland. However, they couldn't get to the mainland because they didn't have visas. Illegal border crossings were frequent but dangerous. Transgressors were shot by border guards. Furthermore, the enclaves remained a haven for criminals who were immune from the justice system of the country surrounding the enclave—exactly as it was back in 1814.

These and other problems rendered the enclaves pockets of lawlessness and abject poverty compared to their already relatively poor motherlands. As the issues of sovereignty, territorial integrity, and especially the unwillingness to let the other side seem to "win" were so sensitive for both India and Bangladesh, the Cooch Behar enclaves were unlikely to disappear anytime soon.

In 1975 I really was not savvy about enclaves or exclaves. I was told in no uncertain terms that specific areas were dangerous. In addition, the relationship between India and Bangladesh was always tense. It was best to stay on the Indian side of the border. The problem was knowing exactly where the border was. Giorgio introduced me to the district health officer in Cooch Behar. He had already warned me in the jeep that this CMO was difficult to work with. However, it was the long, porous border with Bangladesh that was more worrisome to me. Bangladesh continued to have hundreds of smallpox outbreaks. Surveillance would be arduous.

Cooch Behar was not particularly interesting for its geography. It was a relatively flat district, with six rivers that sliced it into sections. The predominant agricultural products of the district were jute, tobacco, and paddy rice (rice grown in waterlogged fields). Yet, Cooch Behar had something that the other two districts did not: Cooch Behar Palace. The palace was built in 1887 in the Italian Renaissance style, along the lines of Buckingham Palace. When I worked in Cooch Behar, only one part of the palace could be visited as the heirs to the maharaja still lived in the rest of it. The vast lawn and the landscaping were extraordinary. The civil administration was located in stunning historical buildings.

There was no time to linger, because we needed to head back to Jalpaiguri before the sun set. We skipped the police station, as I was technically just visiting and not transferring to Cooch Behar.

Dr. Giorgio saved the best for last...Darjeeling!

11

A TRANSFER OF POWER

When we left late in the afternoon, we were finally going to where I really wanted to be. Darjeeling is some seven thousand feet above sea level, and just maneuvering the narrow Hill Cart Road, where the jeep's tires were never more than six inches from the edge of the cliff, was an adventure. Just passing slow-moving trucks and cars was a test of nerves. When I learned to drive back in California, we were admonished never to pass on a curve, but this entire drive up the mountain was curved.

We seemed to be involved in a sport—a blood sport—while twisting our way up. Still, it was heaven leaving the sultry plains and reaching the invigorating climate of the hill station.

I'd been told that somewhere on the trip, we would spot the "toy train" of the Darjeeling Himalayan Railways (DHR). It was called the toy train because of its small size and slow speed. The train has operated on narrow-gauge tracks since the 1800s, providing an important transport link to various parts of the Himalayan Mountains. Riding the toy train was a coveted experience for tourists. Few would bypass the ten-hour ride in the train pulled by a steam engine, which has been accorded UNESCO World Heritage status.

The toy train was unmatched; the little engine made almost impossible moves using sheer engineering ingenuity and creative skills. The train moved at a snail's pace through the hilly terrain, at times so slow that local schoolchildren could hop on and off the train as it was still on the move. They have since replaced the steam engine with diesel, so it only takes seven hours to make the trip now.

The train and vehicles used the same roadway, and our driver always tried to overtake the train in order to avoid being held up by waiting for the train to pass. I missed the chance to ride on the toy train. I just never had ten hours to devote to this treat. When we arrived in the central point of Darjeeling (it took only three and a half hours by jeep), we discovered a different world. The town was surrounded by snowcapped mountains, green tea gardens, pretty villas, large hotels, private clubs, and churches. And there was a mélange of English shops with plate-glass windows.

The maze of the bazaar was teeming with men and women from dozens of different hill tribes, including Gurkha policemen, rosy-cheeked Tibetan women, and sturdy-limbed Bhuttias from northern Sikkim. There were also Indians from the civil administration, proper British men and women, members of the Tea Planters Association, and, of course, tourists. With the invigorating climate and the mash of people, I felt carefree. It was a natural feeling; most people at the hill station were on holiday or leave, so there was a kind of gaiety in the air.

We headed to the Gymkhana Club. *Gymkhana* is an Anglo-Indian expression for a gentleman's club that has both social and sporting activities. I guess over the years they admitted a few ladies. The Gymkhana Club had a few rooms that they "let out" to temporary members. Previous WHO epidemiologists had rented a room and then passed it on to their replacements. If I developed my work plan adroitly, I could try to spend my one free day of the weekend in the mountains. I signed up for a temporary membership, and the administration was told that I would be taking the room.

The club was very British and very male, and it had good food, but lunch and dinner had to be ordered in advance. Of the many things to like in this very civilized club, there were two special things that I adored: the room had a wood-burning fireplace that was lit every evening, *and* a hot water bottle was placed inside the covers at the foot of the bed. When I climbed in at night, I could snuggle down to warmth.

I couldn't see Mount Kanchenjunga from my patio, but just a short walk away was a great viewpoint on the grounds of the club. Early morning was the best time to view it during monsoon season.

Giorgio took me on a quick tour of Darjeeling district as we discussed the smallpox problems in the area. I could understand why Dr. Giorgio wanted Darjeeling to be his last memory of northern West Bengal.

As I suspected, Darjeeling was not a smallpox endemic area. There was little disease threat from Nepal, which also had a smallpox eradication program. In fact, Nepal's problem in the past had been smallpox importations from India, principally from the Indian states of Uttar Pradesh and Bihar. Still, when we reviewed the last smallpox importations into

Sikkim, we saw that they had come from outbreaks on tea plantations in Jalpaiguri or in Darjeeling.

So tea gardens, or tea estates (the term I remembered from my orientation), were important because they imported laborers from other Indian states, and these laborers could potentially harbor the smallpox virus. To maintain current data on the area, it would be important for me to periodically visit tea estates and to ask the managers' permission to talk to the workers about smallpox and the importance of reporting rash-and-fever cases.

We made it an early evening because the next day we were taking Giorgio to the airport to catch the plane for Calcutta. His tour was rapidly coming to an end; mine was just starting.

We left bright and early the next morning to make our descent into the plains. The smallpox team was downcast and a little subdued. Bagdogra Airport looked different to me from my new perspective. There was the rush of getting the bags checked and saying our good-byes. Giorgio took me aside and said, "You know, Connie, I specifically requested Delhi to send an older, experienced, white male epidemiologist to replace me. That's why we didn't recognize you!" He wanted a foreign epidemiologist because of the difficulty in working with the CMO in Cooch Behar.

Stunned, I didn't know what to say. *Damn, I guess he struck out on all counts*, I thought. I was twenty-eight years old and probably looked like I was fourteen. And I had the nerve to think David Heymann looked young. Folks always said, "When you are older, Connie, you're going to really appreciate how young you look." But I didn't appreciate it then. The smallpox team needed to get back to Jalpaiguri town, and Giorgio disappeared into the departure lounge. I wondered what my field team thought of me.

And so went the transfer of power—the king is dead, long live the king!

What is it about moving that unsettles and confuses the mind, causing it to delve into long-suppressed thoughts and feelings? What is the expression that says it so well? Uncertainty is the only thing certain.

12

THE FIRST BIG MOVE

I t all started in Chicago. I was born there. And then one day, my parents made a startling announcement: we were moving to California. I was not enthusiastic. I was to start eighth grade in the fall. Surely, after I struggled to finally be in the top grade and to lord it over all the other grades, we couldn't be leaving.

My dad, an orthopedic surgeon on Chicago's South Side, was approached by Kaiser Permanente Hospital and invited to join its California network. As I later gleaned from side conversations meant for adults only, Kaiser was looking to diversify, although I'm not sure that was the expression used in 1956. Dad went on ahead to California to start his new job and to look for a house. We kids had to finish the spring school term while Mom was packing up. Then we would all take the train, the California Zephyr, to our new home.

Our family included Colbert the Third, the oldest, who was named for my dad and Grandfather Davis. Then, one year and nine days later, I arrived on the scene and was named

Cornelia Estelle. I was the fifth Cornelia in a long family line; obviously it was a name highly regarded by the family. Personally, the name Connie fit me just right.

We were a close-knit family. We were raised Catholic, and as the good nuns were known to provide an excellent education, Colbert and I bicycled every day to Saint Anselm's Catholic Grammar School on South Michigan Avenue. The parochial school was five miles from our house on Langley Avenue, but this was before school buses and student fares for public transport like the elevated train. It was somehow determined that it wasn't that dangerous for us to ride a bike to school.

Oh, I forgot—there was one other child, Edward Henry. I once heard someone whisper to my mom, "Was he a mistake?" Eddie was born five years after me. He was always too young to play in my and Colbert's circles. As the last baby, I thought he was the most favored, but my mom would emphatically state that she hated all of us equally.

It was in the Golden State that we all came of age. For me, Chicago was but a distant memory. I was undeniably a Californian girl.

Our little emigrant group chugged out of Chicago one early summer evening in 1956, headed like millions of other emigrants before us to a new life in the West. Truly, I don't remember the myriad details of the journey. There seemed to be hundreds of folks streaming toward the train platform. I don't remember if anyone came to see us off. There was a very helpful Pullman porter standing beside the steps up into the train. He looked at the tickets in mom's hands and said, "Yes, ma'am, this is your carriage. Let me show you your cabin."

It was incredible what was stuffed into such a small space. There were two sets of bunk beds that were folded flat against a wall, leaving just seats with a huge picture window the whole length of the cabin for daytime. And there was a small bathroom with a shower and a toilet. "I'll let you know when it's dinnertime and show you to the dining carriage," said the porter. "I'll turn down your beds then." And he was gone.

I remember the dining car's white linens and good silverware, and our mom admonishing us kids "not to be acting up" in there. I remember the scenery along the three-day cross-country trip and recognizing for the first time the expanse of America.

I'm not quite sure how we spent our time for the three days we were on board the train. I am sure Mom did not let us traipse up and down the corridor. I'm sure I had books. And Colbert probably had some model plane or car he was assembling. Eddie was likely being cranky and fussy.

This was our great adventure, just as great as the grand European tour I had read about. Although the exact route has faded from memory, I can still see the vastness of the rolling amber wheat fields, the stunning mountain ranges, and that big sky. America was huge, and all I could hear in my mind were the lyrics "Oh beautiful for spacious skies, for amber waves of grain, for purple mountains majesty, above the fruited plains."

What remains a defining moment, etched crystal clear in my memory, was crossing Donner Pass into California. On that last night, the porter knocked on the door and told Mom that we would be arriving in Oakland around 7:00 a.m. the following morning. He asked if we would like to be awakened on the approach to Donner Pass. You bet we did! We didn't care if it was at 4:00 a.m.

Col said, "Look out the window, just look out the window." And then I knew that this was a different land, this California.

Here was a stunning blue lake, with switchbacks slowly climbing up the side of the mountains; the snow was still on the peaks of the surrounding Sierra summits, and the tunnels gave us fleeting glimpses of the scenery. This place was different; this place would make us different. We would never be Midwestern city folk ever again.

Dad was at the station to greet us with our trusty red and black 1955 Plymouth Belvedere. He whisked us through another tunnel to another world called Walnut Creek, California. I had thought we were going to live in Oakland, because that's where we got off the train.

We took something called a freeway for some time, passing Orinda, Pleasant Hill, Lafayette, and finally Walnut Creek. By the time we exited onto Ygnacio Valley Road, I was fascinated by the exotic array of Spanish names in California. As we crested a small rolling hill, we saw farmland and walnut orchards—actually, lots of walnut orchards—to the left. To the right were Eichler homes. *Where is the creek?* I felt like Dorothy and knew that we certainly were not in Chicago anymore.

The San Miguel Eichler homes were the brainchild of a progressive real estate developer named Joseph Eichler. Apparently a social visionary, Eichler commissioned designs primarily for middle-class Americans. One of his stated aims was to construct inclusive and diverse planned communities. He worked to integrate parks and community centers in these localities. He had a brilliant nondiscrimination policy, and his homes were sold to buyers of any race or religion, which was certainly a good thing for us, being both black and Catholic.

I only found out fifty years later that the lady realtor who sold Dad the house was blacklisted and harassed for her daring. So much for policy and practice. I didn't know any of this at the time, but I recognized straightaway that "California modern" was not like any style of house that I had ever seen before. I loved it at first sight.

Santa Fe Drive was only one block long, but it was remarkable. We couldn't have had better neighbors if we had individually interviewed and selected them. We must have arrived a little after noon. Neighbors started gathering at our house soon after. That block was a regular melting pot. Someone told Mom (maybe it was the Driscols), "We're bringing dinner tonight, so don't worry about going out grocery shopping."

And the Fugiokas said, "We have tomorrow covered."

Wow! Where are we? For a week, different neighbors from the block, such as our Jewish neighbors next door, the Abramavitzes, brought us home-cooked meals. This was a really good thing, as our moving van came in the next day, and it seemed we were busy unpacking things forever.

Colbert and I stayed on the block for those first few weeks before school started. Now Colbert was destined, being the oldest and ready for high school, to head into Berkeley for a Catholic education. Catholic schools had not quite penetrated the suburbs, so I would need to go to a public school for eighth grade. Then I would also go into Berkeley to high school.

There was a lot of focus on Colbert going to the Christian Brothers Saint Mary's College High School. So it was only one week before I started at Oak Grove Intermediate that Mom started to prepare me for this new experience. At the time, California had the weird policy of putting eighth and ninth grades together and calling it an "intermediate school." It was certainly going to be different.

Saint Anselm's in Chicago was one of the first primarily black Catholic parishes; maybe 10 percent of the students were white. Oak Grove was primarily white, with a sprinkling of Mexican children (the term "Hispanic" was not yet in use). So Mom said, "I'm not sure how the first days at school will go for you. You will get on a school bus that will take you to Oak Grove. Maybe no one will sit with you on the bus. Maybe no one will talk to you at recess."

"Because I'm black?" I asked.

Mom responded, "Well, you're going to a public school."

My parents thought Catholic schools were more disciplined and integrated, and although we had no experience with public schools, they were suspect.

I already knew about the race thing. Just going to the grocery store was strikingly different than it had been in Chicago. It reminded me of *The Wizard of Oz*, and how the film starts out in black and white and then dramatically changes to Technicolor when Dorothy lands in Oz. Chicago, for me, was mostly black, being from the South Side. Whites weren't rare; they just weren't the majority. But in Walnut Creek, everyone was white, except for us.

When the first day of school arrived, Mom walked me to the corner for the bus. There were kids from our block and also from surrounding blocks. There wasn't much time for last-minute words of encouragement. She gave me a quick hug, and I started up the bus steps. I'm more of a front-of-the-bus girl than a back-of-the-bus girl. So I plunked down in the second row from the front, in the window seat on the right, and smiled bravely at Mom. And the next thing I knew, a girl with a yellow ponytail sat down beside me and said, "Hi, my name is Cathy. What's yours?"

13

FIRST DAYS ON THE JOB

So now I was on my own. I inherited the 1975 gray Toyota Land Cruiser from my predecessor. At least it was distinctive; it was the only vehicle of that type in the three districts. At the last minute, there was a change of staff, and I had a new driver from the terai area, as my focus was to be on Jalpaiguri and Cooch Behar.

When we were in the home district of Jalpaiguri, the driver parked the vehicle at the nuns' house and handed me the key. Then he would make his way home on foot. He was back by 7:00 a.m. the next day to wash the car and get it ready for the day's journey.

I woke before sunrise every day to go outside to look for Mount Kanchenjunga. Usually I could glimpse it for about ten minutes before cloud cover hid the snowcapped peak. I had pretty good luck; I saw it two out of every three days. Then I would head to the kitchen to get some breakfast of tea and eggs and toast. I learned not to order fried eggs, which would invariably come with the yolks broken and cooked hard. I thought yolks should be runny, so I compromised and asked for scrambled eggs.

A typical day in Jalpaiguri district started with my lifeline to water for the day. The cook had my huge two-liter thermos of boiled water ready by 6:30 a.m., when I came down to breakfast. Overnight, I rehydrated myself with water and tea, and in the morning I always made one last toilet run. There was no place for me to pee in the rural areas. Schools did not have toilets. Petrol stations didn't have ladies' rooms in the back. A hospital might have toilets, but they were invariably not usable. The population was so dense that I could not find a tree or a shrub to privately relieve myself without an entourage surrounding me. I worried at first, but it turned out not to be a problem. It was so hot that I was always running a little dehydrated. I had no pee. I rationed my water in the thermos. We typically drank six to eight glasses of chai during the day. Still no pee. Once we got back to the house in the early evening, I would start to drink water again.

After an hour or so, I could finally urinate. Experienced field epidemiologists told me that I would ruin my kidneys and that I needed to drink more water. They were all men. Where was I to pee? And even if I had a wide, long skirt, there was no way I could squat down and pee in plain sight of people. It was a dilemma for as long as I was in the rural area.

Once the driver picked me up, we collected the paramedical assistant at the designated location, and I gave a general direction to the CMO. I wanted to build a little rapport with the team and see how much they knew about Jalpaiguri district before we went on to Cooch Behar.

It was pretty silent in the cab that first day. Dinesh, the paramedic whose first language was Bengali, and whose second language was Hindi, spoke good basic English. The driver, Abdul, had limited English: hello, good-bye, turn right. However, by the end of our time together, Abdul had learned a fair amount of English—certainly more English than my vocabulary in Hindi.

I had to learn about the very real caste system early on because our little team faced immediate complexities. In Indian culture, in the north or in the south, in urban areas or rural, all things, people, and groups of people are ranked according to certain essential qualities. Although the caste system is primarily associated with Hinduism, it also exists among other Indian religious groups such as Muslims (although they sometimes deny that they have castes) and Indian Christians. Castes are ranked and named, and membership in a caste is conferred at the moment of birth. It is impossible to change one's caste.

The system has been severely criticized in modern times, and educated Indians sometimes tell non-Indians that no one pays attention to caste anymore. That statement does not reflect reality. Reading the classified marriage ads in any newspaper is proof enough. In 1975, the caste system was alive and well. This ad, for instance, was typical: "Seeking a high-caste Brahmin girl, wheatish color, height five feet ten inches, who has finished secondary school, to be a bride for our son, who has finished university and is earning a six-figure salary as an engineer in Delhi."

Within any given area, town, or village, everyone knows the relative ranking of each caste and of each individual within the caste. First, one is ranked according to wealth and power. There is this expression: "There are *bare admi* (big men) and *chhote admi* (little men). Big men make the decisions, while little men come before them making requests."

Next, there are rankings within families and kinship. Men outrank women of the same age, and younger siblings never address an older sibling by name but rather use a respectful term like "elder brother" or "elder sister."

The underlying concept, which is extremely complex to explain, boils down to the concepts of purity and pollution. Let me make a sweeping generalization here: high status is associated with purity and low status with pollution. Purity is associated with ritual cleanliness—daily bathing in flowing water, dressing in properly laundered clothes, eating only foods appropriate to one's caste, avoiding contact with people of lower rank. Many castes are associated with specific occupations. Those of the priestly caste, the Brahmins, are high status. Low-ranking caste members, such as the untouchables, work as leather workers, butchers, latrine cleaners, and sweepers.

Historically, the four castes, from highest to lowest, were the Brahmins or priests, who looked after the spiritual needs of the community, followed by the Kshatriyas, or warriors and rulers, whose role was to rule and to protect others. Next were the Vaishyas, or landowners and merchants, who looked after commerce and agriculture. And lastly were the Shudras, artisans and servants who performed manual labor. At a later time there emerged a fifth category, the untouchables, who performed menial and polluting work related to bodily decay and dirt. The untouchable caste has gone through a series of name changes. Mahatma Gandhi termed them Harijans, or "children of God." The government called them the scheduled castes. To be politically correct, these groups preferred to be called Dalit, which means "oppressed" or "downtrodden." Inequality among castes is still considered to be part of the divinely ordained natural order and is expressed in terms of purity and pollution.

Each caste has its own *dharma*, a divinely ordained code of proper conduct. Brahmins are expected to be nonviolent, vegetarians, and teetotalers. Kshatriyas have to be strong as warriors and so are non-vegetarian and can drink alcohol. (Personally, this would be my caste, if I got to choose.)

When one dies and is reborn, one's *karma*, or the sum of one's deeds in this life, is judged by divine forces; and once reborn (reincarnated), one is assigned a high or low status depending upon what is deserved based on past actions.

Maintenance of purity is linked closely with the intake of food and drink, including who prepared it or touched it. As a rule, people risk pollution and the lowering of status when accepting beverages or cooked foods from the hands of people of a lower caste. Even accepting water from someone lower on the caste scale is polluting. There are countless traditional rules pertaining to purity and pollution that continually impinge on the interactions between people of different castes and ranks.

In my opinion, my designation as team leader created taboos right from the start. As a woman, it was taboo for me to be traveling around with two men who were not related to me. Restaurants were few and far between and only found at sub divisional-level towns or higher, and even the simple act of eating was complicated. When we went to eat, neither the driver nor the paramedic could sit and eat with me. The

Muslim driver and the Hindu paramedic didn't eat together either.

The first time I went to a restaurant, we parked the jeep in front. I weighed the negative ramifications of leaving the money bag in the car under my seat. No one knew about the money (hopefully), except my team. Dinesh escorted me into the establishment and talked to the owner, who opened a tiny private room about the size of a voting booth that had a full-length cloth that sealed off the room from prying eyes. It was suffocating inside my *purdah* (seclusion of women) booth. There was one mini table and a chair.

When we arrived at the restaurant, I forgot to ask where to wash my hands. I wasn't going to upset protocol to go search for it. The only choice on the nonexistent menu was *dal bhat*, a spicy mixture of rice and dal (lentils) and a cup of chai. Imagine how I felt, eating my meal in solitary confinement. The dingy curtain might have once been white, ten years ago, but now it was a smoky charcoal hue. It seemed to me that a lifetime passed before the meal was served. Thank God they brought a spoon with the meal, as my hands were not spotless. Sweat was dripping down my face, and rivers of sweat were pouring down into my bra. I ate quickly just so I could escape. I ripped back the purdah curtain to see thirty pairs of eyes staring through the restaurant windows. I quickly paid for my meal and pushed open the door to the restaurant. *Great*, I thought. There were even more people squatting in a semi-circle outside the door, just waiting for the chance to see the foreign woman.

Steeped in recent conversations about karma, I was thinking that I had clearly done something grievous in a previous existence to deserve this brand of torture. At least the outside air was cooler than in my purdah booth. Dinesh and Abdul were already in the jeep.

Dinesh asked, "How was the meal?"

"Interesting," I said. "Why were those people staring at me when I came out of the restaurant?"

"Just curious. They had heard there was a new lady epidemiologist," said Dinesh.

Then we headed to a nearby public health clinic to look for a smallpox worker. Once the smallpox worker was in the jeep, I took out my map, closed my eyes, and let my finger fall on a spot on the map. "Let's go to this village," I said. "You have searched for rash-and-fever cases in this village, right?"

"Aacha," was the response.

So off we went. I learned there were two important caveats about driving in the rural area. First, watch out for kids running to play tag with your vehicle. They didn't see a lot of jeeps, so when one passed, they would run out to tag the bumper or the side of the jeep. The problem was that they were not used to cars, so their judgment about how fast the jeep was going, or how close they could get without being run over, was pretty poor. So the driver had to be alert and able to make quick decisions.

The second caveat? If you hit a child or an adult, you were not to stop! You were to go to the nearest police station and report the accident. We had heated exchanges on this directive in Delhi. Why couldn't we throw them in the back of the jeep and head for a clinic? Delhi staff said that a crowd could gather in an instant, and Indians, who we considered to be rather docile, turned violent in a heartbeat.

Another problem faced on the roads (besides other drivers) were animals. Especially dangerous times were early morning, when it was still dark, and dusk, when everything went black. At these times it's difficult to see a chicken, goat, or, for that matter, a cow. We were told not to stop if we hit a cow, either. They said just to head straight to the nearest police station.

It just didn't seem right to me. I asked Giorgio about that before he left.

He said, "It doesn't matter what you think, Connie. The drivers know that there could be problems, and so they will be getting the vehicle out of the area."

To get to my randomly chosen village, we maneuvered along the dirt track between fields of paddy rice. We saw the huts ahead, but something was decidedly strange. There were no people and no yelling children running up to see the jeep. There were no dogs, either. Had everyone been killed? I got out of the jeep and tentatively pushed open a hut door. A fire was blazing. It looked as if people had dropped their things and run off.

Why? If there was some mysterious illness, where were the bodies? The driver started honking madly. And then off in the distance, I saw a lone boy who looked about ten years old slowly walking toward us. When he got close enough, he read the inscription on the jeep door: Smallpox Eradication Programme.

And then he started yelling in Hindi, "It's the smallpox program!"

Dinesh cleared up the confusion. "They thought we belonged to the family planning program, and they ran off!"

When Indira Gandhi declared the Emergency, she devised a twenty-point economic program. The aim was to increase agricultural and industrial production, improve public services, and fight poverty and illiteracy through the "discipline of the graveyard". It was famously said that during the Emergency, trains ran on time, employees attended to their duties, and work was carried out in government offices.

The family planning program was not initially included in the improvement program. But Sanjay Gandhi, the younger son of Indira Gandhi, was especially concerned with issues of overpopulation. He initiated the birth control program, which chiefly employed sterilization—primarily vasectomies—to reduce the birthrate. Villages and districts were given quotas for the numbers of vasectomies to complete, and Sanjay's enthusiastic supporters worked overtime to achieve the goals. Critics charged that the family planning program involved coercion of unwilling Indians.

What I remember about the family planning program in 1975 and 1976 was that one of the incentives offered was that men who got a vasectomy were to receive a transistor radio. I saw a profusion of transistor radios attached to the ears of men in the area. I don't remember the incentive offered for women to get sterilized.

For a time, the trains did run on time, and civil servants were in the state offices doing work. Slums, beggars, and cows miraculously disappeared from the cities, smugglers and political wrongdoers were jailed, and the illegal black-money economy was controlled. By the time the intensive family planning drive was discredited, millions had suffered harassment at the hands of government officials, and hundreds, maybe thousands, of Indians had undergone forced sterilizations.

The leaders who had willed this program into being were out of power, and the program was in disarray. We were still feeling the fallout from the coercive policies of that Indian family planning program, not only in India but also around the world. The Indian family planning program was eventually forced to change and to enact policies that ensured that participation in the program was completely voluntary.

Once the villagers heard we were from the smallpox program, they started drifting back into the village. I was ever so thankful that I worked in smallpox eradication and not in family planning. We got down to work and visited all four corners of the village. We talked to the people about when the smallpox worker last visited and what he did. We asked about rash-and-fever cases and checked to see if smallpox slogans were painted on the village walls. The villagers were aware of the Zero Smallpox Campaign, and they testified that the worker had been there two months ago.

The light was starting to go. It was after 4:00 p.m., and we had at least a two-hour drive to get back home to Jalpaiguri. This was the most dangerous part of my day. Villagers on the road rarely hung kerosene lanterns on the backs of their dark, slow-moving wagons. As I peered through the darkness, I swore to do a better job of tracking the time, and in the future I'd be sure we started back home earlier.

14

ALL THE COLORS OF PADDY RICE

The rural areas of Jalpaiguri and Cooch Behar were economically disadvantaged and considered very poor. Over 80 percent of the population was rural. The main agricultural crop was paddy rice. Reaching some villages was difficult as they were surrounded by closely packed paddy fields, and no roads or paths led into them. Consequently, there was a considerable amount of walking entailed in smallpox work in these areas. The paddy fields were wet and muddy, and the perimeters of the fields were built up with packed mud. Farmers did not look kindly on strangers traipsing through their paddy fields. The raised perimeters were, at most, seven inches wide and fifteen inches tall; walking on them required a delicate sense of balance. If it had just rained, or our sandals were slippery, there was a high likelihood of slipping off the rim and making a large hole in the paddy by mashing down one or more plants in a field filled with water. To get to the villages, we often had to crisscross the paddy fields, as there was no direct route.

In the beginning it was appalling. I would fall into a paddy, and then villagers would come rushing out to identify the idiot who was messing up their fields. Dinesh would race ahead to pacify the farmers, and once they saw me, they would calm down, probably praying that I wouldn't pay them another visit. When we finally reached a village, I would look a mess. My pant legs would be muddy, my Birkenstock sandals would be caked in mud, and if, as often happened, we had also been caught in a monsoon downpour, we would also be dripping wet. I didn't use umbrellas; there was no way I could walk on the paddy perimeter with an umbrella in my hand. It was way too hot and humid for raincoats.

In some ways, the villagers were honored that a foreigner had trudged all the way to the village, and at the least we broke the monotony of their day. Someone would bring me water to wash my feet, and I would already be dreading the return trip to the jeep.

We would get down to smallpox business without delay. I would show the smallpox card of the nine-month-old boy with a typical rash and scars and ask, "Is there anyone in the village with a rash and fever like this? Do you know of the reward for just reporting a rash-and-fever case?" The reward was a relatively new phenomenon, so it created a good deal of interest. A reward of one hundred rupees (roughly twelve dollars) was more than these farmers could hope to make in four months!

In most cases, I was the first foreigner to ever visit their village, so they would offer tea. I soon learned that accepting chai could take up to an hour out of my day.

The process to prepare chai was lengthy. Water would certainly not be boiling in the hut (and I agonized a lot about its source and quality). Firewood or cow patties (dung) would be gathered to make a fire, and then there was the washing of the teacups and the search for a teaspoon. Sugar was relatively expensive and used only on special occasions. Villagers sometimes put a teaspoon of salt in their tea for contrast. The women would hurriedly discuss among the neighbors as to who had sugar. Then the mother-in-law would gingerly bring out the carefully hoarded supply. I felt horrible that they were going to all this trouble to prepare the tea (not to mention the work they'd need to do to repair the paddy fields after I left). When they served me chai that they would rarely taste sweetened, I felt very humbled to have partaken of their hospitality.

During my six months in northern West Bengal, walking through paddy fields would remain a constant challenge. It always made me intensely nervous. It felt like walking a tightrope thirty feet above ground. I'm sure the villagers were thankful that my balance did improve over time.

The most striking thing to me about paddy fields was their brilliant color. I didn't know what to call the color of the green of the paddy rice. Rice seedlings started out a brilliant electric green with undertones of yellow. As the stalks matured, they turned what I called "India green," because it was the color on the flag of India. Then the stalks mellowed to golden yellow; and when they were ready for harvest, they were the color of dry straw.

In my districts, the plants were hand harvested by sickle and then threshed to separate the grain from the enclosing husks. This was done by bashing the bundles of rice stems on a stone or other hard platform, or by using oxen to trample on the stems. If a road went through a village, people would lay the stalks on the packed dirt road and use our jeep to trample the rice. The last step was winnowing the rice: tossing the rice up in the air, catching the grain in the basket, and letting the chaff and dust be carried away by the wind.

Once, early on, the people of a village insisted that we stay for the midday meal, which took what seemed like hours to complete. This particular village was really destitute. I only saw one chicken running around. When they brought the curry and rice, it was immediately apparent that they had killed the only chicken. The whole village gathered round, staring as my team and I ate. I wanted to refuse and tell them to feed the smallest children, but my team told me that to refuse the meal would be a great insult. I could barely make the food go down my throat. The heat of the chilies caused tears to stream down my face.

"Don't you like the curry?" they asked worriedly. I answered that I liked it, but I was not accustomed to chilies, so the spices made me cry.

That day gave understanding to this quote by Mark Twain: "The Indian may seem poor to we rich Westerners, but in matters of the spirit it is we who are the paupers and they who are millionaires."

After we finally took our leave, I told my team in the jeep, "Look, this can't happen again! All the kids in that village were malnourished."

From then on, when we were asked to stay for a meal, the team agreed to lie and say, "Dr. Davis has a serious allergy to eggs and chicken. If she takes one bite, her face will swell up and she will choke to death. So please don't ask her to eat."

We agreed that it was faster and more hygienic to travel until we came upon a chai shop and then stop for tea. We were also able to get good information on rash-and-fever cases in the surrounding communities from these chai shops due to clients coming to the shop from diverse villages. And we were able to pass on information about the smallpox program.

There were no places to eat in the rural villages; when we came upon a sub divisional town, we were faced with the dilemma involved in eating meals. By the end of the first week, I was extremely frustrated with eating alone and with the feeling that I was always on display, even while hidden by that purdah curtain. Something had to change.

On the way home late again one night, I said, "Something has to change. I'm going crazy. I understand the strict rules of caste, but I have discussed and negotiated with the gods, and I am ordering you both to eat with me!"

I continued, firmly reinforcing that as the chief of the team, I was ordering them to eat with me. I added that they would not be *voluntarily* breaking the taboos. The bottom line was that they were assigned to me as my staff members, my team. I told them that I knew that the first times would be difficult for them and that they would feel uncomfortable. In addition, I assured them that I accepted all the bad karma that would surely follow.

Then I played my trump card, saying, "For me, you are my family." They were stunned. They didn't even eat together. To be absolutely sure they understood, I continued, "And if we go to a truck stop or a restaurant, we will eat together at a table, out in the open. Don't, however, let any other men sit at the table."

I didn't know how they would take it. Uneasily, I wondered if they would be upset enough to report me to the smallpox program, saying I caused them to lose status. Or was I giving them both more status because I was the foreigner and I should have more status? In some instances, a white foreigner was treated as high caste, particularly in the case of a high government official. Since I was a foreigner, technically I was outside the caste system and automatically untouchable.

To be honest, I didn't lose sleep over it. I remember thinking, *They either will kill me and steal the rupees under the seat, or we will develop a real close friendship.* And then, of course, there was the issue of how the wider world would view this transgression.

We were in a new sub divisional town and a new restaurant for our first meal together. There were a couple of tables already occupied, all by men. We settled for the remaining table in the center of the room.

Then we filed out to find the lavatory to wash our hands. In India, food was always eaten with the right hand. Abdul turned on the faucet, and I went first to soap up and then wash off my hands. I shook my hands in the air, because the towel hanging under the basin had seen better days.

I demurely kept my eyes downcast, because there were toilets there in the back that appeared not to have doors on them, and I didn't want to scare any male who stumbled out and confronted our little group. I was happy to hurry back to our table. The owner approached Dinesh and asked if the memsahib (the lady) wanted to be in the purdah room. Dinesh declined the offer, and we ordered.

There wasn't a big selection, but there was some kind of fish dish. Thinking of the famous quote "Fish and rice make a Bengali," I decided that this would be a good meal.

While waiting for the food, I tried to keep the conversation going and said, "I think next week we need to transfer to Cooch Behar. That district is priority." I asked about lodging and accommodation there. Dinesh said there were several dak bungalows in the district.

Dak bungalows! There was a certain ring to the phrase. This was an Indian institution that came into being back in the days of the British Raj. The word "bungalow" originated in India in the seventeenth century and was used to describe a type of shelter adapted from the Bengal peasant hut. This new building form emerged from the need for temporary accommodation to service the influx of British nationals working and traveling in rural India, where the idea of the hotel was still largely nonexistent. It seemed to me that the idea of a hotel in the rural area still appeared to be largely nonexistent.

These structures were first developed to service the *dak*, or mail system, a service administered by the British government. These soon developed into a series of rest houses to accommodate government representatives conducting official business in remote and isolated areas. The distance between them was about the distance that a horseback rider could travel in a day. Each bungalow was outfitted with a cook and a watchman to tend to travelers when they arrived. The typical dak bungalow was a one-story building with a central dining room and veranda and two or three bedrooms, with an adjoining kitchen and servants' godown.

So I asked, "How do you reserve a room?" My team just looked at me. They explained that there was no way to reserve a room; the best plan was to arrive by 4:30 p.m. and hope that space was available. Apparently if there was a room for the sahib (that was me), then there were always quarters for an entourage. I thought that it seemed pretty chancy to just show up and hope that a room was available.

Our conversation about hoped-for lodgings in a dak bungalow was interrupted when the waiter put a shallow dish in front of me that had a mound of rice that could feed all five members of my immediate family back home. Oh, but what was that on top of the mound of rice? It was a fish head, with bulging eyes and an opened mouth seemingly imploring, "Please don't eat me!"

I looked up and said to my team, "Wait, don't touch your food! There is no way I can eat a fish head. It may be a delicacy to you, but it's going to make me upchuck any food I can eat. Whoever wants this, let's exchange plates now." My driver reached out, and we switched plates. Thank God, because the fish in his dish had some flesh on it, but it was missing the head. But Lord, there were millions of tiny bones. I made no dent in the rice. Once again, tears streamed down my face. I couldn't help but wonder if I would ever be able to eat in India without crying.

When we finally left the premises, we broke out laughing about my fish head. Then I asked, "How do you say 'I want a child's portion of rice'?" From that point on, the restaurant cooks would always get a kick out of serving a child's portion of rice to me, and would shake their heads.

We muddled through that first meal together, but with each subsequent meal, it became easier as we grew more comfortable in each other's company. I realized that we really were a team, and we had also become a family.

I don't know what the wider world thought of us breaking these taboos. However, I observed over time that when anything involved a foreigner, it was easiest for the community to just ignore the breaches in tradition. No man ever tried to sit at our dinner table, even when it could seat eight people.

On the way back that night to Jalpaiguri, I thought that I'd better break it to the good nuns that I would be moving on next week to Cooch Behar. I tried to remember if I was supposed to tell the outgoing police station that I was leaving.

15

A RUMOR OF RASH-AND-FEVER CASES

The good sisters were sad to see me go, or at least they said they were sad to see the inquisitive American leave. I thought it wouldn't hurt to ask if they knew of any lodging possibilities in Cooch Behar. They told me that near the capital of the next district was a large Catholic mission run by a Jesuit priest. Maybe he could put me up, and I could use his compound as a base.

It was a good lead. My former university was Jesuit, so I should have an in with this Jesuit director. As we neared the capital, we kept a lookout for the mission. The compound wasn't easy to miss. It looked like a fortress, with nine-foot walls and broken glass placed on the top of the walls to discourage thieves from scaling the enclosure.

When the guard came out and asked our business, I said, "Tell the director that an American wants to speak to him." The gates opened. Father LaFerla, SJ, was the welcoming director of the Caritas mission. He was well known in the surrounding area and had a wealth of information. He also had connections with the armed forces general in charge of security along that six-hundred-kilometer stretch of border with Bangladesh.

A former Jesuit college student? Of course I could use the compound as a base. I explained that I would be moving around a lot, searching for smallpox cases. I doubted I would be at Caritas many nights. I wanted to leave my duffel bag and a small aluminum trunk that I had recently acquired in my room in the compound.

Best of all, I knew that I would probably be able to break my current teetotaler status. At least, I knew that in the States, Jesuits could be depended on to have a reliable stash of alcohol. He did not let me down on that count.

After dinner and over a good brandy, Father LaFerla provided me with a good history of West Dinajpur, which now is split into two districts, and Cooch Behar. This area had a history of *dacoity*, which, while currently reduced, was still present. Therefore, I was told I must *never* travel at night.

"*Dacoity*" is a term for banditry in Hindi and Urdu. In section 391 of the Indian Penal Code, the ingredients of this crime have been set forth explicitly: "When five or more persons conjointly commit or attempt to commit a robbery... every person so committing, attempting, or aiding is said to commit dacoity."

Father LaFerla stated that the dacoits of old were extremely devoted to the goddess Kali. Before leaving to commit dacoity, they would worship Kali. These gangs even offered human sacrifices. Among the dacoit gangs of the past, the Thugis and Pindaris were most prominent. They used to rob travelers of their money and belongings. They would knot a coin at an end of a strip of cloth (*rumaal*), and then fling that knot around the victim's throat in such a manner that it became a noose. And that's how the term "thuggery" came into being. After killing people in this way, they looted all their belongings. Fortunately, at present, these dacoit gangs were extinct.

The tales certainly persuaded me to get off the roads early and not to travel at night. I was delighted with this new forward operating base, and I was ready to go meet the CMO of Cooch Behar and get on with searching for smallpox.

Our little field team headed out early the next morning to visit the Cooch Behar district headquarters to see the CMO and to check in with the police superintendent.

I didn't visit long with the CMO. I just wanted to touch base and say that I would be supervising in the "Blocks" (another term for a smaller administrative unit) that were in the south of the district and would keep in touch. I also touched base with the police to let them know I would be working in Cooch Behar over the next month or so. They didn't seem impressed. Well, at least I had followed the rules and checked in.

We drove past Cooch Behar Palace, and I made a mental note that I did want to visit it soon. It really looked impressive. Then we headed to a lively market that we had passed coming into town to check out rumors of rash-and-fever cases.

Over the years, the smallpox eradication strategy had changed as the epidemiology of the disease was better understood. The mass vaccination campaign from 1962 to 1967 showed that mass vaccination would reduce the incidence of new cases of smallpox but that case detection and containment were also necessary to eliminate the focal points of infection.

From 1968 to 1973, the focus was on surveillance, weekly reports of cases and deaths, and rapid detection and containment of outbreaks.

Indian states were divided into two categories: endemic (areas where the disease or condition was regularly found) and non endemic. Endemic states were the highest priority, and West Bengal was endemic. The next phase was an intensive campaign lasting from 1973 to 1975. Four major endemic states were targeted: Uttar Pradesh, Bihar, West Bengal, and Madhya Pradesh.

At a designated time, every village and every house was visited within a period of one week. This was made possible by mobilizing all health workers, not just smallpox workers. The following weeks were spent in investigating all cases and carrying out containment operations.

In May 1974 India had more than 8,600 villages infected with smallpox. By the beginning of May 1975, there were only twenty-five villages with smallpox in India; eighteen of those were in the eastern states, including West Bengal. The majority of outbreaks were the result of importations from Bangladesh. The smallpox program administrators in Delhi were feeling pretty confident that they were nearing the end of the disease.

The next phase was Operation Smallpox Zero, which lasted from 1975 to 1977. This stage focused on maintaining effective surveillance activities throughout the two-year period following the occurrence of the last reported case. West Bengal was in the intensive campaign phase when I arrived. The focus was on rash-and-fever surveillance, collection of specimens from suspected smallpox or chickenpox cases resulting in death, and the introduction of a cash reward to the first person providing information on a smallpox outbreak and to the health worker to whom the information was given. The cash reward varied depending on the state, but in West

Bengal, the reward was one hundred rupees (around twelve dollars).

Collecting one hundred rupees just for reporting a rash-and-fever case was like winning the lottery. To publicize the reward, wall slogans were to be placed in every village to increase public knowledge. It was hoped that the reward would stimulate both the public and the health staff to search for and report cases. We collected scores of rumors by sitting in strategically located chai shops. We were not just taking tea breaks; it was work. By visiting chai shops and markets, we made it easy for the public to contact my team or the smallpox workers and report rumors. It took good investigative techniques to determine which rumors to investigate and whom to put in our jeep to bring us to the concerned village.

We arrived back at the Caritas compound well before sunset. I was taking no chances with dacoits. The next day I got out the map, closed my eyes, and let my finger fall on the road map. It landed on the border, on a strip of land that looked like a finger extending into Bangladesh. Dinesh confirmed that there was a health center in the general area. OK, that was where we would search that day. We were on the road by 7:30 a.m.

After a while I said, "Let's stop at this village and ask about smallpox and then go on to the health center." A dirt track led straight to the village. Good, no paddy fields for me to negotiate. We went to the first available hut, and I showed the smallpox recognition card to the man who came to the door. "Any rash-and-fever cases in the village?" I asked.

The man did what folks invariably did: he took the card in his hands and stared intently at the infant displayed. He then shook his head and said, "No."

I asked my next automatic question, which was, "Have you heard of rash-and-fever cases in another village?"

To my utter surprise he said, "Yes," and then pointed south, out past the fields surrounding the village.

I turned to Dinesh and said, "I don't think he really understood my bazaar-like Hindi. It's best that you repeat the questions."

There ensued a long discussion. Dinesh then repeated what he had heard. The villager said that he had heard a rumor that there were smallpox cases across the border, in Bangladesh. He could give no further details.

I said to Dinesh, "How did he hear the rumor? Is he sure it's smallpox? I can't believe this!" *Crap! I can't believe this.* In this border area between Cooch Behar and Bangladesh, there were no border demarcation posts that were normally found at official crossing points. The villagers just knew where the border was located. People could easily cross over, but they normally didn't. We decided to head rapidly to the health facility for more information.

The health facility was located twenty minutes away, in a northerly direction. At the health center, there were a few patients sitting in the outpatient clinic. The medical officer heard our jeep and opened his door, indicating we should come in. Dinesh and I introduced ourselves.

The doctor had heard about the new lady field epidemiologist. We asked to see his weekly smallpox reports; this clinic was known for the timeliness and correctness of its reports. I showed the doctor the recognition card and asked again about rash-and-fever cases. He responded that he had seen no rash-and-fever cases, and none had been reported to him in the last six months.

However, he had heard a rumor that there were cases over in Bangladesh, but the rumor wasn't specific.

"Did this rumor give the name of the village?" I asked.

"I'm not sure of the name," he replied, "but it sounded like..." He then uttered a complicated-sounding name—or at least it was to my ears.

"How far away is this village?"

"I don't know."

"Did you investigate?"

He looked at me as if I were crazy and replied, "It's in Bangladesh!"

Right, it's in Bangladesh. I asked if there was a smallpox worker attached to this clinic. When he emphatically answered "No," we left. I wanted to scream. *Damn, damn, damn! I don't believe this.*

We got back into the jeep, and Dinesh said, "What do you want to do?"

"I need to think," I said. "Let's find some shade up the road."

We pulled over to the side. I jumped out and went to sit under a scrawny tree. I could hear Dinesh and Abdul whispering in Bengali in the jeep.

If I could just know with certainty what the rash-and-fever cases were, I could resolve the issue. If they were chickenpox, we could all relax, end of discussion. If they were smallpox, we needed to know where the sufferers had come in contact with smallpox and whether they or any contacts or relatives had traveled to India.

Fact: We knew that importations had occurred from Bangladesh into West Bengal on a regular basis in the past. Should we just wait to see if it happened again? If we heard this rumor about these smallpox cases in Bangladesh, then this village must be fairly close to the border. It seemed pretty passive just to sit and let smallpox reenter.

Fact: India was fairly close to announcing that smallpox was eradicated. What would happen if smallpox cases were imported into West Bengal? God, would Delhi be pissed! And what if these imported cases came into my district of Cooch Behar? It would be blamed on the field epidemiologist in Cooch Behar—yours truly. I could just hear the discussion. "See, you send a woman epidemiologist to do a job, and she f--ks up! Not only that, but she's a black woman and an American." *Surely, God, you would not do this to me.* But why did I have this gnawing feeling in my gut that these cases were really smallpox?

Fact: We knew borders do not stop diseases. So we needed to be proactive. However, this particular border between India and Bangladesh was sensitive, and I had been told not to cross international borders.

Fact: I did have a United Nations Laissez-Passer and didn't necessarily need a visa to enter a country. I could just say if stopped by authorities, "Oh, did I cross the border? I'm so sorry." Well, I guess I decided.

I climbed back into the jeep. I said, "Look, I really need to investigate those rash-and-fever cases. We just have a small problem about this international border. I feel pretty comfortable about crossing over because I have a UN Laissez-Passer. You guys, unfortunately, could get into a lot of trouble if you cross. So I will go alone and just quickly walk to the village and back."

Dinesh said, "Uh, Dr. Davis, how are you going to find this village? And how are you going to talk to them once there? You don't know Bengali."

Abdul said, "We are not letting you go alone!"

My plan for a quick dash over the border was unraveling swiftly, but even I could see when I was defeated. So I said, "Let's get the vehicle as close as possible to the border and hide it in some bushes off the road. I don't feel comfortable driving an Indian-plated jeep into Bangladesh. Then we can walk rapidly to the village. We can see the cases and then quickly return." And that was the plan.

16

What was the likelihood that these rash-and-fever cases would be smallpox? It was now July, and I was only in my second week operating solo in the Tri-Districts with my team. I thought back to a fifty-mile backpacking trip I had led in Colorado. One of the Girl Scout campers had deeply sliced her thumb, and as I was trying to staunch the bleeding, she whispered that she had a bleeding disorder and that it would be difficult to stop the hemorrhaging.

"How can that be?" I asked. "There was no mention of that in your medical record."

"Well, my mom was afraid that you would not allow me to go on the trip if we mentioned that."

I thought, *You're damn right you would not be on this trip.*

As the blood kept seeping through the thick layers of bandage, I grabbed the topographical map. How could I get her out quickly and yet have a chance of returning to lead the other scouts on the rest of their big trip? This was not a cross-country "orienteering game" to see how good I was at reading maps and getting to the finish in the quickest time. This was for real, and the panic I felt was real. But once I focused on the here and now, the panic gave way. I always calmed down once I focused, but it didn't make the fear any less real. The topo map indicated a sawmill somewhat close, and I decided for us to go cross-country and drop down into the mill. Surely, they would have a vehicle to get us to civilization. I carried the scout's backpack out, and after one hour of hard hiking, we arrived dead on target to the sawmill! There was a happy ending here, but it turns out that the sawmill had only been opened up for the summer season two days before our arrival. Sometimes, a little bit of luck is also involved.

Now, faced with crossing the border to find those cases, I didn't have a topo map of the other side, I didn't know where the elusive village lay, and I couldn't be certain of the dangers that lay ahead.

We followed a narrow track due south and passed numerous fields of rice and jute. It was eerie, because we still had not passed a single person from the Bangladesh side. We must have walked three kilometers when the track abruptly opened up to a bustling crossroads with bullock carts and wagons teeming with produce and people. Abdul and I hung back while Dinesh went forward to ask directions to the village.

When he returned, he said, "The village is off to the west, somewhere over there, but it is still some ways away. I think we should take a bullock cart." We jumped on the back of a wagon, our legs dangling over the back end, and started off. We talked quietly.

"Did the people seem curious about us?" I asked, still feeling fearful.

"I'm not sure. I hope they think we have relatives in the village." Fortunately, the driver of the bullock cart was too far away up front to chitchat with us. The ride was uneventful and might even have been enjoyable if we had not been on a secret mission.

It took about forty minutes to arrive. There was a slew of people in the village eager to meet the strangers. So we jumped off the cart, and I asked in English to speak to the village leader. Dinesh translated. An older man was brought to us right away. We introduced ourselves, and I told him we had heard rumors that they had rash-and-fever cases and we were wondering if it was smallpox.

He responded immediately, saying, "Yes, it is smallpox, and it has affected an entire family. I will take you to them."

As we stood in front of the hut, he called out to the family inside. The parents came out first. Their appearance was striking. Their skin had hundreds of small pink patches where the scabs had fallen off, and that contrasted sharply with their dark skin. Then the parents called for the children. All six had the telltale features of smallpox: a dense rash on the face and extremities and a rash on the palms and soles of the feet. *Crap, these are my first smallpox cases*, I thought. I asked excitedly if I could photograph them. They were willing. But I also worried that somehow they had traveled to India and that I wouldn't have time to do proper containment.

"Has a smallpox team from the Bangladesh side been to the village?"

"Not yet," replied the village leader. From the Bangladeshi perspective, the village was isolated in the north and difficult to reach. We stressed that we were from India, that I was from WHO, and that we needed to make sure that they would stay in their village. I asked to collect scabs and quickly lifted eight scabs off the twelve-year-old daughter, who seemed to have been the last one to come down with the illness.

Dinesh talked to the family about where they had been and found that they had recently returned from a wedding in another part of Bangladesh. The father said they didn't have any relatives on our side of the border, and that they didn't travel across the border. I sure hoped that statement was true. We turned to the village leader and stressed that he needed to immediately report these cases to their smallpox workers. They needed to do containment in the village. The headman said that after they saw the rash, no one had visited the family. There were no other cases in the village (so far), and he would send word of the cases to the Thana authorities. We spent less than thirty minutes there.

Our cart was waiting to carry us back to the crossroads where we had started our journey. Now that we had our answer, we were anxious to be on our way. With luck, we could slip back across the border undetected and no worse for the wear. We calculated that our villages on the other side of the border were less than ten kilometers away. They would technically be within this village's rash-and-fever cases containment area.

The return trip seemed faster. We recognized our crossroads and our little dirt track heading off to the north. I paid our bullock cart driver with Indian money. I figured he would be able to eventually exchange it for taka. In any case, the rupee was stronger than the Bangladeshi taka, so he had "gained" on this little voyage of ours. It was only about noon as we approached our hidden jeep. We discussed what our response to these cases of smallpox should be. We decided to take the border as the place to start containment and vaccinate all villages within one kilometer.

I had Abdul drop Dinesh and me off at the border village where we were first alerted about smallpox over in Bangladesh. I sent Abdul back to Cooch Behar to pick up some smallpox workers. We decided he would tell the CMO what we had found over the border. In the meantime, Dinesh and I would call the villagers together to talk to them and to start the enumeration (listing) of all households. The village leader called all the people together to listen to us. I asked if there were any villagers who could read and write in any language. There were two who could write in Bengali.

I snatched some paper and pencils from the jeep before Abdul left, and made a template of the information I wanted them to gather from each family. They were to go from house to house to place a number on each one and to list all the people living within. They were to indicate if each person was currently at home or temporarily out—at the market, for example—or traveling away from the village. I would pay them ten rupees a day to help in this village and two others along the border. I thought, *If we can have the village enumerated before the smallpox workers return, vaccination will be a breeze.*

We explained the situation in Bangladesh to the villagers and told them we needed to vaccinate everyone, no matter their age and no matter when last vaccinated. A young mother asked if her two-month-old child needed to be vaccinated. My instructions in the orientation in Delhi were that everyone in a village should be vaccinated, whether one day old or one hundred years old. The only exception was if a person was ill and looked as if he or she would die imminently. It was prudent to not vaccinate the dying, so that the villagers would not have cause to say the vaccine killed the person. I told her that everyone should be vaccinated, but I would check her child to make sure he was healthy.

I went with the village enumerators to make sure they were going about the process correctly. Of course, they knew how many people lived in each household and could ask where everyone was. I saw the two-month-old child; he was in good health and would be vaccinated. My two workers had finished enumeration, and I was calculating the number that needed vaccinations when my jeep arrived with two smallpox workers.

Abdul reported that the CMO was surprised but would get down the maps and determine exactly how many villages to vaccinate and how many to search for rash-and-fever cases. I asked my temporary workers to accompany the smallpox workers so they would not miss any of the houses. When done, they needed to go to the next village and start the enumeration process. I needed to head into Cooch Behar town and find the telegraph office so I could report these cases. Then I would swing by the CMO's office to see how many villages lay within the ten-kilometer radius.

It was only now, as I trudged up the steps of the telegraph office, that I fully realized I would have to report smallpox cases from Bangladesh. Now, how should I frame this?

Fact: No one in the WHO office in Calcutta had even talked to me on my way up to Jalpaiguri, much less seen me, except for David Heymann. I wasn't even sure if he was still there. So I was this unknown entity working in the Tri-Districts.

Fact: The WHO office did know that this particular epidemiologist was untested. I could just imagine the look of horror on their faces as the telegram arrived stating that there were eight smallpox cases in a village in Bangladesh. Wondering what I had been doing in Bangladesh would cause even more consternation.

Fact: They couldn't even send up an experienced epidemiologist for three more days because of the flight schedule. I could imagine them trying to determine if this report could be relied on. This was going to be more complicated than I had originally imagined.

I walked into the telegraph office and up to the operator and asked for a telegram form to fill out.

He didn't look pleased and said, "Just tell me what you want to say, and I will put it in correct form." *Oh, oh, I guess I am breaking protocol, again.* As most people did not know how to write, filling out the form was his job.

However, I didn't want to alert all the people in the waiting room as to the contents of my telegram. So I said, "I know how to write—just give me the form, please."

He acted as if I had just committed a felony. Slowly he slid the form toward me through the open window slot. I took a seat on a bench. *How do I phrase this so it is not alarming?* I thought. Problem was, no matter how I put it, it sounded alarming.

To: WHO Calcutta: Reporting eight cases of smallpox in one family in Predhanbalabari village in Dinajpur District, Tetulia Thana, Bangladesh STOP Starting containment procedures in Cooch Behar District STOP Have collected scabs STOP Please notify Bangladesh smallpox program STOP C. Davis.

I handed the telegram to the operator. I said, "How much is the telegram?" but he proceeded to read it out loud, slowly and distinctly. Then he counted the words and told me the cost. I gave him the rupees, asked for my receipt, and said sarcastically, "Thank you *so* much!" Then I escaped out the door.

I was guessing the whole town would know the news within an hour.

We headed for the CMO's office. He had a small group of supervisors looking at the maps, calculating the number of villages to vaccinate, and making a line listing of the villages to search for rash-and-fever cases. There were only three villages within the one-kilometer radius for vaccination. Luckily for us, rice paddy and jute fields surrounded the hamlets, and all lay on the Indian side of the border. This area was not densely packed with villages. I brought him up to date on the progress already made with vaccinations in the first border village. I handed over the box with the tin lid that held the scabs, gave him the completed forms, and said, "Please send these on for confirmation."

It was already 5:00 p.m., and I needed to get back to the Caritas compound before dark. I told the CMO I would go back to the border the following morning and help supervise the search in the villages within ten kilometers.

Boy, I needed a drink that night! As I ate dinner later with Father LaFerla, he asked how things seemed in Bangladesh. He wanted to know if the crops were growing well and what the ambience had been. I replied frankly that the crops were growing fine, but I was so scared the whole time there that I didn't ask a lot of questions for fear that they would start asking me questions.

Father LaFerla surmised, "I guess they will send someone up here?"

I responded that I probably had three days to get everything done before Calcutta could get someone here. I said that I would be leaving early and probably getting in late every evening, so he shouldn't worry about me.

The next day we returned to the border. The smallpox workers had finished enumeration of the other two villages and vaccinated everyone on that first day. There were no refusals. The vaccinators had worked late into the night. There were two people who were not present in one of the villages; they had gone to search for work. Otherwise, these villages were safe. The rest of the villages required just a house-to-house search for rash-and-fever cases. The CMO assigned twenty smallpox workers to work on the search, so it would go quickly. With luck, we'd be finished within three days. I traveled to one of the villages being searched and was pleased to discover that they had not found any rash-and-fever cases. I was starting to relax.

I was not totally convinced that those Bangladeshi villagers never came to India. What I knew of Indians was that they certainly walked longer distances and with a more rapid pace than any American I knew. If I could get over to Bangladesh, they certainly could come the other way. We would just need to be vigilant.

I paid my temporary workers off. They had been extremely useful; they knew the people, they knew where the houses were located, and they knew if any villagers were trying to hide anyone. I also gave the one-hundred-rupee reward to that first man who reported the rumor.

I knew that in some states and in certain communities, there was resistance to smallpox vaccination. I found no resistance in these communities. I thought the presence of a woman changed the dynamics. By that I mean the villagers didn't see a woman as a natural threat. The thinking seemed to be, "She's a woman—she's harmless." And I would tease the men, saying, "You men can't be afraid of a little vaccination shot. It doesn't hurt. Look, the smallpox worker vaccinated me, and I didn't cry!"

In each village, I would receive a vaccination to show the villagers that it caused no problems. I received so many vaccinations that I started to worry about overdosing. Maybe it was not such a good idea to be vaccinated fifteen times over the space of a few days.

I was usually vaccinated in a spot that was easy to access. I would pull up the long sleeves of my kurta and turn my arm over to expose the underbelly of the forearm. The worker would jab me five to six times with the bifurcated needle dipped in the vaccine. At the beginning, I let the workers use their own needles. The vaccinator usually had only two needles. I got a skin infection around one of the vaccination spots because the workers could not sterilize the needles until the end of the day. When I went for my first field epidemiologists' meeting, I asked for additional needles. The smallpox unit presented me with a new box of two hundred sterilized needles. Then, whenever I met a smallpox worker in the field, I would check how many needles he had, and I would give him five new needles to add to his collection. If we needed to show the vaccination technique, he would take a sterile needle from my box and then vaccinate me.

At the end of three days, the containment activities were almost completed. I was putting in twelve-hour days going to different locations to check on the work of the searchers. I was exhausted. I longed for the cool air of Darjeeling. It had now been three weeks since Giorgio's departure and that one tantalizing night in Darjeeling. I felt the pull of the mountain. So I told Father LaFerla that I needed a break from the sultry weather and that the work was practically done, with only one more village to search for rash-and-fever cases. I decided to take Sunday in Darjeeling, and I headed off late on Saturday afternoon. I planned to be back in Cooch Behar early Monday morning. And I was off.

It was exhilarating, feeling the air get colder with each thousand feet of altitude gained. And it was like homecoming when I opened my room at the Gymkhana Club. Oh, to gaze at the roaring fire in the room and snuggle with that hot water bottle at the foot of the bed. Pure bliss! We had to leave before 4:00 a.m. on Monday to get down the mountain and back to Caritas by 7:30 a.m. It was a quick trip, and I was rejuvenated.

My jeep pulled into the Caritas compound in good time for breakfast. Father LaFerla intercepted me in the parking lot. He said, "You have a visitor from Calcutta, a WHO doctor. He's in the dining room. I told him how hard you worked doing containment!"

Shit! So they did send someone, I thought. I thanked Father LaFerla for "having my back," and I went in to face the music.

17

CONTACTING THE SMUGGLERS

The visitor from Calcutta looked up and then glanced at his watch as I entered the dining room. It was 7:10 a.m. I introduced myself and said, "Welcome to Cooch Behar."

He said he had arrived on the plane on Saturday and that his vehicle with driver had preceded him to Jalpaiguri. He had gone to the CMO in Cooch Behar, and the CMO had kindly explained how he had found the outbreak and planned the containment activities and that they were winding up the search for rash-and-fever cases in the villages within ten kilometers of the border. The WHO doctor had visited the border villages and noted that the enumeration and vaccinations were well done. The temporary workers talked about the lady epidemiologist and how she had trained them, guided them, and paid them. The CMO told him he hadn't seen me for a couple of days and didn't know where I was.

I was thinking, *Well, thank you, Dr. CMO asshole, for your kind words of praise.* I was about to say something caustic and mean-spirited, but then the WHO doctor smiled and said, "I saw the name on the telegram of who reported the outbreak. This CMO is well known."

The CMO had taken him to visit some of the villages being searched for rash-and-fever cases. They had not found any. The WHO doctor asked where I was lodging and found Caritas. Father LaFerla had kindly let him stay in the compound and said I had taken off late Saturday for a one-day break in Darjeeling.

The WHO doctor told me that as far as he was concerned, everything was under control, and he would be heading back to Calcutta immediately. As he got into his jeep, he said, "Job well done! There is to be a WHO epidemiologist meeting in Calcutta in two weeks. You should start booking a flight." And then he was off. I was immensely relieved. And then I thought, *He didn't say anything about crossing over into Bangladesh.* I wasn't going to bring it up!

This little experience trying to prevent importations from Bangladesh only made me more nervous about that six-hundred-kilometer stretch of border between Cooch Behar and Bangladesh. It just was so long, and there were too many places where people could enter.

I decided I should check out a stretch of border with Bangladesh in the Dinhata block. This subdivision south of Cooch Behar had an international crossing into Bangladesh. I heard rumors that a fair amount of smuggling occurred along this section of the border. However, when I asked questions about what people were smuggling, everyone clammed up.

The actual border crossing did not seem to do a lot of business. I asked the officer in charge if I could put a small-pox vaccinator at the border. Everyone coming in should get vaccinated. He agreed to my posting two vaccinators, one during the day and one at night. As we drove away, we could see people crossing at other places. There were untold numbers of unofficial border crossings. It seemed that more people were crossing at these points than at the official site.

We happened on a local smallpox vaccinator who seemed to know the situation, and I asked him to show us the major unofficial routes that people took to cross the border.

There were at least four major unofficial routes with heavy traffic. I still could not get a clear picture of why folks were crossing at these points and exactly what was being smuggled. In talking about the situation later with my team, I decided it was important to put some vaccinators on these unofficial routes. I was worried, though, about placing vaccinators on the smugglers' routes. If the smugglers thought my vaccinators were trying to "take over their routes," it could be dangerous for them. I needed to try and talk to the head smuggler if at all possible.

I said, "Let's do this like we ask about rash-and-fever cases." We could determine which teashops were on strategic roads and crossroads. Then we would casually drop the hint in our conversations with people in the shops and also with the chai shop owners that "the lady epidemiologist" wanted to talk to the smugglers. We would leave it vague. We would let them approach us. I didn't think it safe to be any bolder in approach.

Personally, I doubted the smugglers wanted anything to do with the smallpox program. We continued to visit busy markets and ask about rash-and-fever cases, and then at the end of the day we would head for one of our strategic chai-wallahs to be available. It felt surreal. I realized we were looking for a needle in a haystack. I wasn't even sure if the smugglers' hide-away was on the Indian side of the border. We got some leads on rash-and-fever cases in several villages, but they were all chickenpox. We had spent a week already in the subdivision, and I had plenty of other areas I needed to visit.

It was an unusually hot day, and we stopped early to get some tea. Abdul was still with the jeep, checking some new noise it was making. I was thinking of talking to Dinesh about moving on to another subdivision the next day. We had tried. It just was not to be. Where was Dinesh? I looked around and saw him outside with Abdul and another guy. I sure hoped the jeep did not have a real problem. That's all we needed. Then Dinesh slipped inside, sat down beside me at the table, and said softly, "Don't look now, but there was a messenger from the smugglers."

"I don't believe it!" I said. "Let me pay for the tea, and I will join you outside." *OK, now what, Davis? Is this a setup? Can we trust this guy? Will we ever come back?* I hadn't really thought about the next step of talking to the smugglers.

So I said to Dinesh, "Does he seem legitimate?" I got the head wobble thing. *Well, here goes nothing. At least we are three against one, so we currently have the upper hand.*

I doubted the guide took us in a direct way to the house. The house was off by itself and had some paddy fields around it; it was just a normal house, except for the high compound walls. There was one small entryway with guards posted inside. Dinesh and I were turned over to another new guide inside the house, who led us to a small waiting room. We sat down in straight-backed chairs. There was nothing on the walls; it was very austere. After five minutes, a door to an inner room opened.

An adolescent boy motioned for only me to follow him. I said, "It's OK, Dinesh. Nothing will happen." At least, I was hoping nothing would happen. I entered a dimly lit room with no windows to the outside. The boy pointed to some cushions on the floor, and I sat down, letting my eyes adjust to the candlelight. I looked up and realized there was already someone else in the room. He was sitting cross-legged, somewhat higher than me on a sort of divan and on some cushions, Asian-type cushions. Chinese? He was Chinese, wearing some short maroon silk jacket with a mandarin collar and silk trousers. *Whoa, this is very strange*, I thought. *What is a Chinese man doing in Cooch Behar?*

I knew that centuries ago, the Chinese, Tibetans, Bhutanese, and Assamese used to rule all the way from southern China to Cooch Behar and had fought a lot of wars over this land, but this was 1975.

I reminded myself, *It's best not to stare directly at his face.* And then I noticed the most amazing thing. His hands were gently poised on his knees, and the silk sleeves of his jacket draped down about two inches below his wrists. His pinkie fingers on both hands had the longest nails I had ever seen. They jutted out two inches with a slight curve, making what looked to me like a backward "C." My mouth must have dropped down to my knees. A boy brought me some green tea. I wasn't sure of the protocol, or, for that matter, which language we would use. I looked up. He indicated that I could start.

"Namaste," I said. "My name is Dr. Connie Davis, and I work for WHO in the smallpox program. I'm sure you are aware of this important program and that India is down to the very last cases of smallpox. Unfortunately, Bangladesh still has a lot of outbreaks. So I'm concerned that smallpox importations could occur from Bangladesh." I rushed on, speaking hurriedly. "I asked to see you because I want to put some smallpox vaccinators on the border in some of the areas that are considered unofficial crossover points."

I stopped talking because I didn't want to exactly accuse him of smuggling, yet I didn't know how else to introduce my concern. "So, look, I don't really care what you *might* be smuggling across the border; it's not my business. But if I put vaccinators on the border, I don't want them hurt. I just wanted to make sure you don't mind. I mean, it won't take long to vaccinate people crossing the border. We don't take names…" My voice trailed off because I couldn't think of anything else to say.

The Chinese man said, "It's OK, you can place your vaccinators." And that was that.

I was so relieved that I jumped up and started backing out of the room. "Thanks for all your help," I said. I really wanted to get away quickly; lingering was not an option. I met up with Dinesh in the waiting room; he was relieved to see me. I said, "Let's go, I'll explain when we get out of here." We climbed in the jeep, and I said, "Let's get going." I then recounted my meeting. Although the head honcho had uttered few words, he did give permission, so we placed vaccinators at four crossover points.

When I later thought about this experience, I kept trying to understand who this person was. To me, he looked Chinese, yet he could have been Tibetan or Assamese. A number of ethnic groups have the epicanthic fold at the eyes. I doubted that a Tibetan would wear Chinese clothes. I was reluctant to ask questions in the community.

Finally I remembered that I had heard about the phenomenon of the long pinkie nail. My aunt Wilma, who had traveled the world extensively, had acquired a large portrait painting, about six feet by six feet, of the Chinese royal court. They all sported the long nail on the little finger. I had queried my aunt about that peculiar custom. She pointed out that the long sleeves of the mandarin robe extended two inches or more below the wrists, and the long nail on the little finger indicated high birth because it was clear that the person could not do any heavy lifting or any type of cleaning and maintain those long nails. Well, at least one part of the mystery was solved.

In moving around Cooch Behar, I had started to use the government dak bungalows. I was staying in one that was close to the municipality of Cooch Behar. We had been lodging there for a couple of days, and as I had signed the logbook earlier and indicated I would be staying for some days, I was not worried about getting in late in the evenings. At least I had a room. I didn't ignore Father LaFerla's warning; it was just sometimes difficult to get in early from the field. One night it was already 9:30 p.m. when we returned to the bungalow because we had eaten late at a truck stop. Though I could order dinner prepared at the dak bungalow, it was difficult for me to say when I would return for dinner. So when we got in, I went straight up to my room. I was tired and wanted to take a bucket bath.

The jeep was in its normal position, parked right outside my bedroom window. There was no lock on the Toyota gas tank in those days, so the vehicle was parked one inch from the wall. This ensured that no one could gain access to the fuel tank to siphon off gasoline. The cook brought up my bucket of hot water. Ah, heaven.

I had just put on my nightclothes when there was a knock at the door. I was instantly on full alert. Who would dare to knock at my door at 10:30 p.m.? I opened the door an inch. A voice said, "Dr. Davis? I work for the internal security police. You have not reported to the police station in the district tonight." He handed me his identification through the open door.

I said, "Do you know what time it is? I was working late in the field, and it was too late to go to the police station. Besides, you can see my jeep outside, and you know I am here. I will report in the morning!" And I closed the door.

Now I am in hot water, I thought. Truth be told, I had not been following the directives about reporting in to the police. *Really, just give me a break. I can't do my job if I am forever taking time to go find the police station, much less waiting around to check in with the superintendent. I'll just have to deal with it in the morning.*

And the morning came soon enough. I consulted with my team, and they thought it highly unusual that I was visited in the night. I knew I had to stop this ridiculousness and decided to go to the district magistrate. He was the highest authority. He would think logically. I would talk to him.

The district magistrate's office was in one of the regal colonial buildings somewhere near the palace. Dinesh and I went in to see his secretary about a morning appointment. We were told to take a seat. Even the waiting room was pretty fancy. *Nice chairs,* I thought. *I could wait here indefinitely.* After twenty minutes the male secretary came to show us into the magistrate's office. I introduced Dinesh and myself and thanked him for seeing us at short notice. I gave a little résumé of my activities in the last month (minus the smuggler visit).

Then I got right down to the business at hand. "I know you probably saw the circular from the federal government that when I leave one district or subdivision and proceed to another, I am to check in with the police and register in the new district. And when I leave, I should do the same." I then explained the little scenario of last night, with the local equivalent of the Federal Bureau of Investigation visiting me at 10:30 p.m. I confessed that I had not recently been following the directives to perfection and explained that once we got news of a rash-and-fever case, we took off immediately to investigate. I always tried to get back before dark, but I did have ten- to twelve-hour days in the field and sometimes forgot about the police check-in.

"Mr. District Magistrate, frankly, I think everyone knows my business. My jeep can't go anywhere without causing crowds to gather. I'm quite sure people know when I have to pee! So I don't think it's reasonable to ask me to check in all the time with the police. Can't you send out a circular that says that it is not necessary for me to continue to register?"

He laughed and said he had heard a lot about the new lady epidemiologist and was happy to finally make my acquaintance. He had heard about the smallpox cases in Bangladesh and the containment procedures on our side. He said he would send out a circular stating it was no longer necessary for me to check in with the police. I thanked him profusely, and Dinesh and I left for the jeep.

Since we were near Cooch Behar Palace, I thought this a good time to check it out. In those days, there were only four rooms the public could visit. But they were stunning. There were the towering ceilings, the durbar meeting hall, the stodgy paintings of past Cooch Behar maharajas, the stuffed tiger, the royal swords and armaments, and a few odd pieces of royal jewelry. I could appreciate the lifestyle!

And then it was time to get back to smallpox work. Also, I needed to get to Jalpaiguri to make sure I was on the flight down to my first WHO epidemiologists' meeting in Calcutta. I was looking forward to some nice urban amenities.

18

DR. DAVIS, WRITE
YOUR MOTHER TODAY!

I had been looking forward to going to Calcutta. First and foremost, it was the big city, and I needed some creature comforts. I was dreaming of staying in a real hotel. Secondly, I would meet my fellow WHO epidemiologists and discover how they handled surveillance activities. Just the chance to go out to dinner and talk about something other than rash-and- fever- cases would be a welcome experience.

The WHO office had booked me into the Fairlawn Hotel on Sudder Street. The WHO administrator suggested I take an official cab from the airport, obtain a receipt, and claim it on my account. I would be turning in all my receipts from my time up in the Tri-Districts, and I hoped none would be rejected.

Calcutta was one of those cities that visitors developed either a love or hate relationship with. As soon as I stepped off the plane, I was inundated by heat. Oh my God, it was only 11:00 a.m., and it was sticky, sultry, and almost unbearable.

Traffic was creeping along the congested byway. Then suddenly, up ahead, there was some type of altercation involving a yellow cab. It was twelve cars ahead, so it was difficult to determine the exact problem. In the space of five minutes, there was a mob of one hundred people chanting and shouting. I yelled at my cab driver, "Let's get out of here!"

He said he was hemmed in and couldn't go anywhere. I screamed at him to do something, scale the sidewalks, shove the damn car behind us, I didn't care what—it was urgent that he do a U-turn and leave. At last he grasped the seriousness of the event ahead and started maneuvering back and forth to get enough space to turn around.

Oh, shit. As we turned I could see that the driver of that other cab had been dragged out, and people were starting to smash the cab! We finally completed a 180-degree turn, and I glanced back to see smoke billowing from the taxi. The mob was going wild!

My taxi-wallah looked scared. Shaken, I said, "What happened back there?"

He didn't answer at first. Finally he said, "The taxi must have hit someone, probably a child." A mob could gather in the blink of an eye and be extremely volatile. They were raging out of control.

I had seen angry before, yet this mob scene reeked of vigilante justice. I willed myself to believe that no one was in the burning taxi, but I doubted the driver's fate was much better outside the cab. I understood now why WHO told us to leave the scene of an accident and go immediately to the police station. It was dead silent in the taxi until we arrived at the Fairlawn Hotel.

I'm not sure anyone could describe the Fairlawn Hotel or its owner/manager. It sure had character. If I said it was built in 1783, that would give a hint of its colonial past. Still, the Fairlawn was totally different from the Claridges in Delhi.

This was no formal five-star luxury hotel; it fell outside classification, a description made with all due respect. It could be described as the home of an idiosyncratic aunt who was frozen in a colonial time warp and yet had decorated each room from a different time period.

Mrs. Violet Smith was behind the desk; she immediately ascertained that I was one of the incoming WHO epidemiologists. From that moment I didn't get a word in edgewise as she recounted the numerous WHO consultants who had stayed at the hotel.

She finally said, "Oh, you must be tired coming all the way from Darjeeling, so let's get you up to your room." And the next thing I knew, I was following a bellboy, who was easily carrying my luggage on his shoulder. I had a room with a view of the busy street, but because I was up one flight, it didn't seem to be too noisy—yet. I wanted to explore the city, but before anything else, I wanted to take a shower, a real stand-up, flow-over-your-shoulders shower. Calcutta could wait.

I suppose I stood in the shower for twenty minutes. Oh, the luxury, the freedom of standing. Then I just wanted to lie on a real mattress that provided some back support and didn't have lumps or bumps. It was several hours before I left my room. Calcutta was always busy, and the streets were incredibly noisy with the honking of cars and trucks. The hotel was in a tourist area, so I thought I would just walk the streets to get a feel for the city. Right outside the door was a rickshaw unlike any that I hired in Lucknow or New Delhi. In Calcutta, the rickshaws were still pulled by men. Not even the Chinese were still pulling these carts.

The memory of that first *haath*, or man-drawn rickshaw ride, would remain etched forever in my mind. The men who pulled the rickshaws varied widely from adolescents to mature adults to old men. Invariably, however, they were all wiry-thin and scrawny, with jutting rib cages. They were dressed in vests and lungis (a cloth around the hips) as they ran barefoot along the roads through rush-hour traffic. My first thought was that hand-drawn carts were inhumane. My first experience of Calcutta was in the rainy season. In the old part of town, there was muddy rainwater swirling down the narrow streets, covering things I didn't want to know about—old shoes, trash, potholes a foot deep, excrement, dead insects, and larger, unidentifiable items. During the rainy season, pedestrians hesitated before crossing the street on foot because of the depth of the water surging by. So although I didn't want to hail a rickshaw, I realized that the wheels of a Calcutta rickshaw would elevate me from the filth of the streets.

I tried to salve my conscience by noting that my puller was just transporting one person, surely an easy load compared to an entire extended Indian family of ten! And I certainly gave him a good tip. Nevertheless, it was inhumane. The city had tried repeatedly to ban the haath-rickshaws without success, due to the outcry from both the pullers and their clients. The rickshaws were everywhere in the central part of the city. I read somewhere that there were eighteen thousand hand-drawn rickshaws in Calcutta; they were ubiquitous and always available.

The WHO epidemiologists' meeting started the next day. When I arrived at the WHO office, I was surprised to see nine junior epidemiologists who were posted in various districts in West Bengal. Most had three-month assignments. The meeting got underway on time.

The regional epidemiologist sent from New Delhi to attend the meeting introduced himself and asked immediately, "Who is Dr. Davis?"

I raised my hand and said, "I am!"

Then he announced, to my chagrin, "Please write your mother today!" He then divulged that my mother had called D. A. Henderson in Geneva, worried that she had not heard from me since my arrival in Delhi back in early June. I'd sent a telex but it was never received, and she had not received any subsequent letters, either.

With the nightly news of the Emergency in India being given priority global coverage, she wanted to be assured that I had arrived safely and was still safe.

The epidemiologist said, "Henderson assured her you were alive and well and working in India." I was mortified. How could my mom call the global smallpox director?

"But I did send a telex the night I arrived at Claridges, and they said they sent it off," I replied. I had certainly paid for the damn telex. And no letters? Not possible. Starting during my student days in Florence, Italy, I religiously sent a letter home each week. It pacified my parents and let them know that I was fine. Mom saved each letter because, as she often said, "One day you will want to write about your travels, and your letters will be like a journal." I sent at least three letters from Delhi. I even mailed the letters in the post office in Jalpaiguri because the dak was notorious for losing mail. Not one letter got through? Impossible.

At the break, I talked further with the Delhi representative. He laughed and said D. A. had even called Dr. Grasset to make sure I had arrived. She assured him that I was alive and well in Darjeeling. He then handed me two letters from home.

I explained again, saying, "I really have written about six letters home, and I wonder what happened to them." For the next two days, my male colleagues teased me unmercifully, calling me "Write-Home Connie." I imagined that all the staff in the WHO West Bengal office thought I was some namby-pamby girl who was missing her mother. I decided to wait to read my letters in the privacy of the Fairlawn Hotel.

As far as smallpox news, the epidemiologist reported that it looked like the last case had occurred in May, and the Delhi office would be announcing India had reached smallpox zero on August 15, 1975, on India's independence day. I silently breathed a sigh of relief that Cooch Behar had no importations to date! He then went on to describe what needed to occur over the next two years for India to be certified free and clear of smallpox.

The Delhi epidemiologist said that the years 1975 to 1977 would be Operation Smallpox Zero. The strategy was aimed at consolidating the victory over smallpox by maintaining effective surveillance activities for the two-year period following the occurrence of the last reported case.

During the meeting we heard some new directives:

- Continue rash-and-fever surveillance.
- Collect specimens from each suspected case of smallpox or chickenpox resulting in death or when there is difficulty in diagnosis.

- Increase the reward for reporting a smallpox case from one hundred rupees to the amazing amount of one thousand rupees.
- Ensure that wall slogans announcing the reward are visible in every village.
- Attend periodic program review meetings with all supervisory personnel at all administrative levels from the central, state, district, and block level.
- Direct special focus on vulnerable areas such as remote regions; border areas; places of periodic pilgrimage, fairs, and festivals; sites with a large number of beggars; and refugee camps. Devise local solutions for each problem area.

The great worry of the national program and the WHO was complacency. They were concerned with keeping the momentum going for active surveillance. At the end of the two-year zero phase we were entering, a special WHO international commission composed of experts in epidemiology and infectious diseases would carefully review the data. The huge jump in the reward was meant to motivate both the public and health staff to search for and report cases.

During the three-day meeting, we also heard from each of the international epidemiologists, who reported on successes and problems in the districts. I reported on the containment activities in Cooch Behar without emphasizing the cross-border aspect, instead focusing on the activities on the Indian side. I also expressed my concern about importations with our long border with Bangladesh and said that I was trying out some new border vaccinations at informal but frequently used checkpoints. This tactic had just been implemented, and

I would let them know if it was successful. I thought it best not to mention the meeting with the smugglers.

I turned in my account with receipts and waited to hear from the administration to see if all my receipts were accepted. Most of the workers were illiterate, so they could not sign their vouchers. In place of a signature, I pressed the worker's digit finger in an inkpad and then onto the voucher. The finance officer noted that I had many errors in addition. Doing financial calculations in my head was not my strong suit. I was relieved to discover that all of my errors were in their favor, so I didn't owe WHO money. Before heading back up-country, the officer bought me a small calculator, which I greatly appreciated. That one gesture would save us both a lot of future time and energy correcting statement amounts. Before leaving, I received a replacement amount of funds to keep me solvent.

The Fairlawn could not accommodate all of us; I was lucky to be one of the chosen few. Some of the guys wanted to find a good Chinese restaurant, so they came by the Fairlawn to collect me for dinner. And so I learned about the Chinese in Calcutta. The first Chinese settler in India came around 1700 AD. The village he founded, fifteen miles south of Calcutta, became a sugar plantation and sugar mill later. Larger numbers of Chinese arrived during the eighteenth century, most of them traders and skilled workers in search of opportunities. The second wave, ancestors of the majority of the present-day Kolkata Chinese, arrived during the 1920s and 1930s. There were two distinct Chinese areas in Calcutta. Those Chinese who settled in Tiretta Bazar opened up Cantonese beauty salons and restaurants, and thus Calcutta's Old Chinatown was born. Later, the ethnic Hakka settled into the eastern part of the city, in Tangra, and went into shoemaking and leather tanning. Their area became New Chinatown.

After the end of World War II, in 1945, those in the Chinese community became more marginalized; they were not Indian, and they could not return to a China they had never known. As a result of a slow exodus to countries such as Canada and the United States, by 1990 the number of ethnic Chinese in Kolkata (note the change of Calcutta's name) plunged to about 3,500 people from more than 19,000. Happily, in 1975 we could go to Old Chinatown and get a good Cantonese meal. So that night, and for most of my visits to Chinese restaurants, we went to Nanking Restaurant, which unfortunately ended its tradition as the oldest Chinese restaurant in Calcutta in 1980 when it closed in the face of a dispute over the ownership of the building. It served good food, and we heard that small groups of discreet guests could ask for some beef dishes. It was not always available, but once the owner did serve us beef. We were all very excited. On one occasion, the owner asked a friend and me if we were interested in seeing his family temple. He took us through the back of the restaurant and upstairs to see an ornate red altar with beautiful Chinese calligraphy and some idols.

Later that night, I quietly read the two letters that my mom had sent. The first one was sent after my parents had returned from their one-week vacation in Britain. Mom was distraught that she had not received the telex from me on arrival. Just reading it made me angry, as I had paid good money to send the telegram. She also gave me the names of two teachers from Berkeley, the Gartenbergs, who were posted on sabbatical in Delhi. They were friends of our family's good friends Alan and Rowena McGregor in Walnut Creek. Mom urged me to look them up whenever I went to Delhi.

Right, Mom, I thought. *Not only is Calcutta on the other side of India from Delhi, but how am I to find the Gartenbergs in that huge city of Delhi with no address?*

The second letter was written some two weeks later, and Mom was explaining why she felt compelled to call Dr. Henderson. The only news coming out of India was bad. She'd heard of people being thrown into jail, and she didn't know where I was posted or even if I was alive. This was really strange. I had written at least three letters in Delhi before leaving for Darjeeling. Surely the letters from Delhi should have made it to Walnut Creek.

I sat down that night and penned a nice long chatty piece about Calcutta and being admonished to write home. I begged Mom to please refrain from calling the director to check on me. It made me look as if I was some fragile girl who couldn't find her way around. I decided I would ask Violet Smith, the Fairlawn's manager, if she could ensure that the letter was posted from the post office tomorrow. If anyone could get it posted, she could!

The next morning I went down for an early breakfast. Violet met me at the entrance to the dining room. She didn't like people sitting at a private table and not interacting with the other guests. So unless guests made a fuss, she would place them with like-minded people so they would not "be alone."

"Oh, Dr. Davis," she said, "I just got in some nice Americans last night who are from Berkeley, California. I was thinking you might know them." Why was it that people thought that just because I was from California, I would know other visitors from my home state? I glanced over at the table to see a middle-aged white couple.

"Violet, I actually didn't live in Berkeley. My parents really lived in the suburbs, so it's not likely that I will know these folks. But I'll join them." She led me to the table, all smiles, where she introduced me as a nice doctor working for WHO and identified the couple as Mel and Dildar.

I smiled and sat down for breakfast. The waiter came and I asked for coffee, and then I turned to the couple and said laughingly, "You know, Violet thinks I know everyone in California. I understand you just got in last night."

Dildar, the wife, said, "Yes, although we are posted in New Delhi, we thought we would take a quick trip to Calcutta before getting bogged down in work."

When I said that I was really from Walnut Creek, not from Berkeley, Mel replied, "Actually, we have good friends who live in Walnut Creek, the McGregors."

My mouth dropped open as I stared at them.

"Wait, the McGregors are good friends of my parents," I said. "Are you the folks doing a sabbatical in Delhi that my mom mentioned in a letter that I'm supposed to look up?" We all burst out laughing. I couldn't believe this!

What were the odds that someone posted in Delhi would be visiting Calcutta at the same time that I came down from Darjeeling, and that we would stay at the same hotel and then be placed at the same table? Crazy. The Gartenbergs were only staying for three days, and they had considered skipping breakfast that morning, but Dildar insisted. Just incredible! Well, I could get an address now. We sat gabbing until I had to leave for my meeting. I guess it was a small world. *Wait till I tell Mom about this.*

The WHO meeting was over too quickly, and then it was time to head back to Jalpaiguri and the field. I just needed to collect my baggage from the room and see if I could say one last good-bye to the Gartenbergs. Well, now I knew some folks in Delhi! As I mounted the stairs, I noticed that my room door was cracked open a bit. As I entered the room I had a clear shot of the bathroom. There, on the floor by the tub, the room boy was filling the in-room thermos with water from the tub tap. Surely that wasn't the thermos marked in bold letters: "This water has been boiled. DO NOT DRINK FROM THE TAP!"

The room boy got up quickly and tried to explain that I had not seen what I just saw. *Oh, shit, I wonder how long he has been putting tap water in the thermos instead of going downstairs and getting boiled water from the kitchen.*

My stomach did a little flip-flop. I wondered how long I would have before I would have an explosion of gastroenteritis! I had taken to heart the admonishments of my fellow epidemiologists and had made a conscious effort to drink more water since I was in Calcutta and had access to clean water.

This was not good. For three days I had really been drinking tap water and an assortment of beer and soft drinks. I glanced at my watch. It was time to get into the taxi and head for the airport. I wondered if I could make it back to Jalpaiguri before the waves of nausea and cramps hit me. Only time would tell!

19

RECUPERATION IN DARJEELING

I was fortunate to have landed at Bagdora airport in Siliguri without incident; however, I was feeling nauseous. I was developing a fever, and my abdomen was making rumbling noises that were progressing rapidly to stomach cramps. I knew I was in for a gruesome ordeal.

My driver took one look at me and said, "You look bad, Dr. Davis."

"Not half as bad as I feel." I grimaced. "Get me to the good nuns in Jalpaiguri, fast." I sure hoped my old room was available.

I just made it to the bathroom. What I wouldn't have given for an American toilet that I could sit on, instead of these raised concrete footprints identifying the standard squat toilet. I will dispense with the gory details of the diarrhea, except to say that I felt like I had a cyclone in my belly that was briskly churning out very liquid feces with blood laced through it. My first thought was, *Shigella dysentery*. The thermometer said 102.5 degrees Fahrenheit, and my temperature was climbing.

I knew I had to prevent dehydration, and fast. Sister Louise came up to see how I was enduring.

"I've made eight trips to the toilet, and this is not relenting," I said.

"I'll bring you up some tea," she said.

As I curled in a fetal position on my bed, I flashed back to the three-month externship I did as a senior medical student on the Apache reservation at White River, Arizona. While I was there, the White River hospital was conducting a study on the treatment of diarrhea with a simple oral rehydration salt solution that any mother could give to her child at home. It was introduced at the hospital, and the child was given the fluid by spoon out of a cup. To my jaundiced eyes, coming from the *premier* University of California San Francisco School of Medicine, this treatment seemed third class. At San Francisco General, we students slipped in an IV rapidly and provided a glucose and salt solution intravenously. We could hold a child for eight hours in the emergency room and rehydrate him or her in order to avoid a costly admission to the hospital.

The director of the Arizona Indian Health Hospital explained that the clinic was conducting an important study for WHO to try to address the problem of infant diarrhea in areas and countries with no easy access to medical care. There was a strict protocol, and I was to follow it exactly when any infant came in. Diarrhea was definitely a problem on the Apache reservation. We had packets that I had to dissolve in one liter of clean water, and I was also instructed in how to make a home solution. I struggled to remember the formula.

There was a knock at the door. Sister Louise came in with another person. "Connie, this is Dr. Mukherjee from the

Jalpaiguri district hospital. I asked him to come examine you."
He quickly looked at my dry, parched lips and then pinched
the skin on the backs of my hands and on my abdomen. When
the skin made a small, pointed peak that slowly retracted back
to its normal shape, we knew I had somewhere between mild
and moderate dehydration. He said gravely, "I want to admit
you to the hospital for IV treatment."

Fuck, he wants to admit me. I remembered only too well the
state of that hospital.

"No, I refuse to be admitted," I said forcefully. "I'll be all
right. I just need to take more fluids." Obviously annoyed, the
doctor left.

Sister Louise returned, and I tersely spit out my defense.
"I've been to that hospital. It is the kiss of death!"

If she really thought I was in extremis, then she should call
WHO in Calcutta and have them evacuate me. The diarrhea
was still in an early stage; I knew I could fight this. I wrote out
the instructions on how to make the solution. This was several
years before oral rehydration salts (ORS) packets were available from or promoted by WHO. I remembered that to one
liter of boiled water, we added six level teaspoons of sugar and
one-half teaspoon of salt.

"So, Sister, I have calculated the amount of liquid I should
consume daily. If you place the glasses on this little table, I will
drink them slowly. Please, Sister, *you must* continue bringing
me the glasses of ORS."

It seemed to me that every time I sipped the solution, I
needed to use the toilet. The diarrhea was pure liquid now,
light brown, and with not too much blood. I was relieved that
the symptoms did not resemble cholera. I was fatigued. It was
way too much trouble to wear the bottoms to my pajamas.

Perhaps I should just squat on the raised concrete feet and not move from the toilet.

Then I saw this insect. I had never seen it before and never have since. It appeared to be eight inches wide and looked like some type of humongous spider. It was on the toilet wall in front of me, but I was too exhausted to push up from the squat and get away. *Please, God, don't let this thingy bite me. I promise to live a better life if I can just escape.* I fell back on my butt and was able to gradually crawl back to the bed.

Sister Louise was awfully good at checking on me and also dealing with the thankless task of keeping the bathroom hygienic. Finally, I was into day two, and the bowel movements were decreasing. Maybe I was winning the battle. Sister Louise brought up some rice soup, basically some water in which rice has been boiled. That did not cause any problem. My stomach seemed to accept it. I continued slowly sipping the ORS solution, despite being totally bored with it. On day three, I progressed to boiled rice with nothing on it. I could sit up in bed and occasionally maneuver to the window to see how the day was progressing. Sister Louise said my team came by every day.

"To check if I'm still alive?" I asked. She laughed and left the room.

I didn't have a scale, but I had seriously lost some weight. I must be approaching my high school weight. Too bad I had to suffer the Calcutta revenge to get there.

I had survived, but I needed a change of scenery. I was still weak and could not envision starting back to work. I asked to see my team when next they came by. I sent Dinesh to the office to tell the CMO that I would like to head up to Darjeeling to rest and recuperate for one week. He asked the SPX program to send a message to Calcutta.

The next morning, Abdul transferred me to the Gymkhana Club for one week of rest and relaxation. The club manager was delighted to see me arrive but concerned that I had been ill. "Memsahib, the mountain air will do you good," he stressed. "Just relax." And I did.

I had a little guidebook on Darjeeling that listed numerous activities like horseback riding and short hikes. I was on vacation. I desperately needed to build up my strength, so I started with short walks to investigate the Chowrasta central bazaar. I coveted the treasures there: pashmina shawls, antique bronze Buddha statues, and priceless silver and turquoise Tibetan jewelry.

I astutely researched the various possibilities to reach Tiger Hill to see sunrise over Mount Kanchenjunga, which was *the* tourist attraction. I also determined the costs to go horseback riding in the hills. The day passed quickly. Before I realized, it was teatime at the club. It was refreshing just to languish in a huge leather chair and be hypnotized by the wood-burning fireplace. The air was energizing, and I was slowly regaining my strength. I ordered dinner at the club but ate lunch outside so I could investigate the myriad types of food available in Darjeeling. I loved the Nepali *momo*, a kind of Chinese wonton. And nothing could beat the wood-burning fire in my room and snuggling down to the heat of the hot water bottle at the foot of the bed.

I wanted to see sunrise on Tiger Hill at any cost, so I made arrangements to share a taxi with some tourists to see this wonder of the world. We had to leave at 3:30 a.m. to arrive at the viewing site of Tiger Hill before 5:00 a.m. It was freezing and dark at 3:00 a.m., but I knew the destination would be spectacular. Of course there was always the chance that fog or clouds would obscure the view, but it was almost the end of the rainy season, and I hoped it would be clear. I knew some tourists made the trek up to Tiger Hill three times before they could see this spectacle. There were about thirty tourists already at the site at 4:30 a.m. We huddled together to block the wind and looked for the first rays of sunlight.

I had heard the experience described as breathtaking, magical, and even mystical. I wasn't disappointed. When the first rays of sun provided a yellow backlight for Kanchenjunga, and then the light quickly turned pink and then a brilliant white, I took four pictures in quick succession with my trusty Olympus and vowed *then* that I would also climb to the base camp of Everest. That morning our little group on Tiger Hill was very silent, almost reverent, and I understood how primitive peoples could worship a mountain. It was an unforgettable experience that I replayed repeatedly in my head. I didn't get to see those slides of the morning sunrise over Kanchenjunga until more than two years later. There were no reliable photography shops in India in those days, so all the slides that I took throughout my entire time in India could not be developed until I eventually returned home. When finally developed, the photos were spectacular, and I enlarged all four and mounted them on the wall in my study, side by side.

In my wanderings around Darjeeling, I chanced upon the Tibetan Refugee Self-Help Center, where, among other things, handwoven Tibetan rugs were created. Instead of buying something ready made, I custom-ordered a special rug, only two feet by four feet, in my favorite color, blue. A weaver started on it right away and measured the warp threads that day. It was magical to drop by every day to see the progress of my rug. Others at the center produced *thangka* religious paintings and ran a Tibetan primary school. I wandered at will in Darjeeling, and everyone was friendly. I wasn't treated as an anomaly, and I didn't have hordes of kids following me. I was free. It was liberating. I walked everywhere.

I was quite taken with the Tibetan culture and the people. I found an Indian tailor to make a typical long Tibetan *chuba* dress in silk brocade from Bhutan, with a white cotton chuba blouse and a colorful woven wool apron that was apparently worn only by married Tibetan women. I liked the look, so I bought it. I thought I would wear it to the next state meeting for smallpox to show that I represented the northern region.

I had always had a love affair with horses, so it was imperative that I ride horses here. Darjeeling ponies were small, sturdy, and surefooted on the steep trails. The owner was always walking or tagging alongside, but I didn't mind. That way I didn't have to remember how to return to town. It was peaceful riding out over the mountainside with row upon row of emerald-green tea bushes in the distance. There were numerous Buddhist temples to visit. I would just hop off the pony, and the boy would hold the reins while I ran in to see the statues and paintings. It was effortless to meet young people and tourists and get their suggestions of other things to do in Darjeeling. I normally didn't go out at night; there were no nightclubs or bars that I knew about.

Everyone urged me to visit Sikkim, the tiny kingdom north of Darjeeling. (Hmm, not likely.) The week flew by quickly; I had recuperated my strength. I was eating normally with no problem. Now I was lean and strong. I probably lost fifteen pounds during those three days of gastroenteritis. It was weird that after that bout of serious diarrhea, I thankfully never had another major episode of gastroenteritis during the rest of my time in India.

20

SURVEILLANCE OF THE TEA ESTATES

It was so fantastic to see my team on Monday at the Gymkhana Club. I assured them that I had recovered, and we were back in business. It seemed fortuitous that we were in Darjeeling and had not yet surveyed any tea estates; we would inquire about rash-and-fever cases in one of the tea estates before descending the mountain.

As in every district, we notified the CMO of our visit and intent. With eyes closed and index finger raised, I chose the lucky tea estate. It was within the Kurseong subdivision. Our first priority was to find the road to the estate and then request the manager to speak to the workers.

The few roads in the Darjeeling high country were notorious for their steepness and narrowness. We finally arrived at the tea estate around 2:00 p.m. I walked up the steps to the manager's house, knocked on the door, and asked the housekeeper if I could speak to him. I was shown into the living room. Managers lived rather well, from what I could see.

I explained who I was and then said, "I don't want to disrupt your operations, but I would like to visit the workers' quarters and see if there are any family members that I can query about rash-and-fever cases." Also, I understood that the workers brought in the tea around 4:00 p.m., and I asked if I could I talk to them about smallpox.

He gave permission and then said, "After you see the workers, please come back to the big house for tea." I wholeheartedly agreed, because I wanted to taste some good Darjeeling tea. Maybe he could enlighten me about where to buy some. I couldn't find one shop in all Darjeeling that carried it, which was strange.

Although I knew that tea originally came from China, I didn't know how tea had arrived in Darjeeling. As I learned, the history was fascinating.

Tea was a state secret of China, as China used it as currency and forbade anyone to give away seeds or slips of plants or even to provide information on how to grow tea to outsiders. The penalty was draconian for anyone who chose to disregard the orders.

Unluckily for the British, who adored tea, China would only trade in silver for it, and that was very expensive. There probably is a lesson here for those attempting to hide something; there will always be those who desperately want to steal it. It took some time to "steal" some plants and then figure out how to successfully grow them, but eventually tea arrived in the Indian state of Assam. In an attempt to break the Chinese monopoly on tea, Britain offered land in Assam to any European who agreed to cultivate tea for export.

A man named Dr. Arthur Campbell decided to try planting some *Camellia sinensis* in the hills surrounding the mountain town of Darjeeling. As Darjeeling was in British colonial territory, the seeds of *Camellia sinensis sinensis* (a small-leaf, hybrid tea only found in China) were brought from Kumeon; and as a result of successful cultivation in the area, nurseries were established by the British government in 1847. The English were delighted; Darjeeling tea was very different from the tea grown in Assam, which was a big-leaf variety called *Camellia sinensis assamica.*

All tea estates were permanently owned by the West Bengal state government, which leased the land to the growers on a fixed-rent basis for a minimum of thirty years and a maximum of ninety-nine years, renewable after expiry of the lease. The leases could be transferred or sold, but for the lease to be renewed, it must be shown that in fact *only* Darjeeling tea was being grown.

The workers in Darjeeling district were mostly Nepali women; this was because they had "the right temperament and a woman's touch."

Were these people of Nepali ethnic background really the indigenous peoples who lived in the district back in the 1800s, or were they Nepali Gurkhas who emigrated from Nepal at the behest of the colonial government to work the tea plantations?

It's complicated, certainly way more complicated than I could explain, but this question was at the core of the Gurkha push for statehood for the Darjeeling area.

Personally, at the time, I was interested only in whether any persons had recently arrived from smallpox endemic areas in Nepal or Bangladesh and could potentially be a source of smallpox importations. Tea plantation workers fell into two categories: permanent, those who lived on the estate with their families in estate lodging, and temporary, those hired during the busy picking season.

One of the supervisors got into our vehicle to show us around the estate. We headed to the lodgings because the workers were still out in the field. We went house to house to show the identification card and to ask about rash-and-fever cases. There were some sick children, but they had coughs and colds and runny noses—the normal illnesses one would expect to see at high altitude, given the use of lightweight clothing. The workers lived in three separate areas surrounded by tea plants. As we walked past the tea trees, the supervisor gave us an impromptu lecture on why Darjeeling tea was so admired and desired.

Tea in Darjeeling was harvested four times a year: around March, around June, in late summer, and in the fall. Winter was the dormant season in Darjeeling, and it began in November. The first harvest was called first flush. The second was called second flush. The third was during the rainy season, so it was called monsoon flush. The fourth was autumnal flush.

"Harvest means that only the first two leaves and a bud are plucked—the word for picking the tea leaves. Pluckers must be careful to pick only those leaves, no other," said the supervisor. "This means that one plucker picks about five hundred grams a day—a little over a pound." That seemed like slim pickings to me.

"First flush does not necessarily mean finest quality. It simply means a tea harvested in the spring. It has a delicate tea color, but with a strong bite," the supervisor continued. "Many of our clients, particularly in Japan and the United States, prefer second flush. That is a darker, stronger tea." Also, generally speaking, it was the most expensive.

We left our vehicle and walked to the next lodgings area. "Where are the children?" I asked.

"The tea plantation provides free schooling, and they are at school," he replied.

The area was very quiet, and no one seemed to be at home. "Where are the men if only the women pick the tea?" I asked. He answered that some men were hired as supervisors—*Typical,* I thought, *no woman can be a supervisor*—and others had to search for work outside the estate. To me, the housing looked good (a bedroom, a kitchen, and a toilet with a free water supply), certainly better than a lot of the poor villages in Jalpaiguri and Cooch Behar. We trudged back to our parked jeep.

Tea cultivation was on steep, hilly terrain, and although I had been up in the mountains for a week, I was still feeling some effects of high altitude. We headed to the area where the women off-loaded the tea they had collected that day into the collection baskets. This was a time-limited operation. The planters didn't want the tea to just sit around.

As soon as the supervisors had the tea, I turned to the women and showed them the smallpox identification card. They listened intently but said there were no rash-and-fever cases. I mentioned they might have family or visitors from outside, and at any sign of rash and fever, they should alert their supervisors or the estate manager.

They started their walk home. In some ways they had it good, with free accommodation and half their pay in cash. The other half was in kind: subsidized cereal rations of rice or wheat, tea, free medical benefits for all members of their family, and free primary schooling. Sometimes, as the season changed, they received blankets or shoes or firewood. At least that was the theory.

Still, it was a sort of indentured labor, and it would be hard for a worker's family to just get up and leave and look for a better job. They were effectively tied here to Darjeeling, and it would be next to impossible to leave this work.

That made me reflect on my own situation. I could stop work anytime and search for a better job. I could seek other positions that were meaningful, important, tantalizing, energizing, and fun. I felt like anything was possible. There seemed to be no limits. In fact, I didn't have to limit myself to working in the United States, where race, color, and ethnicity were too often impediments. Who would have thought that I would have to come to India to gain this perspective?

Meanwhile, I was invited for tea at the big house, and I needed to get going. The manager was highly welcoming. "Come in, Dr. Davis. Tell me more about your smallpox work," he said.

And so I launched in about the work in Jalpaiguri and Cooch Behar. *Wow, what a view*, I thought, as I glanced out the living room window over the rows of tea bushes. The manager handed me a cup of Darjeeling tea, the type that would be described as second flush. It was perfect to savor in front of a roaring fire.

And then I asked him, "Where can I buy Darjeeling tea? My mom goes crazy over this, and I have tried a number of shops on the plaza, but everyone shakes their head no. I mean, you would think it would be sold on every doorstep."

The manager laughed and said, "You can't buy Darjeeling tea here!"

He described the process. The tea leaves were first dried on long wire racks overnight, with blowers that were cool in the daytime and warm at night, in the factory on the estate.

The leaves were then scooped up, curled, and bruised, usually by machine.

The curling and fermentation was actually a second drying process. The curled leaf would produce moisture that oxidized the leaf. How long the leaves were allowed to ferment depended on the nose and judgment of the tea planter. Black tea was 90 percent oxidized, and then it was dried to stop the process and preserve it from spoilage. Then it was sent straight to Calcutta to the tea auctions.

Tea was graded by size. Large, whole leaf tea was generally higher quality. The dust, or "fannings," was sold for teabags.

"Darjeeling tea fetches a high price on the international market and is almost exclusively sold overseas," he explained. And then he gallantly came forward with a kilo of top-quality Darjeeling with the estate logo on the package. "Please accept this gift of tea."

I said, "I know my mom will be thrilled when I tell her that her tea came right from the tea estate. I hate to run, but I must get going, because I need to descend to Siliguri today. Thank you so much for your hospitality and the tea."

Darjeeling was not the problem. It was Cooch Behar. I needed to get back to my difficult districts and see how my vaccinators on the border with Bangladesh were faring. *Christ, I need to pay them,* I thought as the jeep started its descent to the terai.

21

OH GOD, WE JUST KILLED
A SACRED COW!

I checked in with the good sisters, and they were relieved that I looked so much better than the last time they had seen me, when I was practically at death's door. The next day, I went with the team to the CMO's office, where I had several messages. The first was that there was an important meeting in Cooch Behar with all the smallpox vaccinators, and I needed to be there before 9:00 a.m. *tomorrow*. The other message alerted me to a West Bengal meeting of smallpox supervisors. I needed to make arrangements to fly back down to Calcutta in three weeks.

I spent the day doing chores like going to the bank and replenishing funds into the account. I had been carrying the cash from Calcutta when I got sick and was unable to go by the bank. Then I thought that although I didn't need to check in with the police, I should drop by just to let them know I was alive and well.

I picked up some clean clothes that I had left behind in Jalpaiguri. Yes, clean clothes didn't become clean without me, or somebody, to clean them. This someone was the *dhobi*. It was generally a hereditary profession (caste), with most of the washermen's families working in the trade for two or maybe three generations.

Their technique had remained virtually unchanged through the centuries. Soiled clothes were first soaked in boiling water with caustic soda and then flogged or beaten on stones beside the riverbank, or on a concrete slab, to physically rid them of dirt and stains. The clothes were then laid on the riverbank some distance from the flowing water and allowed to dry. After drying them in the open, the clothes were pressed with antique charcoal-fueled irons with heavy wooden handles. To heat the iron, the washerman would open it, place small pieces of charcoal inside it, and then close it. What always amazed me was that my clothes were never mixed up with other people's clothes, and not once was a shirt, blouse, or pair of pants ever scorched by an iron that was too hot. Nevertheless, the beating of the clothes on the stones of the riverbank did quickly age them and make them show early signs of fraying. I needed to start looking for some new replacement kurtas.

The next morning, we left early to drive to Cooch Behar in order to get there in time. It was foggy, which was a new complication. Usually in the terai there was heavy rain, but I hadn't seen fog before. The fog was limiting how fast we could go. This stretch of the road was narrow anyway, so our car lights were on, and the windshield wipers were busily making that whooshing sound. All of a sudden an animal came from the left, bearing down on us from a slope.

"Abdul, watch out," I shouted. He almost simultaneously saw the cow. He swerved the jeep sharply to the right, and the wheels skidded on the rain-slick road. The jeep's left bumper hit the cow, and that impact tossed us skidding to the edge of an embankment.

I remember thinking, *Oh shit, we are going over the side.* Thankfully, a tree was in our path. We slammed into it, and that prevented us from going over the edge. I jumped up on my seat and turned around to see the cow on its side, motionless.

Then I heard yelling coming from the village, and saw about eight farmers running out to accost us. Abdul was smashing the gears and going back and forth to rock the jeep out of the deep groove our skidding tire had made.

"Don't you think we should stop and talk to them?" I said. "If we killed the cow, I can pay for it. What if it belongs to a really poor family? They will be devastated."

There was no convincing Abdul to stay. We tore out of there with the villagers running after us.

Crap, now what do we do? We were still about forty minutes from the smallpox meeting location.

Dinesh said, "The district magistrate or some other official will be at the meeting. You can discuss the accident then."

In one part of my brain, I knew we couldn't stop. I remembered too well the taxi incident in Calcutta. But in the other part of my brain, I was imagining the ruin of a family at the loss of their sustenance for milk, yogurt, and dung for the fire.

Of course, as soon as we got to the meeting, I was ensconced on the speaking platform with other district notables, including the magistrate. We launched into the meeting, and at my turn to speak I gave out the report of what I had seen in the various villages we had supervised. Only about half of the villages had the painted slogans announcing the reward for reporting a rash-and-fever case. Although most villagers could not read Hindi or Bengali, just the act of painting the information would push the people to ask the vaccinator what he was writing. In this way the message was passed on.

We had a good turnout of local administrative people, not just the health authorities, for the meeting. Because the smallpox program was a high priority, the federal government wanted all administrative officials, from the civil service to the railroad to the private tea estates, to know about it and to provide whatever assistance might be needed. This meeting was also an opportunity for the workers to turn in forms and to collect salaries. I had already mentioned that when I arrived in the Tri-District area, workers had not seen a paycheck for three months. So of course they were anxious about whether the funds had arrived.

It appeared that the West Bengal coffers were lean, and it wasn't only the smallpox vaccinators who were without funds. All the civil authorities were in the same fix. So with the funds I had available, I put petrol in the jeeps of supervisory personnel and paid workers doing special containment activities. But I certainly didn't have funds to pay regular wages.

These district meetings had a protocol. First we heard reports from supervisors and field staff, and then the CMO discussed new information from Delhi from the smallpox program. Afterward, we were given something to eat, and then we dispersed. I guessed that the best time to approach the police superintendent was while everyone was relaxed and having tea and samosas.

I gave Dinesh the secret wink to come over to me and said, "Let's tell the police superintendent now."

"Hello, Dr. Davis. I haven't seen your jeep in these parts for a while," said the superintendent.

"Yes, well, I was sick with some gastroenteritis that I picked up in Calcutta, and then I was recuperating in the mountains. But I need to speak to you about something urgent," I said. "This morning we were rushing here for the meeting; it was very early, and there was heavy fog. A cow came out of nowhere, and we hit it, and then the villagers started running after us, so we didn't stop. I want to report it. Now, what should I do to repay the farmer who owned the cow?"

He asked where the incident occurred and then said, "Was your jeep bashed in or hurt in any way? These farmers have to control their animals. If anything, the farmer should pay you to repair any damages to the jeep."

Christ, now I am getting the farmer into trouble, I thought. "No, my jeep is OK," I replied. "There is no need to send your staff to the village."

He went on to tell me that he didn't think there would be trouble.

Well, at least I reported it, I thought, and then I said to my team, "Let's just continue on, contact our vaccinators, and see how they are doing on the border." I tried to put the accident out of my mind.

The deal I had with the temporary vaccination workers was that they were to work daily, except Sundays. I would not know when I would be coming next. If I came and no one was there, then I would assume they had *not* been working and I would not pay for any of the seven or ten days they might have worked. If they were on the job, I would pay immediately.

We started at the official crossing and found that the staff were there. They turned in their lists of the number of persons vaccinated each day. I had made up these little chits, and all I had to do now was to fill in the worker's name, as I understood it, and then take his thumb or index finger and press it on my inkpad and then on the chit. Then I would hand him his wages.

When we got to the informal crossings, my vaccinator would come out of the bushes. Since there were few cars or jeeps, the vaccinator who worked evenings would hear the vehicle and then come out with his simple tally sheets to show how many people he had vaccinated. He would be delighted to receive the money. We would check his supplies to see if he had enough vaccines.

When I asked a vaccinator if he had any trouble, he would say, "The word was put out for everyone to cooperate with us and get vaccinated." Funny, the vaccinators at the informal crossings were vaccinating far more than those who were serving travelers going through official channels. With the business all wrapped up, we headed back to Jalpaiguri.

It was 4:00 p.m. and still light outside, but we had some distance to go. We would have to pass through the village with the dead cow; thankfully, it would be dark by then. Abdul was still adamant that it was not a good idea to stop. We would just speed through.

I was really feeling guilty. I just couldn't live with myself; it would be easy for me to pay the cost of a cow. So I had to pull rank. I said, "We are going to stop and inquire about the owner. I will pay the money, and then we will leave."

The mood in the vehicle was pretty glum. Villages were jet black at night because no one wasted kerosene just to light up a house. We slowed down, and Abdul kept the motor going, just in case.

"OK, just honk once so they know we are here," I said. With the honk, we saw a wave of people coming out of their huts.

There was one older fellow who looked like a leader, so I rolled down the window and said to him, "This morning there was a lot of fog, and a cow came out suddenly, and we accidentally hit it—"

Before I could continue my sentence, the headman started jabbering in Bengali. Maybe this was not such a great idea. Then Dinesh started translating. "He said that he saw everything, and it was not our fault. The cow should have been tied up. And it's OK; it just has a small gash on its right front leg. It will be fine."

The headman said, "Thank you for stopping. Not a lot of *bari admi*"—big folk—"would do that."

I was so relieved it wasn't dead. I smiled and said we needed to be on our way. I was thankful that we had stopped and found out the truth; otherwise, to this day, I would bear the guilt of killing a sacred cow.

22

THE THIRD SEX

I always found fieldwork refreshing and fun. You never knew what you would find just around the corner. Word was getting out about the reward for just reporting a rash-and-fever case, so my team had no end of rumors to analyze and then determine which to investigate. After discussing a rumor with an informer, we would put him in the back of the jeep so he could take us to the village. Instead of trying to search for a village with a strange pronunciation, it was easier just to transport the person with us.

When heading into any village, it was always politic to ask to speak to the headman and tell him why we were there. If a leader accompanied us, we received a better reception from the villagers; they were less suspicious. On other trips, we had the district medical officer, the CMO, or a smallpox worker to show us the way.

The first thing I wanted to know was if a smallpox work-er had been to the village recently and when the last visit was. I remember one time when I was getting less than full cooperation from a medical doctor in a health clinic. By state directive, he was to stop all work and accompany the team if I so desired, as long as there was no pending clinical emergency. I had selected the village with my famous closed-eyes-and-finger-tapping-the-map method, and the physician had shaken his head and said, "No, this is a very difficult village to access. Choose another one."

"But I selected this one, and I want to see it," I countered. Then he went into a fifteen-minute discourse about how far away it was and how we would need lots of petrol. I told him that petrol was not a problem for us. Then he told us that there was a river that we would have to swim across because there was no bridge.

I said, "No problem." Actually, it was a problem if the river was deep; I was not the best of swimmers. My intuition told me that maybe there wasn't a river.

Since I remained unconvinced of the difficulty that lay ahead, he stated that after crossing the river, we would not have a car, and the village was another ten kilometers down the road.

I said, "Well, we'd best get going, because this is the village I want to see."

The doctor was not a happy camper. We got to the river in less than one hour. In truth, the river was about four jeep lengths wide and moving slowly. I looked around to see if I could find a tree branch that I could use to measure the depth. No such luck.

OK, God, let's not have this river be very deep, I thought. *You know I am not really a great swimmer.*

I decided to take off my Birkenstocks so as not to lose them in the water. I put them in my daypack and then started to roll up my cotton trousers. I was guessing the water might come up to my knees. As I started to roll the pants up past my ankles, I noticed that everyone was staring at my legs and getting embarrassed. I recognized that seeing a foreign woman's ankles was somehow erotic, so I quickly changed my mind. Evidently it was better to let my pants legs get wet.

Dinesh and I started out together to cross the river. Thank God it wasn't flowing swiftly. The bottom was firm mud, and there were not too many pebbles or big stones. The first step was above the ankle, and the next steps were to the middle of the calf and then to the knees. We grabbed each other's hands to steady ourselves.

I turned around and said to the doctor, "Are you coming?" We continued and were already at the halfway point before he stepped into the water. Fortunately, the water only went two inches above the knee. We got to the other side without mishap. I pulled my shoes from the pack. Of course my long pants were clinging seductively to my legs. What to do? I reasoned that when we started walking they would dry out fairly quickly.

It turned out the village was not ten kilometers down the road; it was only two kilometers. *What an asshole.* When we arrived, there were plenty of villagers who gathered round. I introduced myself and talked about smallpox.

Then I asked, "So, when was the last time you saw a smallpox worker?"

This elicited a rapid response: "No one has been here for two years!"

Then we heard an earful. Christ, this was one of the most unpleasant villages I had come across. Clearly, no supervision had occurred for at least two years. The villagers were angry. I looked at the doctor quizzically. I was disappointed. This was definitely a write-up to the district authorities and the state.

I initially thought my method of selecting villages was haphazard. But it was crazy how this method found the smallpox cases in Bangladesh, led me to the subdivision with the smugglers, and invariably found the villages that had been neglected. Best to stick to my method.

I was now proficient at walking the perimeters of paddy fields. My balance was perfect, and I rarely toppled into a field (much to the grateful satisfaction of the farmers).

My team had developed a method of evaluating the villages. After seeing the headman and ascertaining if the village had seen a worker, we would roughly divide the village into quarters by direction and interview houses to the north, south, east, and west. We would check to see if the worker had written any slogans on the walls about rewards and if he had vaccinated any newborn children. Usually I could draw a crowd, and after searching selected houses, I would try to gauge their awareness of the program. I was always amazed at the questions they asked me.

Women invariably wanted to know about the baby boy who was depicted on the smallpox recognition card. I didn't know who took the photo, but it was in color, on a laminated five-by-four-inch piece of paper. The front of the card showed the front of the baby, and on the flip side was the back of the baby. The women wanted to know his name, where he lived, whether he was Hindu or Muslim, his age, and whether he survived! The first time I was asked these questions, I was puzzled. Then I looked closely at the photo and noticed that he was circumcised. So I made him a Muslim. Then I thought up a common name for a boy. He was between nine and eleven months old.

I said I didn't know what state he was living in. I didn't know whether to make him survive, or whether I would get more cooperation if I said he had died. So I did a little survey in different villages. In one, I said he lived; and in another, some distance from the first, I said he died. The women would really get upset about a boy child dying, so I subsequently made him live. It wasn't worth the drama.

Men, on the other hand, had lots of questions about the reward: When would an informer get paid? How would they get the reward? What if two people reported the same person in the same village? My team was inundated with rumors.

The all-too-prevalent caste system continued to discompose me. I could never tell when I would be treated as a high-caste male or as an untouchable. Sometimes the poorer, lower-caste section could answer all my questions about small-pox and vaccination. But when I queried the higher castes, particularly the Brahmins, in the same village, they would be clueless. It was decidedly strange, because those who wore the sacred thread across their chest were usually knowledgeable and up to date on information.

One day we stopped at a pukka house, and the Brahmin who lived there was really ignorant about the local smallpox worker and even said he had never, ever seen him in the village. Yet, over in another section, the villagers swore the worker had been coming regularly. I was tired, it was a very humid day, and we had been traipsing through this village for about an hour. The village fanned out over a wide area, and we were some distance from the jeep, where my trusty thermos bottle was ensconced. I was perspiring like a racehorse and really thirsty. I wasn't thinking, and I blurted to the Brahmin, "Can I have a glass of water?"

Immediately I wanted to somehow take back my question. I had forgotten he was highborn, and now there was going to be an incident. He gave me a puzzled look, a quick frown crossed his features, and he withdrew abruptly and closed the door. I turned to Dinesh and was about to make a sarcastic remark when the door opened abruptly again. There was the Brahmin with a tall glass of water in his hand. He held it out to me; I could tell it had come from the earthenware vessel that kept drinking water cool and clean for the family. I was so thirsty I just gulped it down. I smiled at him and said, "Thank you for the cooling water—it was like a gift from the gods!"

He reached out for the glass and took it from my hand. And then he turned to the side and smashed the glass on the doorstep. Without another word, he closed the door and retreated inside. On the one hand, he had chosen to recognize me, the Western woman, and talk to me. So at that moment, the Western woman was more like a regular male. But on the other hand, by smashing that glass, he clearly showed that I had defiled the object, it was no longer pure, and it could never be used again by his family. It made no matter that I was a foreigner and working for WHO; I was untouchable in his eyes.

I wanted to knock on the door again and say, "Look, if it was such a big deal, why didn't you just say you didn't have any water?" Then I glimpsed some lower-caste women hauling dirty water from a stream, and it dawned on me that this village was extremely traditional. No lower caste could use the well that was centrally located in the village.

I would not be changing the mind-set of the people in this village. When we got back to the sub divisional level, I asked about the smallpox worker assigned to that hamlet. Turned out he was low caste. He could not even approach the houses of the higher castes in that place; he knew he was not welcome. No wonder the Brahmin had not seen a worker. I asked the medical officer to send a higher-caste worker to the village to inform them about smallpox.

What I really wanted to do was to put the lower-caste worker in my jeep and return to the village and knock on the doors of the higher castes. It would make me feel good, but I would not accomplish anything but stroking my ego. So I let it go, this time.

There were other villages, mostly Muslim, where another problem would present itself. Since I was a woman, I could go into any house and talk to the women. I was never forbidden, in all my time in India doing smallpox work, to talk to the women. However, in Muslim villages, the women were in purdah.

Purdah comes from the Persian word for "curtain," and it was a religious and social custom of female seclusion observed by some women in Afghanistan, Bangladesh, Pakistan, and northern India. Put simply, it was the practice of preventing men from seeing women.

There were two forms of this custom: the actual physical segregation of the sexes and the requirement that women cover their bodies so as to conceal their hair, skin, and form. Physical segregation within a home was achieved with the astute use of walls, curtains, and screens. A woman's withdrawal into purdah normally restricted her personal, social, and economic activities outside her home. The usual purdah garment was a *burqa*, which may or may not include a veil to conceal the face. The eyes may or may not be exposed.

Historians believe purdah was originally a Persian practice that the Muslims adopted during the Arab conquest of modern-day Iraq in the seventh century. Later, Muslim rule of northern India during the Mughal Empire influenced the practice of Hinduism, and purdah even spread to the Hindu upper classes of northern India. During the British colonial period in India, purdah observance was widespread and strictly adhered to among the Muslim minority. In modern times, the practice of veiling and secluding women was still present in mainly Islamic communities in India. However, the practice was not always inflexible and rigid. Purdah could take on different forms and significance depending on the region, time, socioeconomic status, and local culture.

Some scholars argue that purdah was initially designed to protect women from being harassed. Later, these practices became a way to subjugate women and limit their mobility and freedom. Others claim that these practices were always in place as local custom but were later incorporated into religious rhetoric to control female behavior. Muslim men told me that purdah was a symbol of honor, respect, and dignity. It was seen as a practice that allowed women to be judged by their inner beauty rather than physical beauty. In many societies, the seclusion of women in the domestic sphere was a demonstration of higher socioeconomic status and prestige because *their* women were not needed for manual labor outside the home.

Another important aspect of purdah was modesty for women, which included minimizing the movement of women in public spaces and interactions of women with other males. The specific customs varied widely based on religion, region, class, and culture. For instance, for some, purdah might mean a woman never leaving the home unless accompanied by a male relative; for some Muslims, it might mean limiting her interactions to only other women and male relatives; and for some Hindus, it might mean avoiding all males outside of the immediate family. For Muslims, seclusion began at puberty, whereas for Hindus, seclusion began after marriage.

The rationale of individual women for keeping purdah was complex and complicated and could be a combination of motivations: religious, cultural (desire for authentic cultural dress), political (Islamization of the society), economic (status symbol, protection from the public gaze), psychological (detachment from public sphere to gain respect), fashion and decorative purposes, and empowerment (donning veils to move in public space).

My view of purdah was formulated after working and traveling extensively not only in India during smallpox days but also in Pakistan, Afghanistan, the United Arab Emirates, and Indonesia. By restricting women's mobility, purdah resulted in the social and physical isolation of women. The lack of a strong social network placed a woman in a position of vulnerability with her husband and her husband's family. I saw firsthand how restrictions on women's mobility—and especially that of unmarried girls-limited their ability to access education, health care, and family-planning services. What I found in many Muslim villages was that the women had no knowledge of the smallpox program, and yet they would be most likely to notice if a child had a rash and fever.

I couldn't change purdah, but I could insist that the smallpox worker talk to the village leaders. He could request the village headman to give him a ten-year-old boy from the village to accompany him from house to house. The boy could take the recognition card into the house and show it to the women and ask about rash-and-fever cases. I spoke to the headmen of many of these traditional villages, and none ever refused to allow this practice.

I learned in India that there were really three sexes: male, female, and the Western female. Most often I found I was treated as a male in the rural areas and invited to participate in male social customs. In the big cities, I was treated as a high-caste Hindu woman because I was working for the UN, and I was a foreigner. With my smallpox driver and paramedic, basically I was a male, although they treated me like a sister. With caste taboos and the purdah followed in these traditional villages, the Western woman was viewed as free, independent, and even, in some sense, easy. She was a threat just for being there and introducing another way of living. My team was always around me and was very protective of me, treating me like a sister.

I was never personally confronted by any Eve-teasing, a euphemism used in India for public sexual harassment or molestation of women by men, with the word "Eve" used as a reference to the biblical first woman. It was a form of sexual aggression that ranged in severity from sexually suggestive remarks and catcalls to brushing up against women in public places and outright groping. Sometimes it was used with the coy suggestion of innocent fun, making it appear innocuous, with no resulting liability on the part of the perpetrator.

In the 1970s, most Indian women were raised to be submissive and passive. I didn't fall in either category. When doing up-country fieldwork, I was never alone. One or more of my team was always with me. Nevertheless, I roamed the streets in the urban areas such as Delhi and Calcutta alone. I walked confidently and fearlessly in the street. I think if any male had dared to accost me, I would have turned on the fool and confronted him. I think the men could sense this, and they just left me alone.

My days had a certain routine to them. Now, though, I had the notice about the West Bengal smallpox meeting, so I needed to return to Calcutta. The Tibetan rug I ordered was probably ready for pickup. And surely my Tibetan chuba outfit was ready and waiting. I planned to wear it to the state meeting.

23

PAY IT FORWARD

It seemed a long time since I'd gone to Caritas to see Father LaFerla and to rummage through my stash of clothes there. My kurtas and shalwar kameez were taking a beating, so to speak, on the rocks of the riverbanks. They were starting to look threadbare. As I got closer, I was thinking that Caritas was always getting in used clothing, and maybe I could pick up a shirt or jeans or something just to lounge around in at night.

I liked coming back to Caritas because it felt like home, but not just because all my extra stuff was in the duffel bag there. I missed the good conversation and beer with Father LaFerla.

"Hi, Connie, how has it been going?" asked Father LaFerla. "We have missed you."

I told him about the Brahmin smashing the glass on the ground and the village that had not been visited for two years. "So I see things are going as smoothly as usual for you, Connie!" he said.

And I replied, "Well, that's one way of looking at it. Father, my clothes are starting to look a little ragged. Have you gotten any shipments of used clothes lately?"

"You're in luck," he said. "We just got a shipment this morning from Calcutta. Go take a look. There are some clothes that even we can't give away, things like your American Levi jeans. The men are just not interested, so you have a wide choice."

I headed over to the warehouse section to see the latest arrivals. The work had stopped for lunch. There must have been two dozen tables piled with clothes in various stages of being unwrapped and displayed. Items of clothing were stacked twenty pieces deep, and I had to flip items to the side to see what was underneath. The first pile I came to was of children's clothes. I was searching for another table when something caught my attention. It was just the edge of a shirt, but the hem of the sleeve and the pattern—a fine pinstripe in white and forest green—attracted me. That was all I could see, just the sleeve hem and about an inch of the shirt, but something about it seemed familiar. I started getting this feeling in my stomach.

I tried to pull out the sleeve, but the weight of the other clothes did not allow that. So I rapidly flipped off the top layers. *No, I don't believe it.* This shirt was identical to one that I used to own and that I had worn at Girl Scout camp, when the sleeve hems had gotten frayed. Now what was the likelihood that this was my shirt? Well, there was one way to tell. Mom always ironed a name tag into my camp clothes so I wouldn't lose them. I jerked open the shirt and went straight to the neckband, where I found a slightly worn name tag that was frayed around the edges and clearly read "Cornelia Davis"!

I grabbed the shirt and ran out shouting, "Father LaFerla! You won't believe this in a thousand years. I found a shirt that belonged to me!"

I guess my mom must have given it to Saint Vincent de Paul. I had told her I wouldn't need my camp clothes anymore. But what were the odds that I would find my own shirt in India, in Cooch Behar?

Father LaFerla just looked incredulous and laughed.

"Wait till I tell Mom," I cheered. "She won't believe it." And so I recuperated my own shirt, which had been given away to someone needier than me. I took this as a sign of forces greater than me, of strange currents in the air. It was unbelievable. The next day I headed for Darjeeling. There was some local holiday in Darjeeling, and it would be a good time to head up and collect the items I had ordered.

Up on the mountain, I couldn't wait to ditch my things and head down the path to the Tibetan Refugee Self-Help Center to see if my blue custom rug was ready. My last time here, my rug was just a few warp threads on a loom and a little tag with my name. Now the helper went to search for the finished product. And there it was in his hands, my first oriental carpet. Tibetan carpets are distinctive, because once the design is woven into the pile, the weaver cuts out around the design so that it stands out. It was exquisite. I immediately hired a bicycle rickshaw to lug the rug and me to the club. The rug looked stunning in my room on the floor in front of the fireplace.

Then I went in search of that tailor I had commissioned to make my Tibetan dress. I was a little nervous about the chuba. The tailor had only taken a few loose measurements. There was no room for me to try on the clothes at the tailor's shop, so I said I would take them home, and I privately prayed that they would fit. I put on the white blouse, and the sleeves went eight inches beyond my wrists. I'd forgotten that I needed to roll the sleeves up. And then I slipped the chuba over my head and let it fall to the floor. I closed the bodice and tied the Bhutanese material in the back. And then I added the striped wool Tibetan apron. I thought I looked stunning! Soon enough I'd see what the people at state level thought.

I was heading back to the Gymkhana Club when I ran into Amal, a friend I had met when I was recuperating from my bout of shigella diarrhea. He was an Indian civil servant, and he was young, my age. During my R and R, while I was getting my strength back, he had noticed me hiking around Darjeeling.

He stopped me on the path and said, "Some friends of mine and I are heading out for a lightning-fast trip to Sikkim tomorrow during the local festival. I remembered you were pining to go there; I'm glad I ran into you. We can't stay over-night, for various reasons, but there is space in the jeep. Come with us."

A quick day trip? Tomorrow? I think a myriad of expressions raced across my face.

"Look, Connie, I told you this trip is a no-brainer. We go all the time. You will not need your passport. You can pass for Indian. What is the problem?"

I was thinking of all the problems. What if I was caught crossing the border? Technically, I had the Indian permits. I just didn't have WHO permission. So many thoughts were racing through my mind. This was my one chance. I mean, just running into Amal was providential.

Then he said with a smile, "OK, there is one caveat. Can you demurely keep your eyes cast down like a sweet, submissive Indian woman and let me, a male, respond to all questions? They will stop us perfunctorily, just to make sure we are Indians. I'm not sure you are capable or willing to let me answer for you. You cannot look directly at the border guard, and you cannot answer him directly. Now that will be a feat for you!"

Oh, I did so want to go with them.

He saw the gleam in my eyes. "We will come by the club at seven thirty tomorrow morning. Be ready!" And he was off.

Now I had done it. I had gotten away with the last border escapade because it was work related. But what was my excuse for this? Dr. Grasset could not have been more explicit. I recalled her precise words: "Under no circumstances are you to go to Sikkim."

Despite that, I had been reading some books on Younghusband and his trip leading a British expedition to Tibet and his return through Sikkim. And damn it, what really could go wrong?

I won't say I had a good night's sleep before the big adventure. I had ordered a takeaway breakfast, as I wanted nothing to delay me or hinder my departure. I scarfed it down and headed out to the parking lot. And I tried to look nonchalant.

They were on time. That was a miracle right there, as Indians were notorious for having a different time schedule from Westerners. Amal had a friend with him. "Aanand, this is Connie; she'll sit in the front to have the best view. I was thinking that we would go straight to Gangtok and then stop at Kalimpong on the way back. OK with everyone?"

"It's OK by me," I said. And we took off.

The sun was up, and there were no clouds in sight. It was going to be a perfect day, I could tell. Soon we were flying along on National Highway 31A, heading for Sikkim.

The terraces of tea trees were neat in rows, and as we got farther from Darjeeling, the tea gave way to whole tracts of forests. The road was paved but narrow; there wasn't much room for maneuvering. We were in luck that there was not much traffic on the road, yet. We stopped at a chai shop after an hour, as the guys had not eaten anything before leaving. Why did tea and *chapati* (flatbread) taste so much better when on holiday?

Ah, Sikkim. The name had been coined from *su him*, which means "beautiful home." I think it would be better if it were named something like "abode of the mountains." The snow-covered mountains and lush green valleys not only invigorated our souls but left us in wonder of the extravaganza of their natural beauty. Nearly 40 percent of the total area of Sikkim was forested.

For a long period of time, Sikkim was a Buddhist kingdom, isolated in the Himalayas, populated by Lepcha and Bhotia—two tribes of Tibetan origin—and governed by the Namgyal dynasty from Tibet. Sikkim was declared a British protectorate in 1861. The British government encouraged the immigration of Nepalese workers.

A large proportion of the population was of Nepalese origin. Sikkim was an Indian protectorate from 1947 onward. In May 1975, after various intrigues, the king of Sikkim was forced to resign, and Sikkim became the twenty-second federal state of India.

We had passed Kalimpong earlier, and I was getting nervous. We would soon be coming to the border with Sikkim. Now the fun would begin. Amal could see I was getting nervous.

"Hey, Connie, relax! We will be arriving in Rangpo in about ten minutes. You don't have to do anything."

"Good," I replied. I was watching for a big crossing point, so when we reached the border, I was surprised to see just a few offices and some border guards. Still, I was nervous. I told myself that I had nothing to fear—everyone kept telling me I looked Indian.

A border guard came over to the driver's side, and Amal rolled down the window.

"Namaste. How are you?" said the guard in Hindi as he looked at the three of us. My heart was pounding at 140 beats per minute. I willed myself to continue looking straight ahead with my eyes downcast. I could barely detect the outline of the guard from the corner of my eye.

"So, where are you going?" the guard asked.

"Got the day off for the festival, and we were just going to Gangtok," said Amal.

"And who is this?" he asked, gesturing at me.

"Oh, this is my cousin from Delhi," said Amal. "Her name is Amita. I'm showing her the sights around Darjeeling."

I kept telling myself to just continue to look down.

"How long are you staying?"

"This is only a day trip from Darjeeling; I have too much to do to stay overnight. And actually Aanand also needs to get back tonight."

"Have a good trip," said the guard, and then he indicated we could proceed.

The jeep moved forward. Though I could finally breathe, I kept still until I could no longer see the guard station in the side mirror. Then I looked at Amal, and we burst out laughing.

"This was it?" I said. "And where did you get the name Amita?" It turned out that Amal actually had a cousin by that name, and he was prepared to answer any questions based on his cousin's background.

We got to Gangtok fairly rapidly. At the time, it was a sleepy little town, and it didn't take long to go through it. I wanted to see the view, and so we headed to the Tashi viewpoint. The overlook was about eight kilometers from Gangtok town. It offered a sweeping view of Kanchenjunga's snowcapped peaks on a clear day. On the opposite side, on the mountains, you could see the Phodong and Labrang monasteries.

"So, where is the road to Nathula Pass?" I asked.

Nathula Pass, at an altitude of 14,140 feet and fifty-two kilometers from Gangtok, was an offshoot of the famed Silk Road, and for centuries it was a main trade route between India and Tibet. Lines of mules used to carry silk, gold, and many other items from Tibet to India and take daily essentials back to Tibet. The route in Tibet headed down the Chumbi Valley to Yathung, a place about thirty kilometers away; it once was a major trading township. When the Sino-Indian War broke out in 1962, the border at Nathula was closed. In 1967 a major confrontation took place there between China and India over the placement of border fencing. Many lives were lost on both sides.

Amal said, "Nathula Pass has been closed since 1962, even for Indians. It would take us almost a whole day just to reach the closed area. So you are not going to Tibet today, Connie! Let's head back to Gangtok and get something to eat."

I wanted to eat some good momos, so we searched for a restaurant. It was good to be out of the jeep, and there was nothing like cold beer and momos. Around 1:00 p.m., Amal said, "We best start heading back so we can stop for a little while in Kalimpong."

As we started back, I said, "I'm going to pretend that I am taking a nap on the way back through the checkpoint." Actually, I didn't have to pretend. With a full stomach and the effects of the beer, when I closed my eyes, the rhythm of the jeep created a sensation of being rocked in a cradle, and I was out cold. Two hours later, Amal nudged me and said, "Connie, wake up; we are approaching Kalimpong. We can do a little shopping."

Kalimpong, back in the day, was a main trading hub. It was much reduced by 1975, and the main street was dirty and muddy. But there were a few shops run by Indians, and I spied some dress material for a chuba. That was my main purchase of the day: fabric from Bhutan bought in Kalimpong, and nothing from Sikkim.

We had no time to visit any of the monasteries in the Kalimpong area. I realized that it would take two to three days to do the tourist thing there. Still, I was so high from the trip. *Just wait until I tell my fellow epidemiologists in Calcutta*, I thought. And then I realized I could never tell them. I had been forbidden to go to Sikkim. It hit me that the secret trip to Sikkim was exciting in the doing, but being unable to brag about it meant in some strange way that it never occurred.

Amal and Aanand dropped me off at the Gymkhana Club. It felt good to return to my room, where the room boy had already lit the fireplace. I looked at my Tibetan rug on the floor and my burgundy Bhutanese material destined for a chuba, and I smiled. *Well, I did it. I saw Sikkim, and maybe I can't tell anyone in WHO, but I can sure tell the manager here of my escapade.*

24

OFF TO CALCUTTA AGAIN

Bright and early Monday morning, my jeep and driver were at the Gymkhana Club, and I had all of my things packed and ready. I thought it best to take the rug down to Caritas and not have bits and pieces of my belongings scattered through the three districts.

I needed to check out the flight departure times and pick up my ticket for Calcutta. I could already taste Chinese food melting in my mouth and thought what a brilliant diversion it would be to link up once again with my fellow epidemiologists. What was incredible for me about staying for such a length of time in India was the chance to return to places where people knew me and were genuinely happy to see me again.

Ms. Violet was at the reception desk when I arrived at the Fairlawn Hotel. "Welcome back, Dr. Davis. I hope things are going well for you up in Darjeeling," she said. She called for one of the hotel staff to cart my luggage to my room. I thought it best to dump my parcels and head straight to WHO to find out more about the venue and the objective of the state smallpox meeting. And maybe, just maybe, there would be some letters from home.

The smallpox office was a blaze of activity, with staff members rushing to and fro. The administration officer gestured for me to join him.

"I have some letters for you," he said. *Great, finally word from home.* I searched for a soft couch in some quiet place and tore into the first letter. It was from Mom, as expected, and she sounded uneasy. She wrote:

> Connie, right after I had talked to your nice director, that Dr. Henderson, a packet arrived from India. And there were four letters that arrived at the same time, but they had been opened. You won't believe this, but someone had censored the letters. Everywhere it seemed you mentioned a place name, they had taken something like a black marker and blotted out the whole name. We can get the gist of what you are experiencing, but it is strange that something like that could occur. Someone was reading your letters. Is this correct? Shouldn't you report this?

Yeah, Mom, who should I report this to, the Indian government? Protest to WHO? Still, I was astonished that with all the things the government had to do, they assigned someone to go through my mail. How did they do this? They couldn't know when I was going to write or where I would post my letters.

I complained to the head of the WHO office in Calcutta. "My mom just wrote me that she finally got the letters I posted right after I arrived in Delhi and then from Darjeeling. She said they had been censored. Black marks throughout when I mentioned a place. Every locality was erased completely. Has this happened to other staff, or are they just picking on me?"

From the looks on their faces, I could tell that this was not a usual occurrence. True, this was the Emergency, and anything could happen, but my story sounded so farfetched that I didn't even know to whom to complain. But at least I was vindicated. I did write those letters way back when, like I said I did.

Then I found out more about the meeting to be held the following day. They would be telling us some big news. In the meantime, I had the rest of the afternoon to just relax and explore. I wanted to see if I could take some pictures of typical Calcutta scenes—but somewhat surreptitiously. Taking photos in rural areas was really easy. No one complained, at least not loudly. Yet it was tricky trying to get photos of people in urban areas. I couldn't get a clear answer from any official as to whether I was committing a crime by taking photos. So I planned on finding my special rickshaw-wallah, who was normally parked right outside the Fairlawn, and then slowly go down the streets and little alleys while clicking away with my trusty Olympus camera on my lap. I wouldn't have it up to my face, so it would look like I was just sitting in the rickshaw. At least, that was my plan.

It was early August, and the weather was miserably hot and humid. Actually, the weather was always miserable in Calcutta, if you ask me. I took showers and changed clothes up to three times a day. At least I could stand in the shower there, and the dhobi-wallah had lots of work. After a quick shower, I was refreshed, and I grabbed my camera and stashed it in my purse. My favorite rickshaw-wallah was outside. I explained I just wanted to see the city, and he was to haul me around to inner-city areas that I had not previously visited. I placed the camera strategically on my lap and just aimed it out the side of the rickshaw.

We went down a street and saw a huge billboard that said in English "Keep Calcutta Clean." Spread out right in front of this billboard was a *bustee*, a slum. This one was composed of a few ramshackle huts with some plastic sheeting or cardboard tossed over each one. Pots and utensils were strewn around the area, and some of the women were bathing their little children with a bucket. (I could relate to that.) Others were cooking or just lying around. There was such a contrast between the billboard and the slum below. I took some photos and then started to feel a little uneasy. I told the rickshaw driver to return to the hotel. Enough for one day.

As we were returning, I saw a place that served *lassi*, a yogurt drink, and thought, *I need something cooling, and lassi is always cooling*. Calcutta had its own way of eating yogurt, drinking lassi, and taking tea. They used earthenware cups made of terra-cotta clay that came from the banks of the Hooghly River around Kalighat, a neighborhood built around the majestic Kali temple, where worshippers have trekked for 1,600 years to beg blessings of the black goddess. These clay cups of various sizes were called *bhar*, and the bhar-wallahs churned out cups of various sizes along with earthenware images of the goddess.

Lassi is prepared with plain yogurt, water, sugar, a pinch of salt, and some ice. When we stopped at the lassi shop, the lassi-wallah took a small wooden pestle and rotated it rapidly between his hands for some minutes. Then he poured the lassi into a bhar cup and handed it to me. It was sublime. With the last sip, I smashed the clay cup on the sidewalk outside, a custom I had learned. I loved the taste of the yogurt with the earthiness of the bhar, and I loved the finality of the smashing of the cup. You smashed the cup after taking tea and yogurt also.

The next day we epidemiologists at the Fairlawn were collected and taken to the state meeting. I felt all dressed up and somewhat out of place in my Tibetan chuba and apron. I looked great, if I may say so myself, and it certainly was easy to walk in the dress. I didn't worry that the skirt was going to suddenly fall off.

There were about 150 supervisors there from every district. Several senior WHO epidemiologists were present from Delhi. So what was this big announcement? The representative from the Delhi national program announced that the last indigenous case of smallpox had occurred on May 17, 1975. No further cases or outbreaks had been reported. India had achieved smallpox zero status. The whole audience burst out cheering, yelling, and giving hugs all around.

That is amazing, I thought. *There is no more smallpox in India! And aren't I lucky to have seen those eight cases over the border in Bangladesh?*

The federal government of India was planning big celebrations for achieving this feat, and they were scheduled to coincide with India's independence day on August 15, 1975, which was less than two weeks away. Still, the work was far from over. India could not be certified eradicated until two years following the last case.

The rest of the day we heard reports from various districts. I wondered how long WHO would need us junior epidemiologists if the country had reached zero status. As I was leaving the venue at the end of the meeting, I crossed paths with the director of the West Bengal smallpox program. He complimented me on my Tibetan dress but told me that he hoped I would wear Bengali attire next time. Guess you can't please all the people all the time.

It was time for me to return north. I couldn't wait to tell my team the news.

25

YOU MUST LEAVE IMMEDIATELY!

I started to genuinely enjoy the job once I reached a certain level of familiarity with the work. There was a certain rhythm, and I no longer worried if I was doing things correctly. I just knew. I guess that's when everything starts to fall apart.

I had returned to northern West Bengal some two weeks previously. I made a work schedule and knew where I would search and what subdivisions would be next on my list of priority areas. All was well with my world.

Then one day, we ate a late dinner when we should have been returning to our dak bungalow. It was 9:30 p.m. when we got back that August night. It had been a long day; I was exhausted.

The *chowkidar* (guard) -cook came up to me immediately. "Dr. Davis, a man from WHO Calcutta has been here all day. He's looking for you," he said. "He wouldn't say why. It seemed urgent. I don't see him right now, but he probably went to get something to eat."

Oh crap, now what? I thought. *Just when things are going fine.*

I told my team that someone was looking for us, and they should stay close. I went up to take a bucket bath. I was just finishing putting on clean clothes when there was a soft tap on the door. I opened it to a slight Indian man who looked alarmed.

He introduced himself and said, "I have been searching all day for you. I have been sent by WHO Calcutta with instructions to find you with all urgency. You must leave this place immediately!"

My first thought was that this must be some joke, only he wasn't smiling. He pulled out three letters from his messenger bag.

"Read this one first," he said. It was a plain white envelope, sealed, with my name on the front.

I tore it open and sat down on the corner of the bed. It was on WHO stationary and read: "Connie, this messenger was sent up in urgency to find you at all costs and to deliver this letter. You are in grave danger where you are currently stationed. You are to leave immediately from Cooch Behar and proceed straight to Calcutta. You are NOT to wait for morning. You are NOT to tell anyone. It does not matter what time it is. Leave immediately!"

The messenger was carrying two other letters: one addressed to the top armed forces official in my area, and the other addressed to the Jalpaiguri divisional district magistrate/police superintendent. I was to present these letters if I encountered any problems. The letters were not sealed. They stated that both parties were to give me all assistance in traveling to Calcutta. They were *not* to confiscate my vehicle. They were to provide any assistance I may need.

It does not matter what time it is. Leave immediately! These phrases rolled through my mind. I didn't know how to react. I had read the words, yet I couldn't comprehend that they were addressed to me. I looked at the guy and said, "Do you know what this is about?"

He shook his head and said, "I was told to impress on you the need to act quickly."

"Can you go get my team and ask them to come up to my room?" I asked. I glanced at my watch; it was now 10:30 p.m. and not the time to start travel. My team rushed in, and I said, "Calcutta sent a message that I need to leave this place immediately, tonight!" I handed my letter to Dinesh. "Here is the letter to me; you can read it. We have to get on the road immediately. What is the petrol situation?"

Abdul said the jeep's tank was only half full. I pulled some rupees from my handbag and said, "See if you can get the petrol station owner to open for us. We need a full tank, or we won't get too far!" He left immediately.

I turned to the messenger. "Are you to travel back down with us?"

He shook his head no. "I will find my own way back. Are you leaving tonight?"

I shook my head yes. I just needed to pack. And he was gone.

I turned to Dinesh and said, "We need to pay the folks up on the border. They need their money." How could I disappear in the night without telling at least the CMO that I had been urgently called to Calcutta? But the letter was explicit—I was not to tell anyone. I thought, *Am I to leave like a thief in the night?*

I sent Dinesh to the chowkidar to ask for our bills. I told Dinesh to tell him we had word of a case of smallpox if he asked why we were leaving at this hour.

Dinesh was off on the task. I looked around the room. Dirty clothes were piled in the corner for the dhobi. I tried to remember if I was expecting any clothes back from him.

It was hard to keep my mind on target. What could be about to happen that would be particularly bad for me if I were in the area? Only war between India and Bangladesh, and if that was the case, my goose was cooked. War was not pretty anywhere, but for a woman alone, an area surrounded on three sides by Bangladesh was definitely not the place to be!

OK, I told myself, *Davis, be systematic. Start in the bathroom and just start throwing things into your bag.* I actually didn't have a lot of clothes with me. I had left most of my belongings—including the Tibetan rug, various antique bronzes of Buddha, and a Tibetan thangka painting—at Caritas. The road went by Caritas, though, so we could stop and throw in the rest of my stuff. It seemed pretty certain that I would not be returning anytime soon.

I glanced at my watch again; it was almost 11:00 p.m. The jeep had not returned. Abdul must be having trouble finding petrol.

So I wouldn't talk to the CMO, but I could leave a letter with the doctor's guard, and he could hand it to him in the morning. I tore open all the drawers on the small desk in the bedroom until I found some plain white notepaper. I scribbled hurriedly, "Dear CMO, I was not able to talk with you last night. I received an urgent message to proceed immediately to Calcutta. I needed to leave last night. WHO will provide further information. Sincerely, Dr. Connie Davis."

I heard the rumble of a jeep in the distance. It must be Abdul. I glanced around the room one more time and wondered if I would ever return to the Tri-Districts. Only time would tell. Dinesh came up with the bill and grabbed the duffel bag. I slung my handbag over my shoulder and hit the light switch, and we quietly went down the stairs. I paid for the lodgings and signed out in the big logbook. It was final.

It was now approaching 11:30 p.m. It was the first time I was on the road this late. Before we started, Dinesh said, "We will take you to Calcutta, and we will not let anything happen to you."

I smiled ruefully as I thought, *Well, we've got it covered—a Muslim, a Hindu, and a Christian testing our karma.*

According to Hinduism and Buddhism, there is an inequality of mankind that has a cause. This inequality is due not only to heredity and environment but also to karma. In other words, it is the result of our own past actions and present doings. We alone are responsible for our happiness and our misery. We are the architects of our own fate. So what would be our fate? The jeep swung by the CMO residence, and we woke up the chowkidar to give him the letter to be delivered in the morning. Then we were off, each thinking our own solitary thoughts.

No one was on the road. It was eerily quiet. No one felt like small talk. Personally, I was thinking about dacoits and that I was going to be in deep shit when we got to Caritas. Father LaFerla would be livid that we were on the road this late. That is, if we actually got to Caritas! Besides dacoits, the greatest danger was running into animals that we couldn't see on the road. There was just a sliver of a moon. The trip was uneventful (thankfully), and we pulled up to the locked, barred Caritas gate around 2:00 a.m.

I said, "Just honk the horn once."

A voice in Hindi asked, "Who is it?"

The driver yelled out, "WHO, Dr. Davis."

The guard peered out and sternly asked, "Why are you traveling at night?" Then the big gates swung open, and we drove into the safety of the compound.

Father LaFerla had heard the noise of the gates and came to see what wayfarer had gained admission. He was surprised and concerned to see us.

"Connie, come to the study," he said. He turned to address the guard. "Get the rest of the team settled."

As I entered the study with Father LaFerla, I said, "I can explain. Look at this letter that was carried to me by a messenger from WHO Calcutta! Do you have any idea what it means?"

Father LaFerla read my letter rapidly. He gave a sigh and said, "You haven't heard the news? Sheikh Mujibur Rahman, the president of Bangladesh, was assassinated in the early hours of August fifteenth."

"What?" I said. I had heard nothing.

Father LaFerla had been in contact with a friend in charge of all paramilitary forces in the division. They were to prepare to defend India as it was unclear what would happen in Bangladesh. However, he had no orders for a preemptive strike.

Father LaFerla could understand that WHO would want me out of the area. He told me I should pack up all my things there at Caritas and be ready to depart at 5:00 a.m. He would wake the cook at 4:30 a.m. to prepare breakfast for us. We should fill up the petrol tank before leaving town. I showed him the letters to the armed forces and police, and he thought that they could help, but I probably would not need them. Confiscating a WHO jeep just was not worth the trouble. So I headed to my room and packed my things. I lay down on the bed and wondered how the day would go. Father LaFerla said that if the way was clear, I could be in Calcutta in nine hours.

It was still dark when I rolled off the bed and headed down to breakfast. Caritas staff started hauling my duffel bag and aluminum trunk down from my room to the jeep. I was anxious to leave. I prayed, *Just let this day be over fast, and with no incidents.*

Father LaFerla was there to see us off. I would really miss him; he was a good friend.

"I don't know when we will see each other again," I said. There was a catch in my throat, and tears welled up in my eyes. If there was any trouble, he would be on the front lines.

Father LaFerla said, "Don't worry about us. We will be fine. You know, Connie, you always have a place with us. Come back!"

I responded, "I hope I get to come back up." But my gut said that was probably just a pipe dream. We got in my jeep, and the cook handed in some sandwiches and drinks to take with us. The big gates opened one last time, and I leaned out my window and waved good-bye. I never saw Father LaFerla again.

We headed west toward the national highway and almost immediately encountered a seemingly endless line of military trucks headed northeast to defend the long border.

Shit, I thought, *there is going to be a confrontation.*

I started to count the number of army vehicles that passed us heading northeast. When I reached 150 trucks, I just stopped counting. Vehicles and supply trucks took up most of the road, encroaching on our side. We could only average thirty kilometers per hour. Our task was to put distance between northern West Bengal and us.

Somewhere in the middle of West Bengal, we heard honking and saw lights flashing in a jeep behind us. It was another smallpox jeep and WHO epidemiologist. What a surprise to run into them. We swerved over to the side of the road. I jumped out and ran to talk to another junior epidemiologist from Britain—John.

"I've been ordered out of my districts!" I said. "Have you been ordered to evacuate?"

John shook his head no and said, "I heard about the assassination, and folks are pretty tense, but I've received no word from WHO about what to do."

We commiserated, and then I said, "I have to keep moving. WHO Calcutta wants me down there today. Do you know about any meeting for the WHO epidemiologists?" John shook his head no. He was in the dark.

It was a long, dusty, humid trek down to Calcutta. It had been a couple of hours since the last military vehicle had passed. We were making better and faster time now. The only thing was, none of us had driven to Calcutta before, and we were uneasy about driving into the big city. How were we to find WHO?

I decided to just chill out. I was not the driver; I just left it to the team. Eventually, we meandered into the office. Everyone seemed elated to see us. I went right into the administration office. It was already 3:00 p.m.

The administrative officer looked up and said, "Just getting in? No problems?"

I shook my head no and said, "It was uneventful. So what's up?"

He replied, "You need to go straightaway to the consulate."

"What consulate?"

He looked exasperated and said, "The US consulate."

"Should I get cleaned up?" I asked.

"Just go."

I tried to remember if I'd seen the US consulate, but then I decided to just take a taxi. I left the building and flagged down a cab. As we drove up to the consulate, I started searching for my passport. I showed the marine security guard at the gate my passport, and he waved me in.

At the marine reception window, I explained that WHO had sent me over to see the consul, but I didn't know why. The guard picked up the phone to call the consul's secretary. "Helen, there is a Dr. Cornelia Davis down here. She says she works for WHO in Darjeeling. Should I send her up?" He put the phone down. "Go right up to the consul's office."

As I entered the secretary's office, she said, "You can go right in. The consul is expecting you."

So I walked in and said, "Good afternoon, sir. WHO said I was to report right away to the consulate."

The consul asked me to sit down and offered coffee. "Do you know what this is about?" he asked.

"I have no idea, sir. I was up in Cooch Behar yesterday evening, and a messenger came to my room, telling me I had to leave immediately. So I left! Please excuse my appearance, but WHO said I was to come over here right away."

The consul related that he had received an immediate notification from the American embassy in Delhi when the news erupted that the Bangladeshi president had been assassinated. He had been instructed to find out if there were any Americans up-country who could be in trouble if difficulties arose between the two countries. They called around and talked to the UN.

"It seems you were the only American up north," the consul said. "Also, you were in a sensitive area surrounded on three sides by Bangladesh. We told WHO to get you out by any means possible."

He continued to fill me in on the current situation. "It still is not clear who is behind this heinous crime, but in all likelihood they will start accusing India of having some complicity in this. India might also use this disturbance to annex Bangladesh. So we need to find out everything you saw and heard on your way down."

He picked up the phone and said, "Michael, she's here. Why don't you come down right now?" Then he explained that he wanted one of his political agents to hear my report, so I would only have to do this once.

Somehow I had gone from clueless WHO epidemiologist searching for smallpox in some hapless village on the border to keen observer of the political situation on the frontier.

"I don't really know anything," I said. "Yesterday started out just like every other day. I was in my selected subdivision near some enclaves of India on the border." I explained that after work, we returned late to the dak bungalow to find the messenger with the letter, and then left on the spot. I stopped along the route to pick up personal items left at the Caritas mission. "Personally, I think the interesting thing was all the vehicles and men that the Indian army was sending up-country. I stopped counting after a hundred and fifty trucks. It certainly looked to me like war was imminent, and I just wanted to get out of the area! However, the Caritas director had spoken to the top military commander in Cooch Behar, who was ordered to defend the country but not to invade Bangladesh." The consul just nodded his head and looked at the political agent.

They thanked me, and I headed back to WHO.

Meanwhile I was wondering when, if ever, I could return to my posting. I needed to see about my team and find out what would become of me.

I checked in again with the administrative officer. He said they were working on getting some funds for my team and that the team would be heading back north the next day. I told him I was concerned that we had left temporary workers stranded and unpaid. He assured me that WHO was on it and would send a national to find the staff and pay all debts. I was to say good-bye to my team and head to the Fairlawn Hotel. I would be in Calcutta for some time.

I met my faithful team, relayed to them the news that I would be staying in Calcutta for the present, and thanked them for all their hard work. We all started to choke up with the knowledge that the team was breaking up. I had been in India only three months at this time. In the end, I ended up in Calcutta anyway. Karma had spoken.

26

MAY YOU LIVE IN
INTERESTING TIMES

Everyone always attributes the saying "May you live in interesting times" to the purported translation of an ancient Chinese proverb and curse. However, no Chinese source has ever been found.

Karma had brought me back to Calcutta, and I would now work out of that district office searching for rash-and-fever cases. I returned to the Fairlawn Hotel, my home away from home. I requested another room that would afford a little more privacy and quiet. I had bad memories associated with my previous room due to the incident of the tub water and the thermos bottle and the ensuing illness. With the Fairlawn as my base, Violet Smith made sure I met any interesting folks passing through the hotel.

Early on, I had investigations to do over in Howrah district. The Hooghly River flows between the twin cities of Calcutta and Howrah. The Howrah Bridge was the span that I always took to make the crossing. The Howrah Bridge was a cantilever bridge, a structure projecting horizontally into space from both sides of the river, supported only on either end and with a suspended span in the middle. When the bridge was commissioned in 1943, it was the third-longest cantilever bridge in the world. It somehow weathered the fierce storms of the Bay of Bengal region and carried a daily traffic of approximately 100,000 vehicles and possibly more than 150,000 pedestrians, easily making it the busiest cantilever bridge in the world.

I clearly remembered the first time my jeep negotiated the bridge. There were two lanes for vehicular travel, a central lane for the tram, and pedestrian passageways on either side. The undulation of the bridge scared the shit out of me. The whole span swayed immensely. Fortunately, I didn't get motion sickness. The congestion was so bad in the vehicular lanes that pedestrians could walk faster than the cars and buses were moving. With that amount of traffic using the span, bridge maintenance presented unusual problems. The bridge suffered from the rash driving of motorists, and considerable damage was caused from cargo boats that hit the bridge periodically or had funnels that got caught up under the structure.

My six-month contract was proceeding briskly, and the big festival season was fast approaching. While the rest of India celebrated Diwali, the festival of lights, and worshiped Lakshmi, the goddess of wealth, in Bengal the biggest festivals were Durga Puja and Kali Puja. These festivals occurred in October, and as Indian festivals revolved around the moon, the actual dates varied each year.

There was a WHO epidemiologist meeting scheduled during Durga Puja, and all the foreign epidemiologists were in town. I met a Swedish doctor named Hans, and we roamed the city together to get immersed in the festival.

Durga Puja was the ceremonial worship of the mother goddess. Apart from being a religious festival for Hindus, it was also an occasion for reunion and rejuvenation and a celebration of traditional culture and customs. While the rituals entailed ten days of fasting, feasting, and worship, the last four days—Saptami, Ashtami, Navami, and Dashami—were celebrated with much gaiety and grandeur, especially in Bengal, where the ten-armed goddess riding the lion was worshipped with great passion and devotion.

The beautifully handcrafted idols of the goddess Durga were stunning, and we could see them being crafted in Kumartuli, an area of north Kolkata. Truth be told, Hans and I were arriving rather late in the preparation, and the *pandals*, or podiums where all the idols are displayed, were nearly finished. The highlight of Durga Puja was visiting the many different pandals of the goddess Durga. Each had a unique theme. This activity was routinely referred to as "pandal hopping." Every neighborhood had its pandal, and there were literally thousands of pandals in Calcutta.

We could only visit a fraction of them, and even so it required stamina and speed as they were spread out all over the city. We were hoofing it, so we just visited the best-known displays in north and south Calcutta.

The most popular time for pandal hopping was at night, when they were all lit up and it was slightly cooler. That was also the time to feast!

Durga Puja was the best time to sample Calcutta's famous Bengali cuisine. There was food everywhere—on the streets, at the pandals, and in specialty Bengali restaurants. Pandal hopping was tiring, so eating while we were out and about was a must. Food was offered to Durga at the pandals, and then it was distributed to the common folk. This food is called *bhog*, and it consists of a mixed vegetable curry, a sweet dish, a fried item, and a chutney.

On the last day of Durga Puja, Dashami, the festivities commenced with married women placing red *sindoor*, or powder, on the idols of the goddess Durga and then smearing it on each other. That evening, the idols were taken to the river and immersed in the water. One of the most popular immersion points was Babu Ghat. We were able to follow one pandal to the river to see it submerged.

Hans and I also participated in Kali Puja, a festival for another incarnation of the mother goddess. Kali, the Dark Mother, was a deity with whom devotees had a very loving and intimate bond, despite her fearful appearance. In this relationship, the worshipper became childlike, and Kali assumed the form of the ever-caring mother.

Kali was the flip side, the fearful and ferocious form of the mother goddess. She was portrayed as being born from the brow of Durga during one of her battles with evil forces. As the legend goes, in the battle, Kali was so involved in the killing spree that she got carried away and began destroying everything in sight. To stop her, Lord Shiva threw himself under her feet. Shocked at this sight, Kali stuck out her tongue in astonishment and put an end to her homicidal rampage. Consequently, the common image of Kali shows her in her melee mood, standing with one foot on Shiva's chest with her enormous tongue stuck out.

In the Western Christian-Judeo culture, our God and saints are depicted as white, and they are pure, holy, and kind. I couldn't think of one Western god or saint who was black. Kali was black and fierce! Her black complexion symbolized her all-embracing and transcendental nature, and according to the Mahanirvana Tantra, "Just as all colors disappear in black, so all names and forms disappear in her." She had four arms, with a sword in one hand and the head of a demon in another. The other two hands blessed her worshippers. She had two dead heads for her earrings and a string of fifty skulls as a necklace, representing the fifty letters in the Sanskrit alphabet, which symbolize infinite knowledge. She had a girdle made of human hands as her clothing, signifying work and liberation from the cycle of karma. Her tongue protruded from her mouth, her eyes were red, and her face and breasts were sullied with blood. She stood with one foot on the thigh and the other on the chest of her husband, Shiva. Her nudity was primeval, fundamental, and transparent, like nature. Her white teeth showed her inner purity, and her lolling red tongue indicated her omnivorous nature and her indiscriminate enjoyment of all the world's flavors. Her sword was the destroyer of false consciousness and the eight bonds that bind us. Her three eyes represented past, present, and future—the three modes of time—and this attribute lies in the very name of Kali, which in Sanskrit means "time." However, while I was in India, I always thought Kali meant "black."

Kali Puja came close on the heels of Durga Puja, at the time when the rest of India celebrated Diwali, the festival of lights. Hans and I had heard that we should try and get into the Kalighat Kali temple to see the ceremonies and various offerings to the goddess, but our informants were not sure if foreigners would actually be allowed inside. We heard that devotees offered animal sacrifices and did Tantric rites, and we were advised not to take photos. One could expect that this festival would be very popular and extremely crowded.

We decided to head over to Kalighat early and then leave at some point to visit Mother Teresa's Home for the Dying. We'd heard it was in the same general area.

We arrived around 8:00 a.m. at the Kali temple, and there was already a crowd at the gates. There was no one around to ask if we would be allowed to enter. People had offerings of red hibiscus flowers and fruits in their hands. We bought red hibiscus garlands at one of the stands so we would have an offering to give, even though we were unsure of the procedure. We got into the line, but it was not moving. An hour or so passed. It was getting warmer, and then the line surged forward. Hans and I kept close and hoped that we would not be separated in the push and shove to get through the gates. There were already crowds within the temple compound.

We could hear the chanted prayers of Hindu Brahmins and the soft drumming of instruments, and we could smell the myriad puffs of incense floating in the air. We were swept into an inner sanctum where the air was still and oppressive. It was exceedingly humid, and sweat was pouring down my face and running in rivulets down the inside of my kurta. The garland in my hands was withering from the heat. Normally, I was not claustrophobic, but my interior space was being trampled to smithereens. I was somehow separated from Hans and swept forward, ever forward, like a leaf. I was pressed closely and firmly to the back of a woman in a sari with long, beautiful, glistening black hair falling down her back. Another person, a male, was practically glued to my backside. I could not have extricated myself even if I had wanted to. I understood now, only too well, how people were always trampled to death during the hajj pilgrimage.

I felt fear. My throat and lips were parched. Oh, for some water. I was surrounded in this swirl of humanity. I wished desperately that Hans would miraculously appear, and I would know I was safe. But I could not see him.

The chanting grew louder, and I heard the sound of animals braying close by. Suddenly there was a medieval scene before me of goats and sheep being sacrificed on a stone altar, and the smell of blood and death and perfumed incense of sandalwood and jasmine wafted up into the air, and devotees were bowing and kneeling and chanting.

Then a priest raised a giant skikamor (sword like knife) up high, and in one fell blow, a huge water buffalo toppled. Adherents rushed forward to remove the parts. I felt faint and slightly nauseous. I looked down to see my bare feet sliding around in excrement mixed with blood. More than anything else at the moment, I just wanted to leave.

But how could I leave? I continued to be carried along with the tidal wave of people. We were now before the goddess. I remembered to place my garland before the altar. And then I was propelled along. My next impression was of being in another section of the temple compound. There seemed to be fresher air in this section, and the crush of humanity lessened. I could breathe again.

Someone came up behind me and put his arm around my shoulder, and I looked up to see Hans. I was overjoyed to see him. I said, "I need to get out of here. I'm light-headed. How do we get out?"

And Hans took my hand and pulled me along. We exited the temple and moved to the side so we could sit down. Hans said, "I'm going to find our sandals where we left them!" I just collapsed where I was. He returned in ten minutes with our shoes in hand. It was a miracle. I was drained; I couldn't move for thirty minutes. Finally Hans pulled me up, and we slowly limped away from the premises. My only thought was to put some distance between the temple and us. After a while I turned to Hans and said, "What was that back there at the temple, some ancient rite?" He just shook his head.

27

FINDING PEACE AT THE HOME FOR THE DYING

They said that Mother Teresa's Home for the Dying was right next door to the Kali temple. The hospice was known by many names, such as Kalighat, the Home of the Pure Heart (Nirmal Hriday), or the Home for the Dying and Destitute, but I knew it as the Home for the Dying. It wasn't exactly next door, but still we somehow stumbled to the open entrance to the home. The door was wide open, and no one was around.

The silence was such a contrast to the Kali temple from where we just escaped. I was still feeling unsettled and light-headed. We kept wandering and eventually turned up in the men's ward, which exited onto an open patio that fronted on the river. I lay down on the cool stone slabs, and Hans sat cross-legged beside me. We waited for one of the nuns to drift by. And one sister in a blue-bordered sari did arrive after about fifteen minutes.

"How can I help you?" she asked. I struggled to sit up.

Hans replied, "We are epidemiologists in the smallpox program. We heard about Mother Teresa and her work, and we just wanted to visit the hospice."

"Let me go get Mother Teresa," she said and quietly withdrew.

I looked around the ward, where some twenty patients were resting on mattresses on the floor. It was very peaceful. So this was the hospice for the destitute and dying. With the help of Indian officials, Mother Teresa had been given an abandoned building that had previously served as a temple for Kali and converted it into a free hospice for the poor. I realize there has been a lot of controversy in recent years about the saintliness of Mother Teresa; attacks on the mission and the goal of the Missionaries of Charity; and doubts cast on the very effectiveness of their work with the poor, and particularly their handling of persons with HIV/AIDS. But at the time I met Mother Teresa in 1975, there was no other organization working with the poorest of the poor in Calcutta.

When Mother Teresa walked into the room, there was a presence; I could feel it. She was small in stature, and both Hans and I towered over her. We explained why we were there and that we wanted to donate some small funds to the hospice. She was apologetic and said she was busy just then and could not accompany us personally, but she would have one of the nuns show us around the hospice. She then thanked us for our generosity and silently exited.

The sister we had met previously returned and, in her limited English, explained the running of the hospice. It was spotless. Anyone who has visited an Indian hospital would note the difference immediately. None of the sisters had any medical or nursing training, but their mission was not to diagnose and treat. It was to assist the destitute to die with dignity. The day we were there, the hospice was not crowded. A couple of sisters were bathing some of the women patients. I didn't notice any volunteers at the time. There was not a lot to see. There were two wards, one for males and the other for females. Clean clothes were drying in the breeze, and I could smell the daily meal being prepared in the kitchen. We left our donation and walked out into the brilliant sun.

We were starving, and the only thought on our minds was to find something to eat. However, that visit to Mother Teresa's Home for the Dying left a lasting imprint on my mind of the quiet, peaceful hospice where God's work was being done.

Once the festivals were over, the epidemiologists returned to their districts to resume the search for rash-and-fever cases. Hans left with all the others. I longed to return to my districts up north, where I had operated more independently. My life revolved around similar work as before—tracking down rash-and-fever cases—but I was assigned areas to follow up, rather than choosing what I thought was priority. I returned every evening to my base at the Fairlawn Hotel. Every once in a while, Mrs. Violet Smith introduced me to an interesting guest who happened to cross the threshold. In November I met Libby, a woman who was traveling solo around India. She was from Britain and had a certain facility with languages and a curious mind. I was impressed that she had been traveling alone for some two months. We had an instant rapport, and it was great just talking with another woman—and not about infectious diseases. Finally, I had a companion to go out to dinner with. We agreed to just head out that evening to explore the area and stumble upon an interesting restaurant.

It was already dark by the time I got back from my investigations. I rushed to shower and change into something easy and comfortable. Walking around at night in the urban areas was always fraught with danger. We couldn't see anything. Street lamps were rare and were usually only in front of some grand house or building. The monsoon was over, though, so we didn't have to confront the flowing rivers of mud and other ambiguous items in the roads.

Libby had an aversion to the human-drawn rickshaws, so we were on foot. Libby had already explored Benares, and she gave me her impressions of the city and the ten best places to visit. I was taking note because Benares was on my list of cities I must see once I finished my smallpox work.

I was also intent on where I was placing my feet. "What were the burning ghats like?" I asked, and Libby had just started to reply, "Well, they..." when her voice fell silent. I turned around to see why she had stopped talking. She was nowhere in sight.

Oh my God, now what? I thought. I started to retrace my steps, and then I heard whimpering. I peered intently through the blackness and saw the faint outline of an open crater. I crept forward and peered down. She had fallen down an open sewer hole. Some fool had stolen the heavy iron cover. The top of her head was two inches below the surface, and she had somehow stopped herself from falling farther.

I shouted, "Libby, are you OK?"

"My leg hurts like hell, but I don't think it's broken."

When I said I was going for help, she begged me to stay, saying, "No, Connie, don't. Can't you help me out? I don't want to be left alone."

There was a pungent odor wafting up from the drain. I felt like barfing. I knelt in the dirt and muck and reached down. "Can you get any foothold on the side so you can help pull yourself out?" I asked.

I'd always heard that people find superhuman strength when it is really necessary. I still don't know how I managed to haul Libby up; she was my size and weight. Once out, she looked a sight, but that wasn't the biggest problem; the smell was overpowering. I certainly didn't want to walk beside her, or even be anywhere close to her, but I thought, *What would I want a friend to do?*

That night was the first time in India when no one, not even the poorest of the poor, came close to us.

Then Libby wailed, "Connie, my shoes fell off—find my shoes!"

"They are gone," I responded. "No one in their right mind is going to reach their hand down that hole to try and find some two-bit sandals. Just know they're gone!"

Normally it was a tight squeeze to get past the people who slept on the streets. Usually I had to run the gauntlet of beggars to get inside the Fairlawn Hotel at night. Not that night; it was smooth sailing. People just peeled away from us.

The guy at reception at the Fairlawn took one look at us and motioned for us to take the back stairs. When we got to Libby's room, I said, "Drop all of those clothes. They can come, collect, and destroy them. And Libby, scrub well in the shower. Then do it all over again. I'll go see what antibiotics I have to give you."

After the shower, I examined her leg. It was banged up but not broken. She gulped down some broad-spectrum antibiotics and fell off to sleep. I had learned my lesson: take a rickshaw at night. It was the safest thing to do. Libby was a little traumatized after this event and decided she needed to chill out on a beach in Goa.

Then I got a call from Dr. Grasset. Delhi was pleased with my performance, and although India had declared smallpox zero, the most difficult period was still ahead. She asked if I would be interested in going to Rajasthan for the next eighteen months. Rajasthan was one of the princely states, with lots of royalty and the opportunity to meet princes. I could ride horses as much as I liked, conduct searches in the desert on camels looking for smallpox, and be in charge of a whole state.

Now who could resist that?

I said, "I'll get back to you!" I needed to think clearly and weigh options. Did I really want to go to the desert? India was already too hot for me. But the job was not yet over; India still needed to pass certification. Why quit before smallpox in India was declared truly eradicated?

28

IN THE FOOTSTEPS OF LIEUTENANT COLONEL TOD

I wanted to return to Darjeeling just one last time and take leave of Mount Kanchenjunga, but that was not to be.

I reflected on my six months in West Bengal while sitting in the same departure zone where I had met Heymann and counted rupee notes just six months before. So much had happened that it was hard for me to even fathom it.

I had identified smallpox in a border village in Bangladesh, done outbreak containment on the Indian side, negotiated with smugglers to allow smallpox workers to vaccinate on the border, thought my jeep had killed a sacred cow, found my own green pinstriped shirt in a Caritas NGO donation from the States, met Mother Teresa, surreptitiously crossed the border into Sikkim, and been evacuated from Cooch Behar when the US embassy thought war between India and Bangladesh was imminent. What other adventures were ahead in Rajasthan?

Orientation this time in Delhi was a breeze. I would be in charge of a whole state. This should be easy. The objective remained the same: to investigate all rash-and-fever cases. India had announced that it was down to zero smallpox cases. The issue now was how to keep up the interest in reporting cases and how to get smallpox workers and supervisors to continue to look for it as if their lives depended on it. The primordial question was: where could smallpox hide or go undetected? Each state would analyze its own area for its peculiar vulnerabilities. Urban areas, with their large pockets of slums, construction sites, and railway stations, were monitored on a continual basis. States that had remote areas; borders with other countries; or places of periodic pilgrimages, fairs, and festivals that attracted a sizable number of beggars, nomads, or pilgrims from other states were considered at-risk areas likely to harbor unrecognized outbreaks.

There were always questions about isolated districts in the Thar Desert of Rajasthan. To respond to likely concerns that would come from the certification team, Rajasthan would be asked to conduct special surveys, and I would spearhead those efforts. Rajasthan had many colorful festivals that drew people from far and near. Some of those festivals even involved worshippers offering gifts to the goddess of smallpox, Sitala Mata. When there were still many smallpox outbreaks, people took the sick and infected to the temples to be blessed.

It was important to have health staff at the festivals to look at the sick and to see if any had a rash and fever. That meant, of course, that I needed to attend these festivals to make sure proper surveillance was ongoing. I thought it great luck that I *had* to cover the festivals. The only problem was that Rajasthan was the second-largest state in the Republic of India by area. And I thought I was busy when I just had my three little districts in West Bengal.

I stayed in the Imperial Hotel this time around in Delhi. The Imperial was on Janpath, a major thoroughfare, and was close to Connaught Place. A friend advised me to track down James Tod's *Annals and Antiquities of Rajasthan*, a three-volume series of books about the history and geography of Rajasthan.

Lieutenant Colonel James Tod was an English-born officer of the British East India Company and a scholar of the Orient. He combined his official role and his amateur interests in his books, which featured the area then known as Rajputana— the present-day state of Rajasthan.

He joined the East India Company as a military officer and traveled to India in 1799 as a cadet in the Bengal army. He rose quickly through the ranks and eventually was appointed political agent for some areas of Rajputana. It was during this period that Tod conducted most of the research for his books. Apparently he was successful in his official role, but he had his differences with his superiors. Over time the areas under his authority were significantly curtailed. Tod resigned his post in 1823 and returned to England.

One of the advisors in the Delhi office implied that Rajasthan had not changed that much since Tod's time and suggested I use his annals to learn the area's history and culture. The books would become my Bible; before going out to a district, I would read up on that area's ethnic groups and culture. The advisor was right; the people and customs had changed little since Tod published his books.

Before I left Delhi, I thought it best to touch base with the American embassy. Even though technically I was with the United Nations, and WHO was responsible for me, I let the consular officer know I would be based in Jaipur. I'd heard that Delhi had a very active American Club and a Community

Liaison Office (CLO) that arranged various activities for the diplomats attached to the American embassy.

The lady in the CLO office was friendly and very helpful. Her concern was that Jaipur had a very small expatriate community and that it might be difficult to find domestic help who would be comfortable working for foreigners. She offered to review the CLO's directory of approved domestic staff and find a cook/housekeeper willing to go to Jaipur to work for me. She thought a Muslim cook would be willing to go; she could send him on the bus with money I would advance for transportation.

Because Jaipur was in the desert, it would not have the materials there to make the cheap rattan furniture that all foreigners in Delhi used to furnish houses and patios. She recommended I buy a small table and four chairs and leave it with friends. Once I found a house, I could notify her. She would interview and hire the cook and put him on the bus with my rattan furniture, and then I could meet him at the main bus station in Jaipur. I would recognize him because of my furniture. It sounded like a perfect plan to me.

I had one other housekeeping task to do with WHO. It turned out that Rajasthan was not only vegetarian, but it was also a dry state. That meant that although the luxury hotels would have beer and gin and tonic, it would be difficult to buy alcohol there. However, there was a certain quantity of alcohol that the Indian government allowed United Nations personnel to buy. As I was with WHO, I could transport it to Jaipur on the train.

I filled out a form, and the WHO administration guy made all the arrangements. I ordered red wine, about four cases of beer, ten bottles of gin, and ten bottles of Johnny Walker Red to last the eighteen months I'd be in Jaipur.

And so I was off on my adventure to Rajasthan. Just the name sent shivers up my spine. The Land of Kingdoms, formerly the Land of Princely States, was bordered by Uttar Pradesh and Haryana to the northeast and Punjab to the north. Gujarat was to the southwest, Madhya Pradesh to the southeast, and to the west were Pakistan and the Great Indian Desert.

Rajasthan was very different from West Bengal, which was green and lush and full of rivers to drown in and rice paddies to destroy. Rajasthan was the desert; the light was hot and bright, the air was dry and oftentimes dusty, and then there was the color. I would always remember the riot of colors— in the architecture; in the unique, full-length *ghagharas*, or women's skirts; and in the colorful turbans of the men, which were usually ten to twenty feet long and wound in distinctive styles.

I was based in the capital, Jaipur, which was called the Pink City because of the color of the stone used in the construction of many of its palaces and government structures. And the history of the city revealed an interesting account. In 1876, the Prince of Wales and Queen Victoria visited India on a tour. As pink was the color of hospitality, Maharaja Ram Singh of Jaipur painted the whole city pink to welcome the guests. The residents, who are now by law compelled to maintain the pink color, have faithfully followed this tradition.

I traveled on Indian Airlines and arrived in Jaipur on a weekend. I was saved from finding a hotel, as I had been invited to stay in the mother-in-law apartment at the home of Dr. D. K. Jagdev, the deputy director of Medical and Health Services. I was welcome to stay until I could get my bearings and decide where I wanted to live. In addition, the smallpox program was also under his supervision, so I could ask him anything about it.

I always found it interesting to take a city tour of a new place to get a feel for its history and culture. Of course, district towns like Jalpaiguri in West Bengal were too small to offer tours. But Jaipur was a capital, and there were plenty of tour guides. I decided to take the city tour with E. P. Pram as my guide. I don't know how I lucked into running into Pram. Not only was he an excellent tour guide, but he and his family became my fast friends. The bus had about thirty seats, and there were ten or twelve customers. I was the only foreigner; all the rest were Indians.

The half-day tour did what it was supposed to do: it gave me an overview of the splendors of Jaipur and enticed me to come back asking for more. I saw the Hawa Mahal, the Palace of the Wind, a five-story architectural wonder built with 953 niches and windows as a sort of royal grandstand for the maharaja's harem to watch everyday life and festivals despite living in purdah. The palace was really a facade. It was only one room deep, but it was magical.

We headed for Amber Fort and the palace up on the hill, which were accessible by elephant. Riding an elephant to a palace sounds hokey, but that memory stayed with me long after the trip. After the crowds and the noise of Amber, it was nice to have some quiet moments at the Royal Gaitor tombs, the resting place and crematoria of the Rajput maharajas. The intricately carved white marble cenotaphs were otherworldly.

We zipped through the Jantar Mantar, a stone observatory that highlighted how advanced the Rajputs were in astronomy and astrology. It didn't sing to me at the time, but Pram later put me in contact with an astrologer there who charted my life in zodiac signs and circles that were all hand-painted on a scroll.

We ended our tour at the City Palace, which gave visitors an idea of how the maharajas once lived. The tour put me in a mood to go home and read more from Tod's annals.

On Monday, I headed into the smallpox office to meet my staff and to outline how I could survey this tremendously large state. With this position, I finally had my own Willy's jeep and driver, Abdul Hakim. He drove on all my journeys save one. I've always regretted that he missed that trip; it was the one I almost didn't come back from. Hakim knew the jeep and could fix anything that went wrong. Like in West Bengal, I was assigned several paramedics to accompany me on my travels. Because I would be traveling so much, the state provided Mandal Dutta and Ramesh Chandra, who would take turns traveling with me and investigating rash-and-fever cases.

This would be my team for eighteen months, and I would owe them much in terms of friendship, smallpox knowledge, cultural information, and especially putting up with my idiosyncrasies. They came to accept the fact that I had some strange attraction to camels and they eventually liked that; I became known as "Camel Lady" in western Rajasthan.

I made a vow that I would visit all twenty-six districts of the state. I would come to know the Rajasthan back roads better than I ever learned those of California.

The first step would be finding a house, sending for my cook and furniture, and getting settled in.

29

PAYING HOMAGE TO SITALA MATA

With this move to my new post, the most urgent task at hand was finding a place of my own. Jaipur at the time did not have a resident foreigner community like the big cities of Delhi and Calcutta. There were not a lot of houses to rent. Mind you, I saw some great *haveli*, or mansion houses, for rent, but I was alone, and I knew what my travel schedule would look like. There was no reason to pay a goodly price for a big house and not actually have much time to spend there. I figured I would be traveling up-country about three weeks out of each month.

Eventually I heard about a new "estate" of homes that each had two bedrooms, a bath, and a garage. The area was called Jawahar Nagar. When I went for a look, it kind of reminded me of California's track homes. At least there was water and electricity. I wasn't so sure about the sanitation system, but the houses had real toilets! I even saw telephone poles, or what I thought were telephone poles. In those days Jaipur was not a huge town, and from Jawahar Nagar I could get to the office in no time. In this new housing estate, only half the houses were occupied. After I moved in, my neighbors were curious but self-contained enough to just peer through the curtains at their new neighbor. I wasn't clear on the protocol.

Two houses down on the right, there was a camel sequestered in the garage. And kitty corner across the street, I seemed to be in luck: a single young lady smiled at me. When I later went over out of curiosity, I met Manju, a woman who would turn out to be a good friend. Manju collected artwork and handicrafts to sell to the antique shops in five-star hotels. She taught me all about Rajasthani artisanship and where to find it.

When you rented a house in those days, it didn't come furnished. It didn't even come with a stove or refrigerator or cabinets. WHO did provide me with a mobility allowance, which was intended to help families "settle in." There was one shop in town operated by a Marwari who had a limited but select group of refrigerators and stoves. Marwaris are the caste of moneylenders and merchants in India who became the chief rivals of the Parsis as merchants and industrialists. The term "Marwari" has evolved to be a designation for the Rajasthani people in general, but at that time it was used particularly with reference to certain communities in which the traditional occupation was trading. I bought a refrigerator and a kerosene stove, and I let my driver, Hakim, find out where to get the kerosene canisters. The crazy part was that the stove and refrigerator were delivered by a camel-drawn cart.

What I really wanted was a telephone line so that Delhi or the state government could contact me easily. I thought that as the only WHO representative in the state, obtaining this simple thing would be easy. Little did I know of the difficulties that lay ahead.

Finding the government office responsible for telephone landlines was the first obstacle. Telephone lines apparently were not, in point of fact, for private civilians. But I was a WHO officer stationed in Rajasthan, working on an important mission.

They asked why I felt I needed a phone. I filled out a stack of forms (in Hindi) and drew a map of where I thought I lived, and then asked about how long it would take to have a phone line installed. I got the Indian head wobble; I didn't get the feeling that the reply was in the affirmative. I took it to mean that in due course, a landline would materialize. I put down a small deposit and got a receipt for the money. And then I waited for "in due course" to arrive.

Because I would basically be working as Sitala's representative, I felt I needed to know as much as possible about her. At first I was mystified, because Sitala Mata in Rajasthan seemed very different from the Sitala in Bengal. In almost every part of India there was a goddess, known by a variety of local names, who was concerned with smallpox. In northern India, from Rajasthan and Gujarat in the west to West Bengal in the east, Sitala's primary association was with smallpox, although occasionally she was given other roles and powers, including that of protector of children and giver of good fortune.

If I had to choose which region had the most highly developed "cult" for the goddess, I would have to say Bengal, hands down. This probably reflected the highly developed vernacular religious literature, the highly developed oral tradition, the Sanskritization of the Bengal tradition, and the numerous poems and temples for her.

The mother goddesses of India were well known for their dual qualities of benevolence and danger. Think of Durga and Kali in West Bengal. If Sitala Mata was properly worshipped, she was kind and forgiving, but if she was ignored, beware! She was the potent harbinger of smallpox. If she was angry, she brought heat, fever, itchiness, and the sores of the pox. Sitala was also the cool one and a constant reminder of the necessity of maintaining the proper balances of hot and cold, yin and yang.

In Bengal, Sitala's physical attributes were well known. This goddess rode an ass and carried a broom and a water vessel; she was often naked (or dressed as a married woman) and wore a winnowing fan on her head. Smallpox was generally known as the spring disease in Bengal because epidemics struck in the spring when the air was relatively dry, and miraculously, the illness disappeared with the first rains.

I was surprised when Sitala's physical attributes changed in Rajasthan. All of a sudden she was portrayed as one of seven sisters who sometimes had a brother or other male associate. Sitala Mataji still loved cold and coolness, particularly in the desert. She liked cold food offerings that were cooked the day before her feast was celebrated. It was the measles that was caused by the anger of Sitala Mataji. When I talk about measles and this goddess, it is important to realize that this is a strictly religious understanding of measles. The measles rash represented heat and dirt that had to come out lest the child die. Child talismans of goat, lion, or bear hair warded off the fear that measles brought, and indeed the way measles was thought to frighten children strongly reflected links to the spirit world. Hindus may refer to measles as *choti mata* (the smaller mother) whereas smallpox is *bari mata* (the larger mother). Before the eradication of smallpox in 1977, Sitala was associated with smallpox.

According to Rajasthani legend, Sitala was one of seven sisters who lived in the neem tree and who brought epidemic diseases. She was often in the company of Ghentukarna, the god of skin diseases; Jvarāsura, the fever demon; the Causattī Rogas, the sixty-four epidemics; Olāi Candi or Olāi Bibi, the goddess of cholera; or Raktāvatī, the goddess of blood infections.

For this reason, shrines to Sitala Mata could be found near neem trees. Other talismans against evil spirits and fear included spreading neem leaves and rose petals across a child's bed. Punjabi Christians also spread neem leaves on the floor and used them to brush the measles rash. Hindus placed neem leaves over the entryway to their houses and under infected children's beds.

In Rajasthan a major fair was held in honor of Sitala during March or April of each year. During smallpox time, the fair was attended by over a hundred thousand people in the small village of Seel-Ki-Doongri in the district of Jaipur. This would be my first major fair in Rajasthan, and I was looking forward to it. A number of smallpox vaccinators were assigned to the fair, where in the past they had looked for smallpox cases.

The fair lasted for only twenty-four hours, during which pilgrims visited to pay homage to Sitala Mata. It was believed that if Sitala Mata lost her temper for any reason, the area could expect to be affected by smallpox or other epidemics. It was always amazing to me how people knew exactly when this festival occurred, given that the rural population was illiterate and lacked today's array of communication devices.

The fair was organized to keep the goddess's mood cheerful, and offerings of cash, sweets, and different types of fruits were placed at the feet of Sitala Mata. The temple was on the top of a hillock above the village, and long lines of people hiked up the narrow trail. A beautiful red stone was placed inside the temple as an embodiment of the deity. Many women carried small brass water containers on their heads to throw water on the deity to keep her cool, and people offered cold food made several days before the festival. Inside the temple there were seven large stones in addition to the red stone. People who attended the fair were not supposed to eat until after they visited the sacred shrine. The village also simultaneously held a cattle fair. In the plains below the temple, there was a plethora of colorful activities, and the atmosphere was very festive. Cattle breeders decorated their animals beautifully and transported them to the fair. The best breeder was awarded a prize.

People from all across rural Rajasthan thronged to this festival. The women were colorfully and uniquely dressed, and the men were quite striking in their turbans as they were accompanied by their horses and bullock carts. I got in line, dutifully hiked up to the temple, and observed the worshippers as they went inside. There were no rash-and-fever cases that year, and I wondered how the fair would evolve once people saw that smallpox was eradicated.

I became "enlightened" at the temple, and in a flash I realized how I could clearly let all know that I was Sitala's representative. I needed to go to Jaipur's gold and silver market and search for Sitala's amulet, which showed the seven sisters and one brother. I would wear this amulet around my neck, and that symbol would be even clearer to the people than the program name on my jeep's door.

I shouldn't have worried about how Sitala Mata's legend would hold up after eradication. Of course the festival continued; Sitala Mata always needs to be appeased so that her wrath doesn't bring on other epidemics.

30

BREAKDOWN IN THE THAR DESERT

Rajasthan was generally dry and dusty. The western part of the state lies in the inhospitable Thar Desert. I truly wanted to see the desert districts of Barmer, Bikaner, Jaisalmer, and Jodhpur.

When I was posted in West Bengal, I always felt the pressure of population. It seemed to me that there were always hundreds of people around me. I keenly felt the lack of privacy.

What a different feeling it was in Rajasthan. In its wide-open spaces, there was only one person per square kilometer. In 1976 I met children living in the desert who were ten years old and had never seen rain.

Early on, I planned a surveillance trip to Bikaner. My team was all set to depart, and then I got word from Hakim, my driver, that his youngest child was sick. He asked me to postpone the trip. I told him I understood why he couldn't come.

I decided I would just ask the smallpox program to give me a temporary driver for this one trip. We had already notified the district authorities that I was coming. Although I wanted Hakim due to his excellent driving and mechanical skills, I had looked forward to this trip for several weeks. I felt guilty about leaving him behind, but I was champing at the bit to head out to the desert, and nothing was going to stop me. I would come to regret that rash decision.

Huge herds of breeding camels were the first sign that we were into the real desert region. There were thirty to forty head in each of the herds. During the breeding season, the young calves were so cute; they had the softest fur, like pashmina wool. I don't know why I was drawn to camels. I mean, I was first and foremost a horse lover. When I first came upon camels, I would stop the jeep and jump out to take pictures of the herds. And of course, the herders would crowd around, because jeeps didn't normally stop. Ramesh would explain that I had a thing about camels, and then the herders would help me approach the young calves so that the mother didn't get excited. Eventually I was given the unofficial title of "Camel Lady."

We headed for the district medical office to check in and find out how they were doing as they continued to survey for smallpox. In the true desert regions, the tribes did not live in villages. There were encampments with four or five families living with their camel and sheep herds. Some of the tribes were nomadic, and they followed the good grazing routes.

I realized that it was going to be hard to ascertain anything about the nomadic tribes. The farther we went into the desert, the more difficult it was for the jeep to handle. I got some hand-drawn maps, and the CMO said that the border security force (the BSF) still used camels in their surveillance of the border between India and Pakistan. Maybe they would be willing to lend me a guide and camels to locate and survey some of the more remote areas.

Maharaja Ganga Singh (1880–1943) ruled the Bikaner princely state for fifty-six years and was something of a Renaissance man in improving education and medicine, modernizing the transport and communications network, and carving the famous Gang Canal through the barren wastes (*jangaldesh*) in the north. The Ganga Risala, which the British came to call the Bikaner Camel Corps, included 466 men and camels. It was named after the maharaja. The Bikaner Camel Corps, along with the irregular troops of the Jaisalmer Risala, became the Thirteenth Battalion of the Indian army and saw action during the 1965 and 1971 Indo-Pakistan wars.

Subsequently, this unit was converted into regular infantry, and the camel corps became part of the BSF. The BSF continued to use some seven hundred camels for patrolling the 1,400 kilometers of desert border between India and Pakistan. The Bikaner Camel Corps was legendary, and it was said that Bikaner camels could run up to thirty kilometers per hour and travel one hundred kilometers in a day. I desperately wanted a chance to ride those camels.

At one time, back in the 1950s, India had the third-largest population of camels in the world. During my time in Rajasthan, the desert districts still had a sizable population of camels. Indian camels, as seen in Rajasthan and Gujarat, were mainly the single-humped Arabian camels (*Camelus dromedarius*). In the western part of India, there were four main breeds: Bikaneri, Jaisalmeri, Kutchi, and Mewari. The species adapted to varying environmental conditions, and the Bikaneri and Jaisalmeri breeds of camel were adapted to the climatic conditions of the Thar Desert, where the temperature soared in the summer to 50 degrees Celsius (122 degrees Fahrenheit) and then plummeted to 0 degrees Celsius (32 degrees Fahrenheit) in the winter.

The Mewari breed was adapted to the hilly terrain of the Mewar area in Rajasthan, whereas the Kutchi breed was found in the Kutch district of Gujarat. To my untrained eye, the Bikaneri and Jaisalmeri camels were lean and thin, had small humps, and had short hair on light brown skin. They were bred for riding and racing purposes. And these camels were swift like the wind! The Mewari and Kutchi breeds produced a significant quantity of milk; they were huskier and were commonly used for transport of cargo or pulling water from a well.

The ancient Hindu religious texts mentioned the camel. The *Markandeya Purana* said that the camel was born out of the feet of Brahma, and the only god with a camel as his mount was Virupaksha. The *Goraksha Samhita* said that the goddess Kalakarni (a female guardian deity in the Jain religion known for bestowing fertility and wealth) had a camel as her vehicle. So camels were definitely associated with the gods.

My first sortie out was mainly a rapid information-gathering expedition, not a true search for smallpox. My main focus was to get a feel for the nomads who lived in the desert and to understand the difficulty of accessing them. I still don't know why I failed to ask for a smallpox worker or even someone from the district who knew the area to accompany us. This was my stupidest and least thought-out trip during my whole time in India. In hindsight, I can't believe that my smallpox team just headed out into the desert. We had a temporary driver who certainly was not accustomed to driving in the desert. Ramesh, my paramedic, had been out to the district before but was not from the area.

We made no preparations. We didn't check anything on the Willys jeep (like making sure the radiator was full, or the engine was properly working). We had stopped for lunch in some sub divisional town, but I only had a one-liter thermos and six oranges. We had one ten-liter metal jerry can of petrol, and it sat in a holder on the back of the jeep. I find it hard to believe, even today, that we took off so ill prepared. I can't believe the CMO just let us go.

We had stopped at the district administration building to find out better directions to the BSF camp. There someone mentioned that the track was difficult, but that a water truck went out to the camp once a week. It had left the day before, so there should be fresh tracks for us to follow. And then we took off!

California has three distinct types of desert, and my family had certainly traversed the Mojave Desert in Southern California and Arizona and camped in the Badlands of South Dakota. I was not some neophyte who had never been exposed to the desert. However, the Thar had different ecological systems; and as we moved closer to the Pakistan border, the area changed from scraggly hillocks to dunes. I thought, *This must be what Saudi Arabia is like.*

It was strange, but we passed no encampments or family dwellings. I guessed that people didn't like to live close to a road. The road was really just a sandy track. We could tell it was a track, but I knew that if there were high winds, not much trace of a road would remain. It was 1:00 p.m., a piss-poor time to travel. It was very hot, and the light was extremely bright. It was probably 45 degrees Celsius (110 degrees Fahrenheit).

In all my subsequent travels in Rajasthan, my team never traveled in the heat of the day. We started early, by 7:00 a.m., and pulled over around 11:00 a.m. to find shade somewhere and vegetate until around 3:30 p.m. Then we went back to work until 7:30 p.m.

On this first trip to the desert, no one could hazard a guess as to how long it would take to reach this outpost of the BSF. They said, "It will take probably three to four hours, but it depends." It depended on the quality of the track, on the velocity of the winds, on the quality and strength of our jeep, on the expertise of our driver, and on whether the driver knew how to drive in the desert. Indians were pretty fatalistic; it also depended on the mercy of the gods.

We had been traveling about two hours (and things were going well) when the jeep lurched and coughed, and the engine just quit. Willy's jeeps didn't have a temperature gauge then, or at least I don't remember one. The driver got out and opened the bonnet. I knew right away when he started to fiddle with the engine parts that we didn't have a snowball's chance in hell of getting this jeep started again. He was not a mechanic. I knew that Hakim was right. I just should have postponed the damn trip.

Ramesh Chandra was of the opinion that we should all stay in the vehicle and wait for another vehicle to approach. I reminded him that the water truck only went to the camp once a week. It had already gone the day before. No one would be coming. And no one would be looking for us to return. We were not expected back that evening.

We had planned to stay at the camp, although truth be told, it was not clear if the BSF would let a foreigner stay at the camp. The temporary driver could not tell us what the mechanical problem was; he had resorted to prayer.

I was a hiker, and I felt confident—based on no knowledge of what actually lay ahead—that I could walk to the damn outpost. At least I was not going to sit in this jeep for five days and die of dehydration. So I said, "I think I can hike to the outpost. Ramesh, you can come with me. We will take the thermos and three of the oranges. As soon as the sun sets, the driver can drain the water from the radiator, and he will have a supply of water. We will start hiking at three in the afternoon."

We were between a rock and a hard place. Just staying in the jeep, which was hot as hell and without a tree in sight, was oppressive. We had not passed one soul since we turned onto this track, so running into someone was highly unlikely. We needed to make it to the BSF camp.

I now realized why Rajasthani women and men wore colorful clothes in the desert. The colors can be seen a long way off in the distance. I had on beige cotton pants and a pastel-blue kurta. And I had a dupatta with me. I didn't wear a hat in those days; I thought they just looked too strange on a woman. I could put the dupatta on my head, which was where it was supposed to be in the first place, instead of around my neck. Ramesh Chandra did not have anything for his head. None of us was happy. The driver kept on begging us to stay. But at 3:00 p.m., Ramesh and I pushed off. This was not a packed track, and it was work walking in the sand. I kept promising God that if I ever got out of there, I would not go on a trip without Hakim and at least twenty-five liters of water.

We walked about one hour. It was pretty monotonous. Then we heard someone yelling. We actually didn't see the hut some distance from the track, but this Rakia or Rabari tribal person had seen us. We later found out from him that he thought it strange that two people were out in the mid-day sun, walking. What is the quote? "Only mad dogs and Englishmen are out in the midday sun"?

What a relief. At least we had found someone. But he did not have camels. I had no idea what he was doing in that piti-able hut, but he did have water. It was not a lot, but it was wet—and salty. He said he knew of an encampment just over the hill with camels that could take us to the BSF outpost. I discovered that day that the term "just over the hill" means different things to different people. We started walking. It was not just over the hill. No matter; almost one hour later I saw some camels in the distance and campfires and thought, *Great, food!*

We came upon eight men, alone, with no families. They had been resting and keeping out of the midday sun and wait-ing to break camp and head for home, wherever that was.

According to the hospitality of the desert, passersby must be helped. They agreed to take us to the BSF, who could pro-vide better assistance, and then go after our stranded driver. They offered us their leftover lentils and water and said we would take off as soon as they said prayers. They were Muslims and needed to say either the afternoon or the evening prayer before we got started. I had to remind myself that they were our benefactors. Of course I wanted to take off right away. I was worried about how our driver was coping alone. But I wasn't in charge of this rescue mission.

The sun sets pretty fast in the desert. One minute it was light, and the next minute it was pitch black. Ramesh and I were riding gingerly behind the hump of a camel, with its owner firmly in front. We started off over the hill to find the track to the outpost. After ten minutes, in the distance, we saw two pairs of headlights from two vehicles going down the road. We took off at a gallop to intercept the vehicles. As we got closer, I could see that one of the vehicles was my Willys jeep. Someone got it started? I couldn't believe it!

The vehicles saw us headed their way and came to a stop. There was joy all around when my driver discovered that Ramesh and I were not dead in some gully by the side of the road. I was crying outright, after noting that we were all in one piece. As chief of the team, I was responsible for them. And I was relieved that the driver was not dead from dehydration in the jeep. The camel riders were happy— they could now take off for home. Everyone was pleased as punch.

I thanked the Ribari tribal man who had initially found us and profusely thanked the camel owners for their generosity and hospitality. I had nothing to offer them. Money would have offended their hospitality. I was drained, and we were still not at the outpost. Apparently, the BSF needed something secret—or in any case, not divulged to me—and so they had radioed into the district for it to be brought in today. We were lucky. Ordinarily, a vehicle only went once a week to the outpost.

There was surprise all around when our two vehicles showed up at the outpost. They didn't get too many female visitors during the year. In fact, they didn't generally get any visitors. As I was a doctor, I offered to see anyone who was sick. I was reunited with my first-aid kit, which I always carried in the jeep. I didn't have a lot, but I carried a goodly number of chloroquine pills for malaria, and there were four soldiers who were suffering from that. The outpost had run out of malaria pills early on in the year.

The outpost was pretty Spartan, but it did have radio contact with the outside world. I had been told in Jaipur that the desert got cold at night, and this was true. I had a sleeping bag that I had brought from California. I had never used it in West Bengal, but I put it to good use in Rajasthan. We ate some sort of stew for dinner. With no choice of beds, I got to sleep on the floor of the office with three BSF officers and Ramesh Chandra.

The next day, the officer in charge showed me his maps of the area and where some semi permanent encampments were located. He offered to have one of his staff act as a guide and take us on camels to find the nomad camp. He was aware of the smallpox program and that it was a high priority for the government.

I felt kind of schizophrenic. In northern West Bengal, I was initially treated like an American spy and told to report to the police station. Yet in western India, I was provided with hospitality, food, camels, and a tour of the outpost radio hut.

I learned a valuable lesson in the Thar. This desert was inhospitable, and any team going out needed to be well prepared. Our lives depended on it. We were lucky this time, but we couldn't count on luck in the future. And it became crystal clear to me that I needed to stock my first-aid kit with common medicines like aspirin, chloroquine, and ointments with prednisone to stop itching, because medicine and medical knowledge were more valuable to remote populations than any paper currency would ever be.

31

LITTLE KNOWN FACTS
ABOUT RAJASTHAN

After a close shave with death in the desert, some foreigners would not have wanted to head right back to the shifting sands. However, I felt the tantalizing allure of the desert districts. One fascinating feature of the desert culture was the hospitality offered to the hot, fatigued traveler.

While we were traveling in western Udaipur district and had surveyed several villages for rash-and-fever cases and smallpox slogans on the walls, we unexpectedly came upon fields of colorful, vibrant opium poppies. Blooms in a rainbow of vivid shades of blue, lavender, orange, and red were in exposed fields that were so accessible that anyone could walk into them. It was about noon, and we were hot and tired. I thought the village looked like a good place to vegetate for a few hours until the ambient temperature, which was around 48 degrees Celsius (118 degrees Fahrenheit), started to drop.

My team was invited into the headman's house; the shade was a welcome relief from the unrelenting sun outside. We slipped off our sandals at the door and entered the relatively cool room. Cushions were placed on the floor, on top of woven mats. I stretched out on the separate mat I was offered and curled up on my side.

Ramesh told me that they were preparing tea for us and then asked if I would accept opium tea. As this was a question of accepting hospitality, I heartily said yes. Besides, I was curious about the effects that the tea would have on us.

A contraption was brought into the room. A cotton cloth, so much used that it was the color of dark chocolate, dangled from it. Then powder was taken from a pouch, and several heaping spoonfuls were placed in the triangular cloth. Boiling water was poured into the cloth, and a glass was placed under the makeshift filter to receive the mixture. As each glass was prepared, it was presented to one of the members of my team.

Papaver somniferum, which means sleep-bringing poppy in Latin, is the name for that species of opium poppy. Opium is the source of many narcotics, including morphine and its derivatives heroin, thebaine, codeine, papaverine, and noscapine. The botanical name refers to the sedative properties of some of these opiates, as was so vividly illustrated in *The Wizard of Oz* when Dorothy, the Tin Man, and the Cowardly Lion tried to run across a field of poppies. They fell asleep under a magic spell in a futile attempt to escape the field.

Because the people in the remote regions were wary of outsiders, this was the first time that poppy tea was offered to us; that day was my first glimpse of significant fields of cultivated poppies.

What was the tea like? Well, it was exceedingly bitter. There were many different ways of preparing poppy tea. Most methods required the use of a poppy straw, in which the seed pod and sometimes the stem were ground into a very fine powder to access the bulk of the opium latex, which is within the cell walls of the pod. The village headman had used this fine powder.

What is the best way to prepare poppy tea? Some adherents claimed that boiling the powder rapidly was proper. Others insisted that cold water should be used, and still others swore that steeping the powder in hot water was the ideal method.

Whatever way it was prepared, the effects began around thirty minutes after the tea was consumed, and, depending on potency, the effects could last up to twelve hours.

I first felt a warming sensation in my skin. Given that many of the opioid receptors are located in the spinal cord as well as in the digestive tract, it wasn't surprising that I then felt a sensation of lightness along with a state of euphoria and enhanced well-being. Personally, the sensation of "lightness" was really subtle. In fact, I remember thinking, *Is this all there is?* I lived through the flower-child era of the 1960s, and because I was in medical school, I clearly wasn't the type to be stoned every day, or even most weekends. But for my money, I'd rather have two tokes of Acapulco gold and feel like Alice and her hookah-smoking caterpillar rather than drink any amount of this poppy tea!

The buzz wore off in about twenty minutes, and the headman asked if I wanted a tour of the fields. Ramesh translated as the headman gave me the fifteen-minute overview. Their village had a contract with the government to grow a certain amount of opium that was all purchased by the government.

At the end of the growing season, an official arrived and weighed and then tested the quality of the opium. The government apparently let the village keep a little for medicinal purposes. The villagers were carefully supervised to be sure no opium was diverted into the illicit black market system. I stood that day in the midst of fields and fields of poppies swaying in the wind. They were beyond beautiful. They were stunning.

According to the headman, the whole cultivation process was quite labor intensive. He had a lance, which he used to make a shallow slit from the top to the bottom of the capsule of a poppy, and whitish latex flowed out. I had a flashback to Malaysia and how the workers in the early morning lanced the rubber trees to collect the latex. This was an utterly different kind of latex.

I saw no women during this whole tea-making ceremony. That day was one more instance of me being treated as a male and participating in typically male ceremonies.

It wasn't that I made weekly trips to the opium districts. I was never in the opium production villages during the harvest. In the eighteen months I was in the state, I actually only had poppy tea prepared for me once. However, the memories of that occasion remain vivid.

There is another memory from my supervisory visits. In the district of Bikaner, we stumbled upon a little-known temple where rats are worshipped. The Karni Mata temple at Deshnoke (Karni Mata was a mystic matriarch from the fourteenth century), thirty kilometers from Bikaner town, was completed in the early twentieth century in the late Mughal style by Maharaja Ganga Singh of Bikaner. I mentioned him earlier in the chapter about the famous Bikaner Camel Corps he created. During the Navratri festival, which was dedicated to the goddess Shakti, thousands of people traveled to the rat temple on foot.

According to the legend as I learned it, Laxman, Karni Mata's stepson, drowned in a pond in Kapil Sarovar while he was attempting to drink water from it. Karni Mata implored Yama, the god of death, to revive him. After first refusing, Yama eventually relented, permitting Laxman and all of Karni Mata's male children to be reincarnated as rats.

The temple was famous for the approximately twenty thousand black rats that lived and were revered in the temple. Now, I could not verify that there were twenty thousand rats in the temple, but there were a hell of a lot of them! I never could have imagined the experience of what felt like thousands of black rats running over my bare feet. Among the many thoughts racing through my mind, the most prominent was, *Crap, what kind of diseases do rats carry?*

Well, of course, first on my mental list was the Black Plague, which killed millions during the Middle Ages; and then there was leptospirosis, which could lead to kidney damage and meningitis.

The thought that worried me most was that the rats might also like to nibble on my feet. I had been told that if one of the rats was killed, it must be replaced with another made of solid gold. Although I felt like kicking the rats off my feet, I restrained myself. I also got the hell out of the temple, fast.

There were no other devotees present at the temple when we visited. Eating food that had been nibbled on by the rats was considered to be a high honor. Out of all the thousands of rats in the temple, there were only a few white rats, which were considered especially holy. They were believed to be the manifestations of Karni Mata and her four sons. Sighting them was a special blessing, and visitors put in extensive efforts to bring them forth, offering *prasad*, a sweet holy food to entice them. Due to my nonbelief, there were no sightings of white rats. I just counted myself lucky that I didn't come down with one of the many dreaded diseases.

32

SEARCHING FOR SITALA MATA AT PUSHKAR

Then there was the story of the rattan furniture that I bought in New Delhi and left in a friend's compound until I could have it shipped down to Rajasthan. After I found my little house, I called the nice American CLO lady and told her, "OK, now you can ship my furniture." She had interviewed some cooks who were willing to also be house-keepers, or at least willing to direct an untouchable to keep my house clean.

Simultaneously, I sent a message to WHO that they could ship my alcohol allowance down by train. I was thinking that things were really coming together and that soon I'd be able to eat a decent meal in my own home. I did know how to cook, but at the end of a long day in the field, I didn't have the en-ergy to kneel down in an Indian kitchen and prepare food over a charcoal or gas fire. And I looked forward to gin and tonics at sunset.

The CLO made arrangements to find where I left my furniture, contact the Muslim cook, and put both cook and furniture on the bus from Delhi to Jaipur. I had left sufficient money with the CLO so she could buy a bus ticket for the cook and pay for the transport of the furniture piled on the top of the bus. We agreed on the date when the cook was to start his journey.

Hakim and I were in the main bus square with my Willy's jeep and rope at 3:00 p.m., the time the bus was to arrive. Miraculously, everything fell into place and played out according to the plan. I recognized my rattan furniture piled on top of the luggage on top of the bus. Lord knows how it managed to not fall off.

It was a regular show, getting the furniture off the roof of the bus and then stashing it on top of the jeep. Mohammed, the cook with the name I'd never forget, recognized the only female foreigner at the bus station, so we were both pleased to have found each other. And that night I sat down on my new rattan furniture in the dining/living room and ate a great meal of chicken curry and chapattis with a cold beer. This was the next best thing to heaven.

Work continued, of course, and the next major fair in Rajasthan was at Pushkar. This fair began every year in the month of Kartika (October–November) and continued until the full moon. Two hundred thousand people descended on the fair, which had a religious significance but was also an opportunity for the tribal folks to sell camels and cattle and take a holy dip in Pushkar Lake.

Pushkar is located at the foot of Nag Pahar, or Snake Mountain, and is surrounded on three sides by the Aravalli hills. Toward the north were sand dunes. Ajmer was the district headquarters town and nearest railway station for one of the most sacred and revered religious sites of India. According to *Padma Purana*, a Hindu religious text that explained how India and the cosmos were created, Brahma created Pushkar Lake by combining the holy waters from Badrinath, Rameshwaram, Jagannath, and Dwarka. Pushkar was the site where Brahma dropped the lotus he held in his hand when he was looking for a site to perform a *yajna*, or a ritual offering of oblations involving the sacred fire.

However, to perform the yajna, Brahma's wife Savitri should have been present at the designated time to perform an essential part of the ceremony. Savitri, however, was waiting for her girlfriend goddesses Lakshmi, Parvati, and Indrani. So Brahma married a Gurjar girl, Gayatri, and completed the yajna with his new consort sitting beside him, holding the pot of *amrita* (elixir of life) on her head and giving *ahuti* (an offering) to the sacrificial fire.

When Savitri finally arrived at the venue, she found Gayatri sitting next to Brahma, which was her rightful place. Agitated, to say the least, she cursed Brahma that he would never be worshipped outside of Pushkar. And her curse apparently came true. The temple at Pushkar was one of very few dedicated to the Hindu creator-god Brahma in India and remains the most prominent among them.

The sacred lake at Pushkar was a big pilgrimage site and drew hordes of Hindus to bathe in its healing waters. According to Indian mythology, all the Hindu pilgrim towns and temples should be visited; and if Pushkar was not visited for worship, then salvation was not achieved.

Pushkar was one of the five most sacred pilgrimage places for Hindus in all of India. Although Pushkar was very sacred,

I felt that if I was going to bathe in any waters for my salvation, then I should really do it in the mother of all rivers, the sacred Ganges at Benares. So I vowed that I would wait to bathe until I finished my smallpox work and could bathe in the Ganges just before leaving India.

Any large festival drew people from all over India; and in the past, people suffering from illnesses such as smallpox would also come to bathe in the sacred waters. Cholera and other waterborne infectious diseases could cause outbreaks when the health authorities didn't make adequate provisions for the disposal of feces and the chlorination of drinking water. The district health authorities assigned a number of smallpox workers to be on the lookout for rash-and-fever cases.

In 1976 this festival had few international visitors, and most of the Indians were on religious pilgrimage. I had now been in India for sixteen months. That year we found no rash-and-fever cases, so I concentrated on the finer traits of the richly decorated camel herds.

The Pushkar fair continued for five days, and those five days were a period of relaxation and merrymaking for the villagers. Animals, including over fifty thousand camels, were brought from miles around to be traded and sold. Trading was brisk; several thousand heads of cattle exchanged hands. This fair was one of the largest cattle fairs in the country.

I could not have cared less about cattle. I was mad for the camels. All the camels were cleaned, washed, and adorned, and special stalls were set up selling finery and jewelry for them. Camels at the Pushkar fair were decorated with great care. They wore jewelry of silver and beads, and silver bells and bangles jangled around their ankles when they walked.

Pushkar was not really known for horses, but I saw my first Marwari horse being ridden at the fair. It was said that horses were no ordinary animals; they were created by the gods, born out of the holy fire of Lord Brahma. The Marwari horse was elegant and brave, intelligent and graceful, and had long been associated with Rajput warriors. It had become synonymous with protecting Rajput honor.

There was no mistaking a Marwari horse. With a long head and a broad forehead, the distinctive animals featured large, wide-set, alert eyes; a Roman nose with full nostrils; and a well-shaped mouth. The most distinctive feature of the Marwari horse was its lyre-shaped ears, which curved inward and met at the tips. The ears were capable of rotating through an angle of 180 degrees to not only provide the horses with extremely acute hearing but also to protect them in sandstorms. The average height of Marwari horses was around sixty-five inches. And when they leaped, they could span twelve feet. The Marwari horses were born with a quick, four-beat lateral gait called either *rehwal* or *revaal*. It was smoother and more comfortable than a trot and was used in the desert to cover long distances with greater comfort.

By traditional accounts, the Marwari horses were originally bred in Rajasthan in 1212 as warhorses. They were bred by the Rajputs, the traditional rulers of Marwar, who developed a policy of strict selective breeding. Apart from their use in battle, Marwaris were excellent horses for hunting and racing. Albino Marwaris were considered priceless and used in religious ceremonies. In 1976, these horses were used for mounted safaris, endurance competitions, and religious ceremonies, and they were also in the cavalry of the Delhi, Punjab, and Rajasthan police.

My love affair with horses started when my family moved to California. One of the first people whom my dad operated on in Walnut Creek was the owner/trainer of a horse-riding stable. Mrs. Price broke her hip when one of the horses slipped and fell on her. Dad told her how much I liked horses, and once she was recovered, she offered to train me in Western and English riding. I helped around the stables, currying the horses and acting as a guide, taking small groups of people out on trail rides.

I didn't ride a Marwari horse at Pushkar. It was only later that I came to appreciate that lateral gait, when I rode the horses of the cavalry in Delhi in early morning rides before my smallpox meetings.

33

JAISALMER, THE MIRAGE
ON THE HILL

I'm not sure why so many of my adventures seemed to occur in the desert regions of Rajasthan. I remember my first trip to Jaisalmer district, which was named after Maharawal Jaisal Singh, a Rajput king who founded the city in 1156.

Jaisalmer was sometimes called the Golden City because it stood on a ridge of yellowish sandstone, which was also used in the city's buildings. The whole city had a yellowish-golden tinge. On my first excursion, the city was my sole destination. We had been traveling for some seven hours on the road from Jaipur. The Jaisalmer district was the largest district in Rajasthan; as part of the Thar Desert, it could be described as a sandy waste.

The general aspect of the area was that of an interminable sea of sand hills of all shapes and sizes, some rising to a height of 150 feet. Those in the west were covered with a type of bushy acacia tree, while the sand hills in the east were dotted with tufts of long grass. Water was scarce and generally brackish; the average depth of wells was 250 feet. There were no perennial streams, and the Kakni was the only small river. After flowing forty-eight kilometers, it spread over a large surface of flat ground to form Lake Orjhil.

The weather was hot, of course, and in the normal course of events, I would have switched places with Hakim to offer some relief from the unending monotonous driving. But ever since one of the foreign epidemiologists accidentally hit a young child in West Bengal, WHO had expressly forbidden us to drive. It was for our own safety. When an Indian national was driving, he was insured by WHO, and although there was litigation in the event of an accident, it was settled fairly quickly. There was unending trouble if a foreigner was involved. So as Hakim drove on and on, my head was bobbing up and down, and I was in a sort of trance.

Then I saw a fort up on a hill, shimmering in the light. This was my first honest-to-goodness mirage. We were still some two hours away from the city, but I could see this vision in the distance. We stopped the jeep and marveled at the sight. When we started again, the vision was gone.

When asked about my very favorite place in Rajasthan, I can honestly say that I loved my little desert town of Jaisalmer the best. For one thing, it was remote and difficult to access, so although tourists did occasionally get to it, the majority normally only made it to Jodhpur. Then they usually kind of gave up and went back once they had seen the Blue City.

I appreciated that the fort was not a touristy, closed-off attraction that visitors paid admission to visit. Nearly a third of the population of Jaisalmer lived in the fort. It was an all-encompassing, living structure. And at sunset, when the dying rays of the sun were descending, the fort and the adjoining palace took on a magical, almost tawny golden-honey glow. And when I went house to house, trying to ascertain people's knowledge of the smallpox program, I had brief but fascinating glimpses into the dwellings of those living in the fort. It looked intriguing to live in the fort, but as there was no running water inside the apartments/houses, I figured it was a pain to constantly haul water into the dwellings. The toilet situation must also have posed a problem; fortunately, it wasn't my problem.

Jaisalmer also had *havelis*, the grand private mansions owned by royalty and important people. They featured a blend of Rajputana and Islamic architecture. The city was just an enchanting, bewitching, and enthralling locale.

The lack of water in the district meant that it was not possible to have large villages or communities scattered throughout the area. We relied on the BSF to loan us a guide and camels so we could go out to visit some permanent wells and talk to the nomadic population. In one BSF camp we visited, we commented that they did not have an immense quantity of camels. They replied that most of the good camels were off on a security expedition. In fact, they told me that they were still training one young camel and suggested that it would be better if I rode on the back of the guide's camel. Of course I wanted my own camel, so I pushed the issue, saying, "It's no problem—I'll ride the camel in training. What could happen?"

As it turned out, a lot could happen in the space of a split second. Our three camels were lined up side by side. Two of the camels belonged to the officers who would be going out with us. Ramesh would be riding with one of the guides.

And then there was the third camel. He looked young, and he complained by roaring and growling when the saddle was placed on his back. He kept turning his neck and looking at the saddle; he clearly was not happy about having a rider or about going out.

Normally a *syce* (groom) put one foot on the folded leg of the camel while it was on the ground. That prevented it from jumping up before the rider was ready. For some reason there was no syce holding my camel. As I started to put my foot in the stirrup, the camel leaped up and took off running at a gallop. I tried to swing my leg over the rump to reach the other stirrup. The next thing I knew, I was being thrown off the camel. I landed with a thump, very embarrassed and a little sore from the hard landing on the ground. They caught the camel and brought him back. I should have left well enough alone, but I'd always been trained to get right back up on a horse. So I tried getting on again. Thankfully the camel settled down, and we took off.

Our intent on this trip was to visit a well and talk to whomever was there gathering water about any rash-and-fever cases back at their camps. As we had no idea where people might set up encampments, the strategy was to take advantage of the wells. If we visited the wells, the various communities would find us as they had to come search for water. At that time we could quiz them about rash-and-fever cases. There were about ten people at this well with about twenty camels that were being watered when we arrived. They were also filling big buckets with water to take back to their campgrounds.

We asked about rash-and-fever cases and passed the photo of the child with smallpox around the gathering. No one had seen any rash-and-fever cases at their camps. We decided to call it a day and head back. My camel was still disgruntled about this excursion and continued making disgusting roaring sounds in the back of his throat.

As we got closer to the border patrol camp, the camel turned his neck 180 degrees so he could stare into my face. I thought, *Shit, he is going to try and bite me.* I was mistaken. He took a gulp and regurgitated a gallon of green slime on me. Oh, the smell! I looked around, trying to figure out how I could wipe the mess off me. At the stable, the syce made the camel kneel down and handed me some rags. I got off the camel quickly. Cleaning up was difficult because there was not enough water to take a shower. I got a bucket of water and proceeded to wash my face and arms and hands. I threw away the shirt I was wearing. Even after I washed, the smell lingered.

I learned that camels have distinct personalities and are different from other livestock. They can be very clever. Camels do not spit, as many people believe. But, as I discovered, what they can do is just as disgusting.

When a camel is chewing its cud (which is basically regurgitated grass) and it gets upset about something, it makes loud noises with its mouth open, and the cud comes flying out. Any ruminant animal has more than one compartment in its stomach. Other ruminants include cattle, goats, sheep, llamas, giraffes, bison, buffalo, deer, wildebeest, and antelope. Most of these animals have a four-chambered stomach. The camelids—camels, llamas, alpacas, guanacos, and vicuñas—have three-chambered stomachs. The take-home lesson here is not to get on a camel that seems displeased!

Unfortunately, this was not the end of this story. Of course I was sore from being thrown off the camel; my hip initially ached. It was several days before I was back home in Jaipur and able to soak in hot, hot water in my tub in my little house. My bruised hip mended fairly rapidly, but it took my bruised ego a little longer to heal from the events of that day. I eventually put it out of my mind and forgot about the episode.

Over the next two weeks I picked up a cold, and I had a dry, unproductive cough. Whenever I took a deep breath in, it really hurt. There was a national smallpox meeting scheduled in Delhi, and I figured I would go in to see the doctor at the WHO clinic before the meeting started.

I figured I had picked up viral bronchitis or pneumonia. Who knows what people can catch from camels? At the clinic I explained that I had some type of bronchitis and that the cough was really causing me a lot of pain. He listened to my chest and then sent me for an X-ray.

When the X-ray technician brought up the film, the doctor looked at it, turned to me, and said, "What have you been doing? You have a green-stick fracture of one of your ribs! That's what's causing the pain."

A fractured rib—so that was the cause of my pain. I told him about falling off a camel that was galloping at full speed. It was a relief to know the cause of the problem. Once the doctor taped my rib cage, I immediately felt better. I didn't, however, ride camels for a while after that.

34

CLIMBING TO BASE CAMP OF MT. EVEREST

It seemed like I worked twelve-hour days for 365 days straight. Because of the reward for reporting a case, there were always rash-and-fever cases to investigate. However, I was able to take a few holidays during my time as WHO epidemiologist in Rajasthan. Once there was a three-day holiday, and I managed to hook up with another woman field epidemiologist, Dr. Helen Tom, who was working on smallpox in Madhya Pradesh. We met during a national smallpox meeting and then made plans to rendezvous to see the Taj Mahal.

The Taj Mahal, of course, is a white marble mausoleum located in Agra, Uttar Pradesh. The Mughal emperor Shah Jahan built it in memory of his third wife, Mumtaz Mahal. The Taj Mahal is widely recognized as the jewel of Muslim art in India and one of the world's universally admired masterpieces. It did not disappoint.

Helen was the only woman I met in the field in India. She was from Australia, which at the time seemed pretty exotic to me. We each traveled by train from our respective posts and enjoyed a long weekend in Agra. It was so awesome to meet up with another woman and compare notes of our experiences in the field. Helen was based in the capital in Bhopal, so she had a certain amount of urban amenities, whereas my rural time spent in northern West Bengal was very different. We suffered under similar caste taboos. She came from a small town—Alice Springs—and she regaled me about life in the outback. Helen wanted to visit California. I always planned to visit Australia, but it's a long way from any place! I still have never traveled there. I tried to interest her in climbing to the base camp of Mount Everest, but that was not one of her must-do items before leaving India.

I had always wanted to trek to the base camp of Mount Everest, but it had seemed like an unattainable dream. In California when I was young, I was in an outdoors Girl Scout troop, and we were always off on backpack trips, learning how to rock climb and do rappelling. In the winter, we went snow skiing at Lake Tahoe. We prided ourselves on being excellent outdoorsmen. Mountains were in our blood. So climbing Mount Everest was not so farfetched. It struck me that in India, I was practically in Everest's backyard. Now I needed to find another person who also wanted to make this climb; who would be fun; and who would have the time, money, and vacation time to do it. I thought that one of my fellow male epidemiologists might be up for the trek, so I put out feelers to see if there was any interest.

My eighteen months in Rajasthan were rolling by speedily, though, and it was doubtful that WHO would grant me time off as we got closer to "c-day" (certification day). The Rakhi Purnima celebration had already arrived and passed.

This holiday celebrated the sacred love between brothers and sisters, and on this day, sisters would tie a sacred thread called *rakhi* around the wrists of their brothers. Pram, my Rajasthani guide, had seen to it that a bracelet had been tied to my wrist.

I couldn't just head to the base camp whenever I felt like it. There were two main hiking/climbing seasons that provided the best conditions as far as temperature and climate to attempt the ascent. Base camp climbers went between March and early May, when the expeditions that were attempting to scale the mountain left, or else they headed up between September and the end of November. My best chance was to go in the fall.

There were many epidemiologists who were interested in going with me, but either they had no vacation time now or they had to wait until their posting was finished.

I finally found one enthusiastic hiker, Dr. Paul Rotmil, who had the time and was keen to go. He already had maps of the trail and information about how to get climbing permits. This was something he had wanted to do for a long time. So I asked Delhi for time off in November 1976.

We didn't have time to start the trek from Kathmandu; I probably didn't have the energy to do all that hiking in the lowland terrain anyway. I had my hiking boots, which had been sitting idle all the time I'd been in India. I also had my old sleeping bag from California. It was a good ten years old, and although it was great in the Rajasthan desert, I didn't think it would keep me warm in the low temperatures in the Himalayas.

I read that there were trekking rental stores in Kathmandu where I could rent a parka, sleeping bag, and anything else I needed. According to Paul's guidebook, it wasn't necessary to join one of those high-priced tented tours from the States. We could fly from Kathmandu into Lukla and select a guide and Sherpa porters right outside the plane doors. I regretted that we would not have any dehydrated food for the trek. We could get dried food in Kathmandu, but that would be relatively heavy for the Sherpas to carry.

Paul and I tried to communicate before arrival in Kathmandu, but our schedules and lack of easy access to phones made it difficult. We decided on a date when we could arrive in Nepal and made hotel reservations at a well-known trekkers' hotel. There were a lot of uncertainties surrounding this trip. For starters, we didn't have hiking permits, and we didn't have reservations for the plane to Lukla, because Lukla was a little airport that was not listed internationally. There were lots of things that would have to be done at the last minute. The beauty of youth and inexperience was that we couldn't see the downside. Why wouldn't things fall into place as we expected?

I'll tell you what I was worried about. I was worried about the cold and about freezing up there in the mountains. And I was worried about altitude sickness. Timing was crucial. Were we allowing enough time to acclimatize? Food was so much cheaper in Kathmandu, but still we would need to calculate how much food to buy for the entire climb. Although trekkers could collect firewood to cook meals, we still needed to exactly calculate our needs for kerosene gas for the time we would be above the tree line. We planned three days in Kathmandu to look for camping gear, buy food and a camp stove, and to get our permits for the trek and tickets for the flight to Lukla.

When we met in Kathmandu, the Kathmandu Valley was green and lush, and the temperature was pleasant; but I felt rushed, running around to pick up rental equipment. Getting our trekking permits at the Nepal Tourism Board was pretty easy and fairly cheap. Paul had requested that the smallpox program in Nepal make reservations for us on the plane to Lukla, so all we had to do was to go pay for the tickets. We were hearing disturbing rumors about flights being canceled because of poor flying conditions. The previous week, all flights into Lukla had been canceled due to poor weather. That meant that there were probably scores of hikers desperate to get on the plane to Kathmandu.

So now I started to worry. What if we couldn't leave on the date we wanted for Lukla? If we started late, it would impinge on the number of days we had planned for acclimatization at various heights. The logistics of this trip were looking worse all the time.

We did find the rental stores, and we rented a tent, sleeping bags, and parkas. I was in luck. There had been an all-women expedition to Everest in May 1975, and Junko Tabei had been the first woman to reach the summit. It was customary that at the end of a climb, the climbers would give their gear and clothes to the Sherpa guides and porters who assisted in the climb. This provided additional resources to the Sherpas, who sold the equipment to rental agencies. The guy in the rental shop showed me a nifty down parka that looked incredibly warm and said that Junko had worn it to the summit. I don't know if this was true or just one more story to get me to part with my money, but I needed a parka, and it fit, and the rental was just two dollars per day. I bought capri-length wool pants and three pairs of knee-high wool socks to cover the rest of my legs. I also rented a down sleeping bag. I already had a wool cap from the States and some ski gloves. I guess I had been planning to do this trek all along in the back of my mind.

We rented a kerosene stove and a two-man tent. We still needed to buy food for ourselves. The Sherpas provided their own food. It was tradition to buy tennis shoes for the porters so they would have shoes to wear above 15,000 feet. We weren't sure how many porters we would need, but we were ramping up the weight of our equipment with the tent, stove, and food, not to mention our backpacks and personal supplies. We were not going to have gourmet meals; we'd subsist on rice, dal, and iodide pills to sterilize the drinking water. We also carried medicine—antibiotics and Diamox for altitude sickness—that we would leave at the volunteer-run first-aid station at Periche, which is at 13,910 feet.

I ran into a woman who had just recently returned from Everest. She gave me good advice. She revealed that the Sherpas would not heat water for me to wash my face and hands. Because the streams were fricking cold, she just used a small jar of cold cream on her face the entire time on the trail. She could wipe off the cold cream, and her face looked clean. She also said, "Basically, during the fourteen to eighteen days on the trail, no one washes, so just leave the deodorant and shampoo with the things you are leaving at the hotel." I packed sufficient underpants to periodically have a fresh change and enough clean thin socks to put next to my feet. I didn't want blisters forming. I knew it was necessary to protect the feet at all costs.

And then it was the day to leave for Lukla. I woke up with the sniffles and scratchiness in my throat. Darn, I really didn't want to come down with a cold now. We were at the airport early for the flight with all our gear. I had offered special prayers for no rain or dense clouds. Of course, it was the weather at Lukla that was crucial. Apparently the approach was nerve-racking, because the plane turned into the landing strip and ended at the foot of a mountain. Wonderful!

I looked at all our gear and hoped the airline would accept it all. We would probably need three porters, because the only thing I was planning to carry was a tiny daypack that had my camera, a small water bottle, some hard candy, and a Swiss Army knife.

There was only one morning flight per day in November. It was a small plane; we were only twelve people. And then we were off. The sky was clear. It took around forty minutes to get to Lukla.

The only aircraft that could take off and land on that short runway were called STOL planes (short takeoff and landing). The runway at Lukla was only 1,510 feet long and sixty-six feet wide, and it had a twelve-degree slope. Landing in Lukla left no room for error. Pilots threw their propellers into hard reverse before they touched down.

The approach was through a maze of spectacular mountain peaks, and the air was often strewn with clouds. The plane had to clear a high ridge, bank left, descend steeply, and land before hitting the big mountain at the end of the landing strip. Navigation was by sight only on this landing strip, and in my opinion, it was one of the scariest in the world.

Our plane had barely stopped when there was a rush of what seemed like hundreds of hikers clamoring to be first to board the return flight of the plane. Because of the week of canceled flights, they were all stranded. The pilots asked us to deplane quickly because they wanted to shut the doors swiftly after us.

The luggage compartment was quickly emptied; our baggage and equipment was just thrown to one side of the runway. We quickly pulled our belongings into a tight circle. We depended on basic honesty when we left our stash of supplies to go find a guide. Paul and I agreed to meet at our pile of equipment in fifteen minutes. Between the hikers shouting and fighting to get on the plane, and us being accosted by independent guides looking for their next trip, I was a little bewildered. I just kept on walking, trying to get out of the crowd. And then I spotted a Sherpa a little ways off from the mob. I walked up to him and started talking.

He said he had been on the Japanese women's successful expedition the previous year. He had his porters off to the side. He needed to look at our supplies, and then could tell us how many porters we would need. I said, "Come with me to meet my partner."

Paul also had someone in tow. We quickly talked about our finds. We settled on my guide because he had better English, and we counted on hearing some great tales relating to the Japanese climb. His name was Sonnam Temba. He told us we needed three porters. We discussed the daily wage for the estimated trip and shelled out half the cost; the rest would be paid when we arrived safely back in Lukla.

We grabbed our daypacks, and the porters divided up the baggage. Apparently, neither the guide nor the porters lived in Lukla, so the plan was to stay with one of the Sherpa teams along the main trail while they gathered their personal kits. The first night we would eat and sleep with Temba's family. The porters took off to drop our baggage at Temba's house and then quickly race to their own homes, tell their families they had a trek, pack up their gear, get enough food for the trip, and then join us on the trail. We were off in forty minutes.

Lukla was already at 9,000 feet, and we had come from Kathmandu, which was at 4,600 feet, so we had some acclimatization to do. We started drinking water and began walking at a leisurely pace down the trail. I was just ecstatic that the plane had arrived in Lukla on schedule and that things had gone smoothly. We'd found a guide and porters, the cost was within the range that other hikers had told us, and we were on the Everest trail. Hallelujah!

We had allowed ourselves plenty of days to reach our ultimate goal, and we left ourselves time to go to Namche Bazaar for the Tibetan market on Saturday and take a slight detour to Thyanboche Monastery to get a blessing for our trek from the head lama. The trail meandered through a forested area, and there were a number of teahouses scattered along the way.

We stopped early on for some chai and something light to eat. It was at this rest stop that we discussed our plans for acclimatization days at 11,286 feet at Namche Bazaar and then at the Periche First-Aid Station. Then we would rest at base camp before attempting Kala Patthar, which was at 18,513 feet.

Sonnam Temba asked, "How do you want your meals and wake-up calls? You can get coffee in your tent at six in the morning and then eat breakfast and follow a Western style of day." He explained that this meant eating breakfast around 7:00 a.m. and getting a later start, having a light lunch in the afternoon, and setting up camp and eating an early dinner around 4:00 p.m. The Nepali style of day started with coffee in the tent. We would get dressed and start hiking the trail. The porters would break camp, pass us on the trail, and go ahead to fix the main meal, which they would serve around 11:30 a.m. This would be a combined lunch and rest stop, and then we would resume hiking around 1:00 p.m. and then break at about 4:00 p.m. for a light dinner.

Paul and I discussed the options and came to the conclusion that it was best to stick to the Sherpa timetable. They were the ones who would be lugging our supplies, and we could just adapt. By the time 4:00 p.m. rolled around, the sun would be behind some clouds, and the temperature would be dropping precipitously. Lunch would be our biggest meal, and we would have a long time to eat and check out the scenery while there was plenty of sunlight and it was warm.

That settled, we started back on the trail, and within an hour we came to our guide's village and found his house. His wife seemed happy to have us and that her husband had the work. This was early November and near the end of the season, so this might be his last paying gig. We were excited to see the inside of a typical Sherpa house and knew that soon enough, we would have to start using the tent.

We only walked about two hours that day, but we had started early that morning, faced the uncertainty about whether we would even fly, landed heading straight into a mountain, and searched out our guide and porters. I was exhausted.

Sherpa houses had two stories and were built of stone and wood logs. They were simple affairs. The roofs were flat and usually made of wood weighed down by heavy stones. The lower level was used to house livestock—in this case, several cows—as well as fodder, food, and firewood; and the upper story was a single large room that functioned as the living room, dining area, and sleeping area. The floor of the living quarters was wooden, covered with carpets and rugs. The heat from the animals below gave some additional warmth to the living area. We just unrolled our sleeping bags there. I don't remember much furniture; maybe there were benches for sitting. The meal was simple, just some type of gruel with tea. The rest of the family joined us on the wood floor. I nodded off around 8:00 p.m. Paul stayed up talking with Sonnam for a while. There was a small room off to the side for an altar. Incense and butter lamps were kept burning before the shrine.

The next day, Paul and I climbed the trail to Namche Bazaar, the Sherpa capital of the Kumbu region. Most trekkers arrived with foreign trekking groups that had tents, food, and yaks, and were self-sufficient. They camped along the side of the road and used wood to cook their meals. There were a few intrepid independent hikers, like us, who hired their own porters and generally stayed with their team's family lodgings until they climbed above the permanent villages. We lodged one other night with the family of one of our porters before we shifted to our tent.

There was a large expedition with about ten tents about a day ahead of us. The trail from Lukla to Namche was like a highway, but the traffic was mostly Sherpas heading for Namche, their capital city. Paul was a strong, fast hiker. Though we started off in the morning together, he soon outpaced me. The thing I kept reminding myself was that I had to find my pace and keep to its rhythm. If I tried to speed up, I would never be able to keep up that pace. Consequently, for most of the trek, I was a solo hiker. After about an hour on the trail, Sonnam Temba would catch up with me and walk with me a short ways. Then he would push on to go search out the best lunch site and make sure Paul was not too far ahead.

On the way to Namche Bazaar, I had to descend to the river and cross two bridges before I started a rather steep ascent. The most difficult thing for me on the Everest trek was having to continually descend toward a river and then regain the altitude that I had lost—and then climb an additional 1,500 to 2,000 feet on the other side.

Backpack trips in California and Colorado involved a slow ascent in elevation. We would reach a plateau and keep that altitude until we peaked over a mountain pass and started the long descent to the final destination. On the base camp trek, my knees and my lungs complained at the constant ups and downs. And the cold I'd picked up in Kathmandu was thriving. It was an irritation to be sniffling and spitting out mucus along the trail, and I worried how these cold symptoms might complicate recognizing the early symptoms of altitude sickness.

After I'd been on the trail about two hours, all three porters would pass me, clamoring up the track and encouraging me to keep up the pace. Lunch was ahead in two hours or so. Actually, it was kind of nice to be traveling solo. My mind could wander, and I could take in the gorgeous scenery without having to make small talk. It was already relatively cool hiking through the forest, but I knew that after we passed Namche, we would get above the tree line, and it would be cold.

Hiking was work, and I was certainly building up a sweat. After climbing out of the sleeping bag in the morning, I would put on a cotton turtleneck shirt, a woolen sweater, and then my parka. If the trail meandered out in full sunlight, off came the parka, and I tied it around my waist. If the sun went behind a cloud, or a switchback took me back into the shade, then I would get a chill and put the parka back on. It seemed a never-ending process of peeling off and packing on the clothes.

We had been warned to keep an ear out for the sound of yak bells, and we knew to get out of their way and to be on the uphill side of the trail. A number of tourists had inadvertently been swept over a cliff due to the bulging baggage on the yak saddles. Even the uphill position was not that safe, unless there was also a place to get out of the way to avoid being trampled.

I could not believe the heavy loads of supplies that the Sherpas carried on their backs. They were not tall; I towered over them. Yet they could carry seventy pounds on their backs with no problem. Going up the trail, a Sherpa woman passed me carrying a gigantic pine log about six feet long and sixteen inches in diameter. I was huffing with my small daypack of five pounds.

I loved lunchtime, which started whenever I dropped in. We had a hot meal of rice, dal, and whatever veggies the Sherpas had managed to buy in a village—while there were villages. Then there was some kind of cold drink, usually with flavored powder to camouflage the taste of the iodine tablets. We always had sunshine at lunch, and I would peel off my layered clothes to reach the cotton turtleneck, which by lunchtime was sopping wet. I would lay out my sweater and parka on the rocks to dry. Over lunch Sonnam Temba often regaled us with some event of the Japanese women's expedition. Sonnam gave credit to Junko Tabei, but he said, "You know it was a Sherpa who reached the summit first. Then he pulled up Junko."

"It doesn't matter who was first—what matters was that she made it," I replied. "And by the way, how high did you climb on Everest? Did you make it to Camp Four?"

There was silence, and then Sonnam said, "I carried equipment to Camp Two."

After lunch, I had time to rest and relax, digest my food, and close my eyes for a little nap. Everyone rested, and then the porters packed up the gear and started off. We discussed where we would camp that afternoon, and our tent would be pitched and a light dinner ready by 4:00 p.m. In November the days were short, and once the sun went down, it was damn cold! We would eat quickly and get in the tent right away. There was no campfire to sit comfortably around for warmth and companionship. I would quickly pee and then run to get into my sleeping bag. I would take off my somewhat damp wool socks and put them in the bottom of my sleeping bag, hoping that they would get dry by morning. If I spread them out over my boots, they would be damp and frozen in the morning. Paul and I would talk for about ten minutes, and then I was out like a light.

We were looking forward to Namche Bazaar, and not just for the famed Tibetan market of goods that were brought over the mountains from Tibet. We were planning two rest days there. When we arrived, Paul scampered all over the town and queried those descending about the trail. I was conserving my energy. I figured I could visit the town or see Edmund Hillary's school at Khumjung when we were coming down. We visited the Tibetan market early on Saturday, and I was able to find some treasures: an antique wooden teacup with silver engraving around the base and a beaten silver lining, a man's turquoise and bronze earring, and a bronze *dorje*, or thunderbolt.

35

CAMARADERIE ON THE TRAIL

The rest days were over in a snap, and then the real climb began. I'd been up to 11,600 feet in Colorado, so I knew I wouldn't have any problem with altitude at the level of Namche Bazaar. But now all bets were off.

We started off early for Tengboche, which was at 12,696 feet. It was on this part of the trail that I first saw Ama Dablam, a mountain that was part of the grouping with Everest. While hiking to the base camp from Namche, it was Ama Dablam that was constantly in our sight. Personally, I think it's a prettier peak than Everest.

Our plan was to visit the monastery at Tengboche and present the two white silk *khatas*, ceremonial scarves, that we had bought in Namche to the lama and ask for his blessing.

There were other people in line to visit the lama, but the line was moving. The presentation of our scarves was disappointingly anticlimactic. We asked for a safe trip and exited the monastery. We were barely back at our campsite before one of the porters ran in and excitedly gave a message to

Sonnam. Someone had gotten altitude sickness on the trail before base camp, and he was being brought down.

That information quickly sobered us up to the ever-present danger of the trail. Paul and I had made a pact in Kathmandu. If either one of us started having altitude sickness symptoms, we would descend to a lower altitude and wait for the symptoms to subside. Then we would try to ascend again, together. We swore to never leave the other hiker with the porters and ascend alone. We had factored in extra days to avoid feeling any pressure or need to continue climbing because of time constraints. Usually people got in trouble because they were on a fixed time schedule with a group, and so they pushed themselves to go on even if they were not feeling up to it. Now someone on the trail was being evacuated.

Altitude sickness occurs when a person cannot get enough oxygen from the air at high altitudes. This causes symptoms such as a headache, loss of appetite, trouble sleeping, weakness, dizziness, nausea, and vomiting. It happens most often when hikers who are not used to high altitudes go quickly from lower altitudes to eight thousand feet or higher. Mild altitude sickness is common. Experts cannot predict who will become ill and who will not. A hiker's fitness level, sex, age, or previous experience at high altitude do not indicate whether he or she will experience acute mountain sickness (AMS). As air is "thinner" at high altitudes, when climbers ascend too high, too fast, their bodies cannot get as much oxygen as they need, so the breathing quickens. This causes the headache and other symptoms of altitude sickness. As the body gets used to the altitude, the symptoms go away.

The best treatment for altitude sickness is a rapid descent to a lower altitude. Oxygen and medicines such as Diamox and dexamethasone are helpful. It is easy for climbers to over-look the symptoms, making it important for climbing buddies and the guides to check each other frequently.

More information on the evacuee filtered in later. He was a foreign leader of a climb who had brought clients to base camp at least three other times. I guess he felt responsible for getting the clients up the mountain and ignored his own symptoms.

It was the Sherpa porters who noticed and took over and then carried him down the mountain. We were particularly vigilant about checking with each other to see how we all felt that night.

We were fine, with no headaches. I normally ate less on a backpack trip, but I was eating and drinking a lot of fluids on this trek. My cough was lingering, but at least it was not worse. I was hesitant to take anti-cough medicine, which might mask the severity of any altitude symptoms. We had two more days to reach Periche, a planned rest stop to acclimatize to the new higher altitude.

I could feel the effects of elevation. My steps were already slow. Taking my camera out to take photos was becoming a major effort. It was also getting colder.

When we arrived at Periche at 13,910 feet, I was grateful that we were there and could rest the following day. I just let the sunlight hit my body, and I relaxed. I was so tired that I could hardly take my daypack off and peel off my parka and sweater so that they could dry. One of the porters brought me a bowl of dal baht, and, although bland, it was hot and hit the spot.

Paul had already searched out the Periche aid post and re-ported that there was an American doctor from San Francisco manning it. He was doing some research on the effects of high altitude on the eyes, and he wanted to look at our optic nerves. I thought, *I'd rather not know what the high altitude is doing to my eyes,* but what I said was, "Let me rest some, and then we can go over to the post before it gets dark."

Paul woke me up from a nap, and we trudged over to the aid post, which was basically a little yak hut. We introduced ourselves and told the doctor about the smallpox eradication efforts in India, and Dr. Peter Hackett told us about coming out to Nepal in 1975 and loving it and staying on to volunteer in the aid post.

He was also very interested in AMS. We told him we had a shitload of medicines that we would drop off on our way down. He seemed very happy about that. He eventually got around to peering in our eyes, and he said they looked good so far. When I asked if he had seen the guy with AMS, he told me he had helped to stabilize him for the trip down. He was doing fine. Normally it was one of the clients who had problems. This guy had been on this trail four times.

It was fun to just relax and laugh and talk and hear all the problems that had passed through the clinic. Peter invited us to come back around in the evening after dinner, and said that if we could gather some yak dung, we could sit around his "stove." His stove looked like a battered old oil drum that had been roughly modified. That sounded great to me—an actual campfire, sort of. It would be my first in the Himalayas. He handed us canvas bags to help in the dung-collection task. I thought, *So this is how he stays warm in the evenings.*

Luckily, Periche was on the main yak trail to base camp, so it was not that difficult to collect the yak dung. The philosophy of the rest day was to rest and not do a lot of walking. We were to just take in the scenery. This was a barren landscape; I hadn't seen a tree since Tengboche.

It was funny; I had never collected dung, even in India, and here I was scouring the environment for yak dung. We were back at 6:00 p.m. at the yak hut and found some chocolate and hard candy to take over to Peter's. We did not have any alcohol with us. That was one of the reasons we were looking forward to getting to Gorak Shep; the lodge there was supposed to have beer. Our luck was holding with the weather. There was no snow, but once the sun set each evening, it was damn cold, so it was heaven to go inside a hut.

Peter had a roaring fire going, and we plunked down our contributions of dung. Our conversations that night were nothing earth shattering; we just shared our smallpox world and he shared his existence manning the aid post on the way to Everest. It was warm; I even took off Tabei's parka and basked in the warmth. Then Peter brought out some alcohol. I don't remember if it was scotch or brandy, but when he poured it into small cups, it was like a heavenly elixir.

Paul and Peter energized me, and I was confident I could make it to base camp. It was difficult to tear ourselves away from the fire, but we had to get to Gorak Shep tomorrow. We promised to pass by the aid station on the way down so Peter could check our optic nerves. And then we reluctantly departed.

As usual, we left early on the trail. This was the beginning of the difficult section for me. Above fourteen thousand feet, the trail was a bitch. My mantra was: *left foot, right foot, on the way, follow the drinking gourd.* I remembered the words from my guitar-playing and singing days, from an old folk song of the slaves following the North Star to freedom. We planned to have tea and food in Lobuche and then push on to Gorak Shep. It was supposed to be relatively easy. "Relatively" was the interesting word. I caught up with Paul and Sonnam at the one and only teashop in Lobuche. They had been there some time, waiting for me to get in.

I said, "Sorry, it's all I can do to just put one foot in front of the other. But I plan to savor this tea." They planned to press on and get to Gorak Shep and set up our camp.

"Connie, be sure and fill up your water bottle here, and don't loiter long. Keep on coming," said Sonnam.

"No problem," I answered. I planned just to take a fifteen-minute stop. I went out with them to the trail and waved good-bye.

Then I saw a bench on the side of the teahouse in the blazing sun. I stripped down to my cotton turtleneck and laid out the sweater and parka to get dry. *I just need fifteen minutes*, I thought, and then I stretched out on the bench facing away from the trail. I took off my wool hat and placed it over my face to keep the rays from burning me. I soaked in the sun and drifted off.

The next thing I knew, some fool jerked my hat off my face and said, "Are you going to lie there all afternoon?"

I opened my eyes but was blinded by the blazing sun. I could only see the back of some hiker with longish hair pulled back in a ponytail going into the teahouse. Damn, my nap was more than fifteen minutes, and I knew I had to push myself if I wanted to get into Gorak Shep anytime soon. In my rush to get going, I forgot to fill up my water bottle.

The trail was not particularly difficult; it just seemed unending. I stopped to pull out my water bottle for a drink—and realized that I had failed to fill it at the teahouse.

How dumb could I be? I thought.

And then a hiker came up the trail and stopped. *He must be the one who pulled off my hat at the teahouse,* I thought. *At least the ponytail is the same.*

"Hi, I'm Larry," he said. "Looked like you were enjoying your nap back there."

"I was, but someone ruined it for me," I said. "I guess it was for the best; I probably would still be there."

He offered me his water bottle with a contrite look.

"Oh, thank you! Are you hiking with a group?" I said.

"No, but I have a porter." Before he pushed off, he said, "I hope I see you at the lodge tonight in Gorak Shep."

I smiled and said, "I'll see you there."

I wondered who this guy was. He certainly saved my life with the water. I couldn't believe I didn't fill my bottle. I returned to the path. By the time I got into our camp, dinner was past ready. We were camped not far from the one and only lodge. It was hard to know how many people were camped inside that place. I wondered where Larry was staying.

"Hey, Paul, did you see a hiker earlier? His name is Larry—I think he's an American."

Paul said, "Yeah, he got in about an hour ago. He said you were walking slow, but you were on the way."

I said, "So, are we all heading to the lodge tonight?" It seemed like this was the place to meet those trekkers who were a day ahead of us and to have some fun.

When Paul and I trudged over, the lodge's main room was packed. I'd say about thirty people were inside. Where had all these people been hiding?

It was a gregarious group; they were singing folk songs from around the world and drinking beer and other stuff. I looked around to see if I could find my savior from the trail. Larry came up behind me and said softly, "Do you want a beer?"

"God, yes, do I ever." I followed him to a makeshift bar. We both got a beer and then looked for a place to sit among the mash of hikers on the floor.

Oh, it was *warm*! There was no electricity, but there was the soft yellow glow of kerosene lanterns and a fire in a makeshift stove in the middle of the room. I took off my parka.

Then we just started talking: about the trail, how tired we were, where we were coming from. Larry was from Seattle, where he did research at Kings County Hospital.

Funny, I had interviewed there and might have interned in pediatrics there, but I had checked out the weather and saw that it rains nine months of the year in Seattle!

I talked about India and smallpox. I nursed my one beer. I was feeling pretty high from the altitude and didn't need alcohol to complicate things. Larry was planning on climbing Kala Patthar tomorrow.

My group was to continue to base camp tomorrow. It hit me that I probably wouldn't see Larry again. Shit! "So, after you do Everest, what are your plans?" I asked.

He was going on to the Seychelles Islands. He was taking off work for a few months, and after Everest he wanted to go someplace warm, with white sandy beaches, where he could scuba dive. Then he asked if I was interested in joining him.

I didn't even know where the Seychelles were exactly. We knew the following day was going to be busy and difficult for us both, and we were heading in different directions. Then Larry was planning to take another trail back to Lukla, while Paul and I would just retrace our steps. I always seemed to be going in different directions as far as men were concerned.

So he walked me back to my cold, forbidding tent. I was shivering from the cold. Larry said, "Connie, I think we will overlap two days in Kathmandu. I'm staying in a rented apartment, and I think it's only a short distance from your hotel." He took my hand and placed a piece of folded paper in it. "Let's meet in Kathmandu. Here is my address." A quick hug, and he was off. I unzipped the tent flap and stepped in quickly.

Paul was already in his sleeping bag. Great, I didn't have to come up with any small talk; I could just dream. But dreams at high altitude were more like nightmares. Morning came too soon, and then we were in the final push on to base camp!

This was the most momentous day of the entire trip. It was supposed to be an easy hike to base camp from Gorak Shep. I kept discovering that easy was relative. Since we had hit fourteen thousand feet, every day had been bone numbing.

I found my mantra, I found my rhythm, and I finally arrived! I looked around and wondered why we had wanted to make it to base camp in the first place. It was the middle of November. We were lucky that the weather had held. It was a frozen wasteland with a few scattered tents from expeditions climbing to the top. There was a lot of garbage—used oxygen canisters, packing material—strewn around.

It was overcast and cold. The Khumbu Icefall looked impressive and was dead straight ahead. For those climbing to the summit, the icefall was extremely treacherous. Huge blocks of ice were continually breaking away and crashing down to base camp or causing landslides.

Back in Kathmandu, before we understood the difficulty of the trek, we had planned to stay a few days at base camp. Sonnam had offered to take us closer to the icefall. We could also climb Kala Patthar, as Mount Everest wasn't visible from base camp.

But frankly, I was dead tired. We had made it, and I could see no reason to stick around. My cold had never gone away, and I still had the cough, which seemed worse at night. I was having frightening dreams in Technicolor at night, although I couldn't remember them at daybreak. We decided to stay overnight and then reassess the possibilities in the morning. I stayed up half the night listening to the sounds of ice blocks breaking away; it sounded like the blocks were crashing directly in our path. I had to get up in the night to pee. It was a real pain to open the tent, walk a short distance, and then pull down my pants. *Oh my God, deliver me from this cold,* I thought. As I climbed back into my sleeping bag, Paul asked if I was OK.

"Yeah, it's just deadly cold outside, trying to pee!" I said.

Morning took its time coming. As we were dressing, Paul said, "Connie, I think we should head down. Last night you were Cheyne-Stokes breathing. You would stop breathing and then eventually cough, take a big breath, and then start breathing again! It was really scary for me."

Cheyne-Stokes respiration is an abnormal pattern of breathing characterized by progressively deeper and sometimes faster breathing, followed by a gradual decrease that results in a temporary stop in breathing called an apnea. It sometimes occurs in otherwise healthy people at high altitudes.

"Are you kidding?" I asked.

He shook his head no.

I looked at Paul and said, "You know, we did it; we trekked to base camp. We did everything we set out to do. Let's not push it. Let's head down today. I'm sure our porters will be happy; they have to be freezing. Their clothing is really light-weight compared to ours."

The camp was packed up in a flash. We practically tore out of base camp. It was incredible how I felt descending the trail. It almost felt like flying. With each thousand feet of descent, I felt like bricks were being taken off my back. We were in Periche in no time.

We decided to camp there and then push fast to descend to Namche Bazaar the next day. We found Peter Hackett at the aid station. He grabbed his equipment and checked out our eyes and found no problems in either of us. Great. We handed over the meds that we had hoarded during the whole trip. I never did take any Diamox.

As we headed out of Periche, the first snowflakes started to fall. All I could think was that I was so glad to be heading down. We really didn't need snow. I wondered how Larry was doing on his trek. It was amazing how fast we could go down-hill. I could keep up with Sonnam and Paul going this way.

As we passed Namche Bazaar, the first of our porters peeled off. The night before, we had paid the porters the bal-ance of the funds and had given a generous tip to Sonnam to divide between the porters and himself. I couldn't give much else, because the equipment was rented. The trek had been hard, but in the end, it was an immense accomplishment for me and gave me bragging rights forever over my older broth-er, the trekker! Eat your heart out, Colbert!

All I could think about was a hot shower back at the hotel in Kathmandu. Paul and I had planned a dinner at the fa-mous Yak and Yeti Restaurant, which was attached to the hotel of the same name. Lukla looked so different now that we were the departing passengers. At least flights had been regular since our arrival more than two weeks ago, so there were no crowds trying to storm the planes. It was a bittersweet feeling, leaving our mountain paradise.

The big city quickly brought me back to earth. I was so ready for our hotel. Paul was a dear, and he returned all our rental equipment and my sleeping bag and parka. I would miss Junko's parka, which kept me toasty warm, and I would forever regret not buying it. It was the best down parka I have ever worn. I went straight to my room. I was tearing off clothes on the way to the shower. I just stood in the hot shower for forty minutes. I looked down at the water exiting the drain and saw that it was unbelievably filthy. I was at least four shades lighter once all the dirt had washed away.

I had left some clean clothes behind in hotel storage. My jeans were definitely hanging on me. I weighed twelve pounds less than when I started the trek. I felt like I could run and bike around town with all this energy. When we met to go to dinner, I noticed that Paul had also lost the "tan" he had acquired on the trail, and off we headed to lighten our wallets at the Yak and Yeti. I had a steak, medium rare, and let the blood run. And there was some good red wine! Our conversation did turn to smallpox, and we wondered what was happening in our respective states back in India. Paul said, "Well, we'll find out soon enough!"

Paul was off the next morning, headed back to India. I had planned two days of decompression in Kathmandu before returning. And I knew exactly how I wanted to decompress.

I found the note from Larry with his address and remembered the directions to his apartment. All I had to do was to walk out my hotel door, turn left, and go straight down the street for about three blocks. *Well, here goes nothing.* I rang the doorbell, and the door opened immediately! Fortunately, Larry was on the other side. We both felt rejuvenated after our return to Kathmandu.

I could tell you that we sat around and discussed the trials of the trail, but no words were exchanged then. We did communicate in other, more intimate ways, which I will leave to your imagination. I was just happy that the living room was warm. I didn't need a parka, and clothes were optional. The wait was worth it! I didn't see any Kathmandu attractions on that visit to Nepal.

Both of us were leaving in less than thirty hours. I had an open invitation to come visit and stay in Seattle. And Larry was invited to visit me in Rajasthan before my carriage turned into a pumpkin in May 1977.

After that, I didn't know where I would be. I kind of knew he would never come to India. But I did eventually get a letter in Rajasthan several months after his Seychelles adventure. He wrote that the water was warm and crystal clear and a dazzling blue, but he regretted that I was not there. And I didn't get to Seattle until some thirty-six years later, when I arrived to attend my daughter's college graduation. At that time I figured Larry had long since moved or was attached to a spouse and family, among other things. Let sleeping dogs lie. I still had the memories!

36

SPECIAL DESERT SEARCH

I was on a plane headed back to Jaipur from Kathmandu. I felt rejuvenated and in great physical shape after the successful climb to Everest base camp. As it was necessary to change planes in Delhi, I planned to spend one day in consultation at the WHO smallpox unit before heading on to Jaipur. The senior epidemiologists had reviewed the status of the former endemic states and were trying to determine the concerns of the certification team.

Rajasthan was always a cause for particular concern due to the isolated and inaccessible areas in the Thar Desert. Delhi had previously intimated that Rajasthan would need additional checks; and after long, hard thought, they proposed the state undertake a special desert search. As the WHO epidemiologist in Rajasthan, I would be intimately involved in leading and executing this search. And there wasn't much time to prepare, because Delhi wanted the results well in advance of the proposed visit by the global certification team in April 1977. I knew what I would be doing in December.

The first day back in the office in Jaipur was hectic. Besides catching up on all the reports submitted from the field, I had some planning to do at the state level for the special desert search. The state smallpox unit had been pulling records and maps and already discussing the wheres, hows, and whos for the search. There was fairly unanimous agreement that the most inaccessible districts were Bikaner, Jaisalmer, and Barmer; their western borders all abutted the frontier with Pakistan.

The next task was to choose primary health centers (PHCs) in the isolated districts that had poor smallpox search records. Eight PHCs were identified by those criteria. Then we worked with the district medical officers to develop a list of all villages and *dhanis* (hamlets with one to ten huts) to be included in the ten-day search.

We determined that nine mobile teams, each consisting of a medical officer, three vaccinators, and a driver, would be needed to conduct the search. In addition, three state-created assessment teams, each with a medical officer and one paramedical assistant (PMA), would appraise the overall quality of the special desert search and evaluate the vaccination status of a subset of the population in the PHCs. Finally, we were to determine if the practice of variolation had occurred and if there were stored scabs that could still be harboring the smallpox virus.

I also had the thankless tasks of calculating the budget needed to support the search and obtaining the funds from Delhi. I was working late into the evenings at the office trying to make sure I had correctly calculated and recalculated the costs for petrol, unexpected repairs, and the special pay for the staff involved in the search. I needed to get those numbers off to Delhi—like, yesterday.

I had just finished a late dinner at home when a massive truck that had been converted into a bus pulled up to my house. Out jumped Pram, my resident guide to Jaipur and Rajasthan, and two guys I had never seen. Pram said, "Connie, you have been working overtime these days, and I thought you needed a diversion. This is Paul and Joe; they are leading an Australian group of overlanders across Asia."

The Asia Overland Route was the name given to the journey from Europe to South Asia, usually to India and Nepal that was taken mostly by members of the hippie subculture and others from the late 1950s through the 1970s. These two guys were the guides/drivers of the converted truck, and they were traveling with about twenty Australian clients. They had started in Europe and driven overland through Iran and Afghanistan and then down into India. They had already been on the trail for five months. In Jaipur, they picked up Pram to show them the Rajasthani sights. They were only staying two nights in Jaipur. They brought a case of beer, and I offered my gin and tonic and the Johnny Walker Red. These were my first overlanders, and it took a while to understand their Aussie accents.

We hadn't gotten too far into their tale about heading into Iran when Paul said, "Hey, mate, there's something wrong with your gin. It tastes like water."

"What do you mean? Maybe the tonic is flat," I said. "Pram, you taste it."

"Can't taste the gin at all, Connie."

I picked up the glass, and I couldn't taste the gin, either. So I went to my storage room and brought out the last four bottles of gin and four new glasses. Paul and Joe tasted the lot. It all tasted like water!

"I can't believe it," I said. We examined the bottles closely. Joe said it looked as if someone drained about half the liquid from the bottles and then refilled them with water. The first bottle had been opened carelessly. When we looked carefully at the last four, we could see that they had been opened and then carefully closed again. There were only two people living in this house.

I said, "My cook told me he doesn't drink—he's a Muslim!" The Aussies cracked up and started rolling on the floor.

"So you think that's funny, heh? All my bottles are diluted," I said. OK, it was true that I was traveling three weeks out of four for work, and I had been in Nepal the last three weeks. But I just couldn't believe that he drank all my bottles of gin. Now what was I going to do? I couldn't keep him. He had stolen and cheated me. He would plead not to be sent away, but how could I ever have control over him or trust him again?

There was no gin and tonic that night. The Aussies and Pram tried to make me laugh, and we loaded up on beer as they continued to relate their adventures in Afghanistan. I was glad Pram brought over the overlanders, but I was not looking forward to the next morning.

Mohammed was up early, and my breakfast was waiting for me. I went to the storage room and brought out all the gin bottles. Then I explained my discovery the previous night and asked Mohammed if he had opened the bottles and drunk them.

First he denied the deed. "No, madam, not me. I do not drink!"

"Well, I didn't drink five bottles. I'm never here."

Then there was much gnashing of teeth and begging for redemption. "I have a family of eight children—we will be destitute," he cried.

"Should have thought of that before you did the deed."

"Oh, madam, just one more chance. I won't do it again."

You bet you won't do it again, I thought. In fact, I had thought about how I would keep Mohammed busy, since I was not in Jaipur a lot. Oh, how stupid was I to think that he wouldn't drink my liquor. I had put all the booze except for one bottle in a closet in the guest room and had put a lock on the door to which only I had a key. In retrospect, I guess he had all the time in the world to get someone in to make a duplicate key, and then help himself. I had to hand it to him, he was very clever. *Christ, I hate sacking the staff,* I thought. *Besides, he is a good cook.* But it was not feasible to keep someone who had blatantly stolen from me, and I still had months ahead when I would be out of Jaipur more than I'd be home. Still, I couldn't believe I was firing the cook.

However, the truth was, I had to supervise domestic staff and watch them like a falcon. I'd learned that domestic employees from Delhi were wise to the ways of the world. I should have hired my staff in Rajasthan and just taken the time to train them, however long it took. I learned a hard lesson; I couldn't cut corners.

I suppose some employers would have sent him away for dishonesty without paying him. However, he did need to get back to Delhi, and I wanted him gone. So I paid for the bus ticket and paid his wages. There was no bonus for work well done. I was without a cook, again.

I had no time to cry over spilled milk. I needed to go out to the selected districts for the special search to see if there were any problems in the preparation phase. The medical officers in the districts had no problem with the methodology of the survey, but no one had heard of variolation.

Variolation was the method first used to immunize individuals against smallpox (variola). It involved taking material—like smallpox scabs or fluid—from a person with smallpox and rubbing it into superficial scratches in the skin of another person, in the hope that a mild but protective infection would result. The patient would develop pustules identical to those caused by naturally occurring smallpox, but they would be less severe. Eventually, after about two to four weeks, the lesions would subside, indicating successful recovery and immunity and leaving the telltale facial scars.

Variolation was first used in China and the Middle East before it was introduced into England and North America in the 1720s in the face of opposition.

How did variolation differ from vaccination?

Vaccination is the administration of antigenic material (a vaccine) to stimulate an individual's immune system to develop immunity to a pathogen. The active agent of a vaccine can be inactivated (non-infective) or attenuated (reduced infectivity) forms of the causative pathogens, or purified components of the pathogen that were found to be highly immunogenic. Those who receive a vaccine develop immunity to the disease without coming down with the disease. With variolation, patients came down with the actual disease, and some could still die from it. If you survived, you had immunity.

Before there was a vaccine, certain areas of colonial India administered by the British practiced variolation. It was also known that in the desert regions of Pakistan and Afghanistan, variolation had been a common practice. The smallpox virus could survive in scabs for ten years or more. The certification team was concerned that there could still be viable scabs out there, buried in the ground or elsewhere, that could act as foci for reinfection. If the practice of variolation had occurred in the desert region of Pakistan, what would have prevented it from occurring in India? We knew that borders didn't keep out diseases or practices.

None of the young district medical officers had even heard of the practice. They looked at me as if I were demented and telling a crazy, fantastic tale. I was leading one of the assessment teams, and my personal mission was to determine if indeed this practice had occurred or was still occurring. I needed to find out who did variolation and talk to the last person who had done it, if humanly possible.

I knew that to investigate this practice, I would need camels to get around the desert. I had already used a number of the camels from the BSF. I just needed to make contact and make sure the BSF could support us again.

The special desert search was conducted from December 13 through December 23, 1976. The nine mobile teams had their survey instruments and would collect both demographic data and smallpox vaccination data. The teams collected data on age, sex, religion, and language, along with information on smallpox vaccinations, scars, and facial pockmarks. The health interview also asked about variolation and determined the population's knowledge of the smallpox program: if they had seen the recognition card, if they knew about the thousand-rupee reward for reporting a confirmed case of smallpox, and if they knew where to report suspected cases.

We gained immense knowledge from the special desert search. The districts selected—Jaisalmer, Barmer, and Bikaner—were also the three largest districts in Rajasthan by land mass. Their population density was sparse: four, twenty-seven, and twenty-one people per square kilometer, respectively.

In Rajasthan as a whole, the composition of the religious communities was 90 percent Hindu, 7 percent Muslim, and 3 percent other. In the desert area, there was a higher proportion of Muslims, with 24 percent in Jaisalmer, 12 percent in Barmer, and 11 percent in Bikaner. Furthermore, there was a high concentration of Muslims along the border, and they maintained close ties with relatives in Pakistan.

The survey results confirmed that variolation was a well-known procedure in the desert area and that it was confined exclusively to the Muslim community. Variolators were members of the Bardi-Fakir sub caste. A *fakir* was regarded as a religious priest/saint and credited with having supernatural powers. He was involved in various religious ceremonies and was skilled in healing the sick.

Initially it was difficult to get any answers about variolation or who did it from the Muslim community leaders, as they were fearful of reprisals by the government. I had to repeatedly reassure them that no one would get in trouble if I spoke to the fakirs. Finally, we obtained the names of three fakirs. Then we discovered that two of the three were deceased. Trying to get directions to the remaining fakir's dhani was like trying to find water in the desert.

At first, I thought I was being led on a wild-goose chase. I kept hearing that the fakir's dhani was just over the next hill. I had heard that before. We were on camels, and I had a guide from the BSF with us. For three days I followed rumors. The fakir had gone for a wedding in another place, or he had headed home and we had just missed him, or someone was sick over that hill and he had gone just a few hours before we arrived.

On our third day of searching, we finally found his dhani. There was an old lady vigorously sweeping the area in front of the hut. She confirmed that the fakir lived there, but he had just left that morning to attend to a sick child. She was his spouse. I couldn't believe that we had finally found his camp-site. She welcomed us and invited us for tea. We dismounted from the camels, and I said to Ramesh, "Let's see how much his wife knows." Turned out, she knew a lot.

Once we all had tea, I asked Ramesh to translate and tell her I was a WHO doctor and I was interested in whether her husband ever did smallpox variolation.

She looked up and said, "Yes, my husband did smallpox variolation for many years."

I asked, "Do you know how he performed it, or can you describe the process of variolation to me?"

She laughed and said, "I used to help him in getting things prepared." And then she went into a lengthy description of the procedure. "Back in the old days," she continued, "when a smallpox outbreak occurred in a dhani or among a nomadic group, it was the custom for the community to send a camel to collect my husband. I often went along. When we got to the dhani or the village, my husband would collect scabs from an infected person. He would look at all those sick with small-pox and try to determine who had the mildest case. He would then take scabs from that person.

"Then I took over with the next part. I would place the scabs in a medium-sized seashell and dissolve the scabs and pus in human milk by grinding and mixing it. Once this mixture was liquid, I would give the seashell back to my husband. I had already prepared seven needles—like sewing needles—bound together with a thread. My husband dipped the needles in the scab fluid and then jabbed the right hand of the person numerous times."

The old woman then took my hand, and with a jabbing motion, she indicated the area of my hand that medical doctors called "the anatomical snuffbox." The snuffbox is located between the thumb and the first finger.

"Then," she said, "the leaf of the *beri* fruit was placed on top of the puncture wound and bandaged in place. Eight to twelve days later, the smallpox rash usually occurred. Anyone who was unprotected or who never had a smallpox infection was brought forward for variolation."

Then I asked coyly, "Is the fakir still doing variolation?"

She looked at me like I was crazy and laughed. "He stopped a long time ago," she said.

"Why?" I asked.

"Because the government came out with vaccination, and he wasn't needed anymore."

I had one last question. "Did your husband keep the scabs in a safe place so he would always have some scabs ready in case he was called?"

The fakir's wife shook her head, smiling. "There was no need to keep scabs; there was plenty of infection!"

And so we had our answer. We need not fear that children playing one day would unearth some scabs and smallpox would rear its ugly head again. What a relief! And so we thanked the fakir's wife profusely, climbed back on our camels, and headed to the BSF outpost. I needed to check on how the mobile teams were doing on the survey.

Realistically, there were probably a number of factors that brought variolation to an end. The villagers in the household study confirmed what the fakir's wife said. With the start of the government program of smallpox vaccination, there was no need for variolation.

The incidence of smallpox was decreasing rapidly in the desert, helped in large part by the low population density. The virus had no new, large populations to infect. From smallpox records, by 1970 smallpox was approaching zero incidences in this area. In addition, government vaccinators probably exerted pressure on the fakirs to stop the practice. And lastly, after the 1971 Indo-Pakistan war, most of the Bardi-Fakir sub caste appeared to have left for Pakistan. The mystery of variolation in the Rajasthan desert was finally solved.

37

CERTIFICATION TEAM VISIT TO RAJASTHAN

Christmas 1976 and New Year's Day 1977 came and went like lightening. Once the special desert search was completed, we had to analyze the data and get the report off to Delhi. I had also been assigned to assist the state of Gujarat, which was adjacent to Rajasthan, prepare for the certification team.

My territory for smallpox surveillance suddenly expanded in the four months before the International Certification Team was to arrive in April 1977. Each state was assigned the task of writing up the history of smallpox in their area. Since I had such a good command of English, I was also charged with assembling the history of smallpox in Rajasthan. It was a very busy time for me, to say the least. Yet there was an undercurrent of excitement that, in fact, India had done it. And if India could eradicate this dreaded disease, then global certification was a done deal.

We were feeling pretty smug, and I was reviewing the state report on smallpox activities when the unthinkable occurred. Bad news always seemed to transpire late in the day. The state smallpox team received a telegram about a case of rash and fever located somewhere between the Jodhpur and Udaipur districts. It was February 1977 and only two months before the certification team was to arrive.

This is not good news, I thought as I packed my little travel case. My team started out around 4:00 p.m., calculating it would take between four to six hours for us to reach the village. We were met by the district staff, who had visited the family. Rumors were swirling hot and heavy.

Of course no one wanted a rash-and-fever case this late in the game. Apparently, this one involved only one person, a boy around eight or nine years old. He had not traveled.

The District Health Officer (DHO) did not think it was smallpox; however, the rash had just started, and it is always difficult to distinguish between smallpox and chickenpox early on.

Night had fallen by the time Ramesh and I went into the hut to look at the child. The light of a kerosene lantern spread a weak yellow glow, and I had my flashlight with me. The boy was miserable, with a high fever and lots of congestion in the nasal passages. There was no rash on the palms of his hands or soles of his feet. He had developed a fever first, and the rash was very early. Actually, I couldn't see much of a rash anywhere. I took my ballpoint pen and circled the faint papules. They were sparse on the front and back of the trunk. I couldn't see much on the face and arms. Still, chickenpox progresses rapidly, so I knew that if we came back in four to six hours, we would have more to go on. Right now the whole village was gathered outside with the village leaders, and of course everyone wanted to know what the WHO epidemiologist was thinking. I decided that we should use this as a teaching moment.

I congratulated the person who reported the case, and gave him the initial hundred rupees. It was great publicity and high drama. I talked about how alert the community was and how we appreciated the swift response of the district and administrative people. I said that right now I didn't see any rash on the palms of the hands or soles of the feet, but I planned to stick around so I could examine the child again in four hours to look at the progression of the rash. Meanwhile, I was starving, and we needed to find a place to eat. And off we went.

We were back at 1:00 a.m., and the rash had progressed on the trunk, particularly on the back, with some vesicles and papules sprouting up in crops. There were different types of rashes in the same area. There was still no rash on the palms and soles, and nothing so far on the face. This case was progressing fast, and we had our answer. It was chickenpox. The smallpox rash was slow moving and developed all in one stage. I discussed the situation with the DHO and said that he should take samples of the vesicles in the morning and check if there were any scabs; if so, he could expedite them to the laboratory so we could have confirmation of chickenpox.

He should also call Jaipur and let them know the good news. Jaipur could talk to Delhi. All I wanted was a shower and a bed. The DHO said he had booked rooms for us at the government circuit house in the district town of Udaipur, so we should take off. I told the young DHO that he had done the right thing. He reported the rash-and-fever case early and got other opinions. Now was not the time to hide any case, however ordinary. Tomorrow, he would talk again with the community and the village leaders about the case and send off the specimens. Nothing like a rash-and-fever case to get everyone excited.

I slept well after we finally got in. It was 10:00 a.m. before I woke up and looked out my window and saw the stunning view of the Taj Lake Palace Hotel. The Lake Palace was a luxury hotel featuring white marble walls located smack in the middle of an island in Lake Pichola. Even in those days, the hotel was expensive. The hotel operated a speedboat that transported guests to the hotel from a jetty at the City Palace. In the right light, it looked like the hotel was shimmering in the lake.

I'd vote for the Lake Palace Hotel as one of the most romantic hotels in India. Being in the middle of the lake did keep the riffraff from roaming the hotel corridors. I thought I deserved to celebrate the chickenpox case, and so I had my team take me to the jetty. I was going to eat lunch at the Lake Palace. Lunch wasn't memorable, but I remember the ambience. There was a great antique shop in the hotel. The owner of the boutique told me a story that stoked my love of horses.

Once upon a time, in the pre-Vedic days of old, the Rajput king would hold a ceremony called the Ashvamedha Yagnya. A white Marwari stallion was consecrated and then left to wander through the king's domain for a year, attended by warriors, priests, and magicians. In its free wandering, the horse could do what he wanted. He could eat the crops and have his pick of any breeding mare; in short, he was like a god.

He might enter the territory of other rulers, in which case an armed struggle could ensue for the possession of that territory, because whatever lands were traversed by the sacrificial horse fell under the sovereignty of the king who was performing the Ashvamedha rite.

While the horse wandered, the people honored the king with continuous festivities and celebrations, until the end of the year, when the horse was returned to the king's city and sacrificed at the climax of a highly elaborate ritual to the sun god.

Of course if you were a king in an adjacent kingdom, you didn't take kindly to this ceremony. And the poor were probably not enthused about the hordes of people who would need to be housed and fed descending in their area.

After hearing the story, I fell in love with an antique carved wooden stallion that the shopkeeper sold me. I'm not really sure of the significance of the ceremony, but it was for the greater good of the kingdom in some ancient fertility rite. Personally, I thought that this ceremony was a lot healthier than *sati*.

Sati (also called *suttee*) was the practice among some Hindu communities (particularly the Rajput royals) by which a recently widowed woman, either voluntarily or by use of force or coercion, committed suicide. The best-known form of sati was when a woman burned to death on her husband's funeral pyre. However, other forms of sati existed, including being buried alive with the husband's corpse and drowning. Over the centuries, the custom died out in the south of India, only to become prevalent in the north, particularly in the states of Rajasthan and Bengal.

Historically, the practice of sati was found in many castes and at every social level, and it involved both uneducated women and the highest-ranking women. The common deciding factor was often ownership of wealth or property, as all possessions of the widow devolved to the husband's family upon her death.

Let me say that India was a country that was harsh on widows. Sati was considered the highest expression of wifely devotion to a dead husband. It was deemed an act of peerless piety and was said to purge the widow of all her sins, releasing her from the cycle of death and rebirth and ensuring salvation for her dead husband and the seven generations that followed her.

I'm not sure that there was much of a choice in some cases. I doubt a widow would get much sympathy from her husband's family if she decided she was not quite ready for an early death. There was no question; I deemed the horse sacrifice a better ritual than sati.

Now that we had confirmed that the rash-and-fever case was chickenpox, my team hurried back to Jaipur. Rajasthan was notified that the certification team had chosen the state for review. I knew that would be the case when we did the special desert search. Rajasthan was just too fascinating, too huge, too isolated to think that it could just scoot through without a visit. The WHO epidemiologists out in the field were notified that we would come into Delhi to meet the certification team in India from April 4 to April 23, 1977. The team members would then disperse to the various states, and the field epidemiologists and state officials would accompany them wherever they wanted to go. As we had no idea what area the individual team members would want to visit, every district needed to be prepared to receive the visitors.

That meant they needed to have all their records on smallpox available for the team to review. In this way the state could not concentrate on any one place to try to improve the reports. The certification team would see the real situation. We didn't get a lot of advance information. The international commission was composed of sixteen members from as many different countries, and they first assembled in New Delhi to plan field visits. Each member would visit two states, and national and WHO personnel would accompany him or her. They would then all return to Delhi to give their reports and decide if the country met WHO global certification requirements. Delhi called in the WHO field epidemiologists a couple of days before the arrival of the international commission to go over last-minute plans. The National Smallpox Programme and the WHO SEARO office provided an overview of the program and briefed the certification team.

I was anxious to find out which team members would be assigned to Rajasthan. Delhi finally announced where the members would visit. Rajasthan would get two members: Dr. Frank Fenner, an Australian who would play an important role on the India Commission and the Global Eradication Commission, and Dr. W. Koinange, director of the division of communicable diseases in the Kenya Ministry of Health.

Finally the state could start making lodging and administrative preparations to support the team members' visit. We still didn't know where they would want to go. We would find that out when they arrived. I knew they would want to go outside Jaipur and would pick the desert districts to visit to get an idea of the difficulty of surveillance. They had received the advance copy of the Rajasthan state report on smallpox eradication activities, which had started back in 1962. I felt my role now was just to help the state smallpox unit to present the facts and to help clear up any lingering doubts regarding special surveys or districts that had weak reporting of rash-and-fever cases. I felt really confident that Rajasthan had done its job and had stayed the course, and we had the data to prove we had no more cases of smallpox.

Drs. Fenner and Koinange arrived in the second week of April for a one-week visit. After the state presentation of the Rajasthan data, they were feted at an evening reception at Amber Fort and Palace, the main landmark and top attraction of the Jaipur region. I had visited the fort my first weekend in Jaipur, almost eighteen months earlier, so it seemed only fitting that I should experience it all lit up by soft lights and reverberating in an amber-yellow glow. Incredible India. I wore a sari for this occasion, securely held by a safety pin in the skirt to ensure I wouldn't have a wardrobe malfunction. The gods were on my side.

The next day we took off to visit the areas handpicked by the certification team. They wanted to see the desert districts, as I had surmised. The district authorities presented their region and the smallpox activities in the office. The team could go to any PHC or stop in any village to ask smallpox questions along the way. I think they appreciated the field visits. I knew that they needed to experience the long distances, the heat during the day, the blessed coolness that came at sunset in the desert, and the hot meal in the evening. We planned it so that we stayed in major towns at the end of each day. There were no surprises. The smallpox workers and the health staff had done their jobs well.

It was the last field visit day, and we were heading back on the long five- or six-hour trek to Jaipur. It was about 2:00 p.m., the hottest time of the day to travel. We were on a pukka road heading out of the desert from Jodhpur. About forty meters off to the left, there was a single hut in the middle of nowhere. Dr. Fenner turned to me and said, "Connie, do you think we could stop and go visit that hut off there in the distance?"

"Why not?" I said. So I told Hakim to stop on the side of the road.

Fenner, Ramesh, and I started on foot to the hut. I was dreading this encounter. What was the likelihood that whoever was in this hut, in the middle of nowhere, would know anything about smallpox? What possessed him to even put up a hut here, far away from any water source?

Before we could reach the hut, a man came outside alone. He was a typical, ordinary man with a turban, and he looked at us inquiringly. I pulled out the smallpox recognition card and asked in Hindi, "Do you know what this disease is?"

He said, "Yes, it's smallpox."

"Do you know what the reward is for reporting a case of smallpox?" I said.

"Yes, the reward is one thousand rupees."

Ramesh was translating for Dr. Fenner as I asked the questions. Dr. Fenner was impressed and said, "Wow, even in the middle of nowhere, they know about smallpox."

I was impressed, too! To tell the truth, I was not at all certain this tribal man would know the answers. It brought a few tears of joy to my eyes, which I hid behind my sunglasses. Finally, I could relax. We drove straight back to Jaipur.

The team recounted what they had found on the field visits to the state authorities. Everyone was happy. The doctors departed on a plane back to Delhi, where they would meet up with their fellow teammates and discuss their findings. I would be heading back to Delhi in a few days to hear—in person—the certification team announce that India had officially eradicated smallpox!

38

SMALLPOX IS ERADICATED. NOW WHAT?

I t was hard to describe the excitement and anticipation of the announcement by the certification team that India had eradicated smallpox. We had been working so hard for this day. The announcement was almost anticlimactic—*almost*, but not quite.

Smallpox had totally engulfed two years of my life. The reception and dinner for the certification team sped by. Old hands in WHO said there would never be a success like this program, ever again. They told me I would be hard-pressed to find another project that would be as irresistible and tantalizing as smallpox eradication.

I sure hoped that it was not all downhill from here. Surely, other diseases and opportunities would prove as captivating and alluring.

Of course the naysayers had to chime in. "So what if you eradicated smallpox? The child will just die of some other dreaded disease."

"What's all the hoopla about one disease eradicated?"

"Now what are you going to do about measles or malaria?"

All of a sudden, I was responsible for saving the world. I thought, *They are just jealous because they didn't work on smallpox.* Truth be told, for years after, the smallpox mafia—this little group of golden boys—seemed to have the Midas touch. They were offered numerous opportunities. And yes, there were a few women included in that mafia, including me.

No matter what was said, nothing could dampen my spirits. We did it! And India's certification put in motion the global certification of the eradication of the disease, with international commissions in the remaining twenty-one countries.

Now the question before me was what to do next. What was I going to do with the rest of my life? I thought back to my meeting with D. A. Henderson in Delhi back in October 1976. The WHO field epidemiologists had been having a meeting and presenting our state activities. D. A. was in town looking over precertification activities for India with the SEARO office. While he was there, he graciously met with all the junior field epidemiologists. It was exciting for me to finally meet the chief of the Global Smallpox Programme, and he asked me if I was writing home to my mother! I guessed I would never get past that incident.

He also had wanted to know if I had any interest in working in a new WHO program called the Expanded Program of Immunizations (EPI), which had been unanimously approved by the World Health Assembly in 1974 and was picking up steam. I said at the time, "You know, D. A., it sounds like it would be a great program to work in after smallpox. However, I think I need to go back to the States to look at clinical medicine and see if I truly want to go into pediatrics or international public health. I'm going to have to turn down this offer until I make up my mind." What I knew right at that minute was that I needed to take a break after smallpox, and I wanted to take the long way home.

Once again I was sitting in the Delhi airport, waiting for the flight back to Jaipur. I had just been a part of history, smallpox history, and I knew I would look back on these days, these past two years, as a very special time. In the departure waiting room, I had time to reflect on my adventures and on the lessons learned.

Eleven Things I Learned from Smallpox Fieldwork

1. You have to take risks sometimes. I would never have seen smallpox cases if I had not risked crossing the border and searching down the cases in Bangladesh. I looked another eighteen months for smallpox. I never saw another case in my lifetime.

2. Don't go it alone. My smallpox team in West Bengal and in Rajasthan never let me go off alone to solve a problem. As a team we had expertise, companionship, and safety in numbers.

3. Be grateful for all the opportunities. I have been immensely fortunate in life. My studies in Florence, Italy, introduced me to new cultures and languages. Working on smallpox in India presented both challenges and once-in-a-lifetime opportunities. I learned about true hospitality, the joy of a stand-up shower, what one would do for a mouthful of water, the smoothness of a Mewari horse's gait, the smell of green camel slime, the empowerment that comes from conquering the highest mountain in the world, and the wonderment of helping eradicate a deadly disease.

4. Collect adventures instead of things. Early on I vowed to travel while I was young and healthy and not wait until I had the money. I saw too many seniors in Europe who were too tired to climb the castle steps or enter the tourist bus. I wanted to hike to Everest while I was young, and I knew there were other adventures out there. I would have the memories for old age.

5. Treasure friendships. It was the friends I met along the way who enriched the journey.

6. Whatever doesn't kill you really does make you stronger. I thought that bout of shigella dysentery would kill me, yet after that episode, I never got another bout of gastroenteritis in India. My immune system really got stronger!

7. Appreciate time alone. Today, we are surrounded by many activities. We are bombarded by TV, computers, iPods, and cell phones, and the list could continue. Yet, on reflection, it was wonderful to have the time to read a book, to trek alone on the trail and commune with nature, and to get a good night's sleep.

8. Being friendly and open to new people in unlikely places can lead to cool adventures. I never knew who I would meet on a mountainside or in my own living room. Those Australian overlanders made me want to see the Asia Overland Route. I was so close to Afghanistan and Iran. Now was the time. There might never be a better time.

9. Don't take no for an answer. The Delhi office doubted the wisdom of placing a single woman in the rural area. I begged Dr. Grasset to place me in a rural area, and she did. Everyone said there was no variolation in the Rajasthan desert, but the desert survey proved otherwise. They said we couldn't eradicate a disease. Yet we did. Don't take no for an answer.

10. It's OK not to know what you want to do for the rest of your life. I was young! I didn't have to have every second planned out in advance. I was learning to leave some space for the totally unexpected to happen.

11. All that truly matters in the end is that you had fun on the journey! As I looked back on my various exploits in India, I realized that I had fun. I was not the same Connie Davis who had left California two years before. I had changed; India had changed me.

Oh, oh, what's the loudspeaker saying? Go to door three—the Jaipur flight is departing.

Why was it that it took so long to settle into a place, yet it took only two days to pack up and leave? I had planned a leisurely departure. I didn't want to be running around willy-nilly. My neighbors knew I would be leaving, so it wasn't that hard to divest of beds and the refrigerator and stove. Despite my caveat about collecting adventures and not things, I hadn't listened well to my own advice. WHO agreed to ship a very limited amount of goods back home, so I ran out and promptly bought another aluminum trunk. I would be taking the long way home, and that meant I needed to pare down the things I was carrying with me. I packed up the Tibetan rug, the thang-ka, the antique wooden horse, all the undeveloped film that I had taken for the two years, and other Rajasthani "treasures," and I trusted that I would one day be reunited with them.

WHO was giving me a great return ticket on Pan American Airways, and I requested as many open stopovers as possible. When I signed on for the smallpox eradication effort in India, my best friend from medical school wrangled a teaching position in the medical school in Nairobi, Kenya. I kept in loose contact with Kathy and her husband, and I let her know when my contract was up. She enticed me to come to Nairobi by pointing out that as I had done Everest, why not climb Kilimanjaro? The only caveat was that they were leaving Nairobi for home leave; I needed to get to Kenya by July if I wanted free board and lodging.

My tentative plans were to fly to Kabul and stay for a few days, as the overlanders told me it might be difficult, as a single woman, to get around in Afghanistan. Then I would fly on to Tehran to see the shah's Peacock Throne, among other things, and then continue on to Nairobi.

I had a friend to visit in Frankfurt who had been an au pair in Jaipur, and I planned to visit her and have stops in Paris and London before finally arriving home in five to six months.

It was hard leaving the smallpox unit, especially my team. I was well feted by the state and given a twelve-inch brass replica of the famous Chittor Tower of Victory, an imposing structure located in Chittorgarh, Rajasthan, to commemorate a Rajput king's victory over Muslim armies. I guessed this symbolized our victory over smallpox.

I said a tearful good-bye to Pram, the tour guide who tried to keep me entertained, and several other friends I had met in Jaipur who were horse or art lovers. I booked the early afternoon plane to Delhi and asked not to have a big, official send-off. I just wanted my smallpox team to see me off.

We were putting my duffel and suitcase in the jeep when a government truck rolled up in front of the house. I thought, *Now what?* I'd paid off the landlord; everything was taken care of. There was a crew in the truck, and the supervisor walked up and asked, "Dr. Davis-ji?"

Warily I replied, "Yes, I'm Dr. Davis!" He handed me a chit. Apparently that was the day I was going to finally get a telephone landline! Eighteen months after I made my request, it was finally being fulfilled.

I said, "Wait—please, I'm leaving now, today, on a jet plane. Don't put the phone in!"

"So sorry, madam, but this paper says to install a telephone at this residence. And we must do it." I just shook my head and jumped in the Willys jeep. My last view of the house was the telephone company installing my landline. Well, I wasn't going to pay for it!

39

TAKING THE LONG WAY HOME

The flight was on time for Delhi. *Good-bye, team, and good-bye, Pink City. I will miss you all.* Now I was just a regular person. My WHO contract was ending in two days, and I just needed to pick up my airplane ticket for the return home.

Nevertheless, I couldn't leave India before fulfilling some promises I had made. I would be staying with a friend in Delhi who had a huge apartment and a nice guest bedroom. Indian Airlines was running a special promotion. Foreigners could fly *anywhere* in India for one week for a hundred dollars. The only conditions were that travelers could not "backtrack" and revisit places they had already seen, and that they had to start and end in Delhi. I couldn't pass this up. I planned to fly Indian Airlines for two weeks for only two hundred dollars. The ticket had to be paid in dollars, but that was not a drawback for me. The airline was going to lose on this deal.

Although I had been posted in some of the most stunning areas in India, like Darjeeling and Rajasthan, India was enormous, and I wanted to see some other sites.

When I first arrived, I could not fathom the plethora of Hindu gods and goddesses, the cycle of death and reincarnation, the principles of dharma and karma. But now, the wheel of life didn't sound all that strange. *Bhavacakra* (the wheel of life) was the symbolic representation of *samsara* (cyclic existence) found on the outside walls of Tibetan Buddhist temples and monasteries in the Indo-Tibetan region. In the Mahayana Buddhist tradition, it was believed that the drawing was designed by the Buddha himself in order to help ordinary people understand the Buddhist teachings. I was keen to visit some of the important Buddhist sites in India before I departed. I was just a stone's throw from the famous Silk Road that connected the East to the West through trade and cultural disseminations. And I was going to see the famous standing Buddha in Bamiyan, Afghanistan. And finally, I had promised myself that I would bathe in Mother Ganges in Benares before I left India.

I planned my route so that I would start in Goa. It was a minor Buddhist site, but I wanted to see the beaches and experience a little of the hippie trail in India. From Goa I would set off for Sanchi stupa, located in the state of Madhya Pradesh. From there, I would fly to Benares, and just outside Benares was Sarnath, an important Buddhist site. From Benares I would travel to Kashmir, collapse on a houseboat in Dal Lake, and vegetate for a week. Once I returned to Delhi, the real trip would begin.

I wasn't a tourist now, but a traveler. What was the difference? Well, tourists were people who went to a country to see the top attractions and photograph them, and then return home to regale their friends. Travelers also visited a country and may well have seen the same top attractions, yet they wanted to go deeper. If possible, they wanted to blend in with the locals, learn some of the language, and interact with the native residents. It would be a whirlwind trip—four locations in two weeks—but I didn't know when, if ever, I would be back in India.

I left my duffel with friends and headed south. I was going out of my comfort zone, as I would be traveling solo. At least I felt I "knew" India and was more comfortable staying in Indian hotels of the two- to three-star persuasion.

Goa was hot, and very humid, and the light was different from Rajasthan. The Indian Tourist Organization recommended an Indian family hotel that was right on the beach, meaning I could walk out the front door and be on the sand within a block. It was around 2:00 p.m. when I arrived. I was locking my suitcase before running out to see the beach when all of a sudden there was a huge commotion outside, far louder than the usual Indian background noise. Something was going on.

I rushed outside to see a crowd of thirty Indians looking out to the sea and gesticulating excitedly. I asked someone nearby, "What's happening?"

He shook his head slowly, and said, "There has been a drowning."

An Indian family had arrived at Anjuna Beach and were looking at the sea when their toddler, about three years old, walked into the surf. The undertow just swept him away. The mother rushed in to grab him, but she also was swept under. It happened so fast that there was nothing anyone could do.

It was then I saw the signboard warning visitors about the undertow. Anjuna Beach has a rather steep decline, and the undertow in Goa was well known. In fact, I had planned to just wet my feet and not do any serious swimming.

I just walked the beach until I came to a cabana restaurant with a bar full of locals and some hippie types. May was not really the best time to travel in Goa, because it was hot. I slumped down at a reed table, and a waiter soon came with a menu. Everyone was very friendly, and a local joined my table and wanted to know how long I was staying. I told him about the drowning. He said it happened all the time. Many Indians didn't know how to swim, and the sea engulfed them. Even strong swimmers should beware the undertow. His advice was to get a tan (not my priority), eat some fish curry, and listen to the disco music that would start at sunset.

I smelled a strong odor of hashish in the air; it seemed to be easily available. I only planned two nights in Goa, but I could see why the hippies loved it. Goa was a state of mind, with delightful beaches, cheap but excellent local food, clubbing at small bars, and Kingfisher beer that was cold and reasonably priced. It turned out that my local informant was a drug dealer. He readily shared his merchandise with those around, so I didn't know how he made any money. It was a laid-back life, but I had Buddhist sites to visit, so I left for Sanchi.

Sanchi was a sleepy little town; there was not much there besides the Great Stupa. It was the oldest stone structure in India and was originally commissioned by the emperor Asoka the Great in the third century. A stupa was a mound-like structure containing Buddhist relics. Asoka was one of India's greatest emperors, an empire builder who embraced Buddhism after witnessing the mass deaths of the Kalinga War, which he himself had waged. What impressed me most was the carved decoration of the northern gateway to the stupa. Although made of stone, it was carved and constructed more like wood, and the gateway was covered with narrative sculptures depicting the life of Buddha.

Over the centuries, Sanchi was vandalized and ransacked by invading Muslim armies. With the overall decline of Buddhism in India, Sanchi was forgotten until 1912, when it was rediscovered and restored by British archaeologist Sir John Hubert Marshall. Truthfully, I was disappointed in Sanchi. I should have realized that it would be more of an archaeological display than an expression of vibrant Buddhist art. And I didn't meet any locals who could give me insight into Buddhism. I guess I ended up being a tourist in Sanchi. What would I find in Sarnath? I went on to Benares.

I truly looked forward to Benares. My friend Libby, the one who had fallen in the open sewer in Calcutta, had raved on and on about the burning ghats, and WHO staff had said it was a must-visit city. I arrived at my hotel in the early afternoon, threw my suitcase on the bed, and headed out the door. I wanted to see the Ganges. Benares was the spiritual capital of India, the city of Shiva. And it just felt different. As the holiest of the seven sacred cities, it was important to three religions: Hinduism, Jainism, and even Buddhism. I was heading for Dashashwamedh Ghat, the main ghat in Benares. *Ghats* were steps of stone slabs that descended the embankment and led down to the river, where pilgrims performed ritual ablutions. Normally, there was a huge temple in the background of the steps. There were two types of ghats: those where Hindus stood waist high in the water and took a ritual bath, and those designated for cremation, the burning ghats.

My intent was to head to the river and then make my way to Dashashwamedh Ghat for the evening fire ceremony to Shiva. However, my plans changed when I was overtaken by events.

As I was strolling down the street, I ran into a funeral procession and decided to follow at a discreet distance. Women were not allowed to participate in Hindu funeral processions or any of the ceremonies at the burning ghat, so I couldn't "blend in" with the procession.

Photos were strictly forbidden. The white-shrouded corpse was on a wooden pallet, and about eight male relatives were carrying the stretcher. As we continued toward the Ganges, the streets seemed to get narrower and more claustrophobic. The sun was starting to set as the procession slowed right before the ghat. We had arrived at Manikarnika Ghat, the place of Hindu cremation. Smoke was billowing up from several pyres already lit, and there was a slight wind. The procession I was following was motioned to wait.

I made a wide detour around to my right, going in the opposite direction from the smoke, and stood some distance from the two pyres that were burning. I was too late to see the eldest son lighting the pyre and circumambulating it.

One pyre was almost extinguished, but the body was only partially burnt. I could clearly see the ribs. Attendants from the untouchable sub caste of Dom were stoking the dying embers, and I guessed the family was too poor to put on more wood.

The other pyre had a goodly amount of wood and was burning briskly. I could see the white shroud in the center going up in smoke. The male relatives were still surrounding the pyre. They told me it took about three hours to cremate a corpse.

The Doms were working on the first pyre and gathering up ashes and bones to throw into the Ganges. There was no ceremony at this point; the remains were just thrown in. I was seriously reconsidering my plans for bathing at sunrise in the Ganges.

The heat of the fires, the smoke, and the billowing ashes were starting to affect me. Truthfully, the thought of my own death was painful to accept. I had so much to live for. I decided against making my way to the fire ceremony at the main ghat. It was dark now, and I had no idea how to get back to my hotel. I hailed a bicycle rickshaw and told him the name of the inn.

I knew the Ganges was polluted, yet it was striking to first see the dark, murky water, which was flowing more swiftly than I had imagined. It was impressive. This most revered river started from the Gangotri glacier in the Himalayas and traversed some 1,580 miles across the teeming plains of the Indian subcontinent before flowing east into Bangladesh and from there spilling into the Bay of Bengal. All along its banks, ashes from the deceased and dead animals were thrown into the river.

Hindus believed that if you were fortunate enough to die and be cremated in Benares, and if your ashes were scattered in the river, then you would escape the endless cycle of death and reincarnation. If a person died in the Ganges or had Ganges water sprinkled on them as they breathed their last breath, it was believed they achieved absolute salvation, escaping the toil of reincarnation to be transported immediately to Shiva's Himalayan version of heaven.

The Ganges was extremely polluted from septic wastes from villages and municipalities along its route and from the other more toxic liquids flowing from various factories along the way. I thought I would wait to bathe and see how I felt at sunrise. Tomorrow was another day.

Morning came early, very early, at 5:30 a.m. The hotel receptionist told me I would want to be on the banks of the Ganges before sunrise in order to get the full effect. I had not slept well. I think I was mulling over the decision to bathe or not to bathe in the river. It was not necessary to die to gain the effects of the Ganges. Hindus also believed that the Ganges was pure and purifying, so immersion in the river wiped away the sins of the bather—not just those sins of the present but of a lifetime. True, I'm not a Hindu, but I doubted God was so selective that he wouldn't show a little mercy my way.

The receptionist told me where I could take a boat out on the Ganges. Apparently the water was cleaner in the middle, and some people preferred to take a dip from the boat. As I got closer to the bathing ghats, there were flower sellers hawking their wares of marigolds and small votive candles that you could cast into the river. I bought a small offering of four marigolds tied around a candle.

I eyed the boats at the dock. I had my doubts about their river-worthiness; however, one already had about six Hindu pilgrims and was ready to cast off. I climbed aboard. The sun was starting to cast the first reddish-gold hues of the morning on the shoreline. We cast off and soon reached the middle of the river. One man in a dhoti went over the side but stayed close to the boat. The water didn't look any cleaner out here to me, and it definitely was deeper than at the shore. I decided the better part of valor was just to cast my flower offering on the river and watch as it was swept away. I cupped my hand and splashed a handful of water over my head. If a few drops of Ganges water could admit the dying into paradise, surely my fistful of water could wash away my sins. As I gazed at the river, I understood the sentiments of Prime Minister Nehru, who wrote that the Ganges was "a symbol of India's age-long culture and civilization, ever changing, ever flowing, and yet ever the same Ganga."

As the boat started back to the shore, I could see the myriad throngs on the banks standing waist high in the waters and bathing. There was a sprinkling of *sadhus* perched seemingly immobile on outcrops of boulders. A *sadhu* was a religious ascetic or holy person. The sadhu dedicated himself solely to achieving *mokṣa* (liberation), the fourth and final stage of life, through meditation and contemplation of Brahmin. Strolling slowly along were two *digambara*, sky-clad (naked) sadhus who wore their hair in thick dreadlocks called *jata*.

Because my boat was full of devotees, I didn't feel right about taking photos. It would have broken the meditative spell on board. We had an uneventful landing, and my first thought was that I was starving and I wanted a vegetarian breakfast—certainly easy to get in Benares. Then I would be off to Sarnath.

The Dhamek Stupa in Sarnath was said to mark the spot of a deer park where the Buddha gave his first sermon to his five disciples after attaining enlightenment. At the end of the twelfth century, Turkish Muslims sacked Sarnath, and the site was subsequently plundered for building materials. I was struck once again by the blandness of the archeological display. I didn't know what I was seeking, but I wasn't enlightened that day. So it was on to Kashmir.

I fell in love with Kashmir. As the Mughal emperor Jahangir once said, "If there is paradise on earth, it is this, it is this, it is this." I was headed for Dal Lake in Srinagar, the summer capital of the state of Jammu and Kashmir. It was here that I planned some rest and relaxation, thinking I would take a deluxe houseboat for three days and then go up to Gulmarg in the mountains. During the times of the British Raj, the colonial administrators would move their headquarters out of the lowlands and go up to hill stations to escape the heat. Even though the Dogra Maharaja of Kashmir restricted the building of houses in the valley, the British circumvented this rule by commissioning lavish houseboats to be built on Dal Lake. I flew into Srinagar and hailed a taxi to take me to the *shikara* (water taxi) station.

The shikara assigned to my houseboat awaited me. I was instantly transported back to colonial times when I stepped into the houseboat. It had three bedrooms, a large living and dining room, and a cook assigned to the quarters. The houseboat was not moored to the busy side of the lake and was some distance from any others.

If I wanted to go out to see something like the Mughal gardens, the houseboat shikara was there at my command. A shikara was a small taxi boat that was paddled and had no motor. Deluxe houseboats had their own private shikara to take clients around. Most shikaras had a colorful canopy to cover the boat and provide shade. They reminded me of Venetian gondolas but were smaller. Vendors selling everything from vegetables to Kashmiri rugs would slip up beside our boat and bring out their wares. You didn't have to leave your houseboat for shopping.

Fate intervened when I went to see the Shalimar Gardens. I saw a handwritten note on a bulletin board. It said, "Two French women looking for two others to share expenses to

Ladakh! Leaving in two days. Come to our houseboat in the evening for more information."

Ladakh, or the Land of High Passes, was a Buddhist region in the northernmost part of India, in the state of Jammu and Kashmir. Bounded by two of the world's mightiest mountain ranges, the Karakoram to the north and the Greater Himalayas to the south, it was inhabited by people of Indo-Aryan and Tibetan descent. It was initially a restricted area but was suddenly opened up to foreigners in 1975. It was now said that Ladakh was more Tibetan than Tibet. Did I want to go? Yes! I arranged with my shikara to find the women's houseboat.

The French women were flight attendants and had to be back in a week's time. They had contacted a tour agency; the four-wheel-drive jeep with a driver/guide was already arranged. They just needed two more travelers to share the cost. They had heard from a guy who was coming over later; and with me, they had their group of four. We arranged that on Thursday they would pick me up at my houseboat, and then we would head for land, where the jeep would meet us. I couldn't believe my luck. Another one of my dreams was to visit Tibet, and Ladakh was the next-best choice.

Their shikara picked me up at 6:00 a.m., and then we went to pick up the last passenger, a German guy named Jürgen. He was ready and hopped in the boat. We were at the pier in a heartbeat; we settled into the roomy vehicle and took off almost immediately. It would take two days to reach the capital, Leh, and we would overnight at a place called Kargil—that is, if we could make it over the famous Zoji La pass at 11,640 feet. The pass was always iffy, and we were traveling in late May, when the Srinagar-Leh road had just opened for the season.

The guide said there was snow on the gravel road, but it was open, and traffic was getting through. However, that area was famous for landslides, so he warned us to not get our hopes up.

We traveled through gorgeous country, climbing steadily to Sonamarg, a well-known picnic and hiking area. We ate a packed lunch hurriedly because we wanted to reach the Zoji La pass early and get over that first hurdle. We continued climbing ever up. Our group was not initially talkative due to the early start. We turned a bend in the road and then saw it—a roadblock that had stopped twenty vehicles, including a bus, trucks, and numerous cars.

Our driver got out and said, "Let me go up ahead and see what the problem is." When he came back, he said, "There's been a landslide. The road is completely covered. The army is out in force and shoveling madly, but it was a good-sized landslide!" He added that he doubted that they could get the road open that day. The driver said, "We have to turn back to Srinagar." We were distraught.

"So will it be open tomorrow?" I asked.

The driver said, "They will keep working to clear off the rubble, but the weather may drop some new snow tonight!"

Gloomily we returned to Srinagar. We all agreed to stay together in a three-star houseboat and leave early in the morning. At least by staying in the same boat, we were able to eat dinner together and get to know each other. However, no one was in the mood to talk, and we went to bed early. We headed off the next morning for our second attempt to cross Zoji La pass. Unfortunately, there had been more snow during the night, so it was uncertain if the pass would be clear. It wasn't. *Crap, what a bummer!*

We had started this journey so sure we would have smooth sailing. It was a grim little group that returned to Srinagar and checked into a two-star houseboat. We didn't want to waste our money on houseboats.

In 1977, the only way to get to Ladakh was by road. There were no flights. Even military flights were apparently rare. Our little group was now resigned to our fate. If we could not ascend Zoji La pass in the morning, the trip was canceled. There was no way to do the five-day tour in Ladakh and get back in time for our scheduled flights out of Srinagar. It was a decidedly downcast group that left Srinagar for the third and final try. As we rounded the now-familiar bend that would show us the roadblock and the landslide, you could have heard a pin drop. And then we saw that the line was moving! There was just enough rubble removed to allow for one lane of traffic.

The army up ahead would let about twelve cars on our side advance and head over the pass, and then stop our side and let those coming from Leh get through "the eye of the needle." Our vehicle was in the next group of twelve to advance. We just needed to wait for the Leh traffic to get through the one open lane.

Then it was our turn! Our vehicle was the last in our group. We inched forward, and the driver put us into four-wheel drive. No one was talking. We had to get through about thirty meters of tenuous gravel, but we could see ahead where the road widened to its regular width. Scores of men were continuing to widen the landslide area. When we cleared the one lane and were once again on solid road, we all started yelling and crying and laughing all at once. We were through; we had made it! The third time was the charm, and we were definitely on our way to Ladakh. Getting to the top of Zoji La was almost anticlimactic. It was already 2:00 p.m. by the time we reached Drass. It was a straight run to Kargil, and we got in by 3:30 p.m. We rolled into a guesthouse and immediately went to have dinner. Kargil was technically a part of Ladakh, but 90 percent of the population was Shia Muslim, and only 5 percent was Tibetan Buddhist. Kargil was definitely a way station, a means to an end. We knew that the next day, we would be in Leh.

We were excited. We had made it past Zoji La, and although we had higher passes to negotiate, apparently they would present no obstacle. As we headed out of Kargil, we could see that the landscape was changing. Ladakh was a high-altitude desert. The main source of water was the winter snowfall on the mountains. Summers were short, though they were long enough to grow crops. It looked to me like the moon—dry, barren land, no vegetation, with *chortens* dotting the landscape. *Chortens* were Buddhist monuments standing singly or in sets of three. Some were erected for religious merit, some for protection, and others as memorials or even as tombs of spiritual masters.

We had two passes to negotiate, but after reaching the highest point on the Srinagar-Leh road, which was Fotu La at 13,479 feet, we rounded a bend and came upon a stunning sight. The day had been gray and overcast, but before us was a monastery seemingly stuck on the side of a mountain with high mountains surrounding it. It was illuminated by a shaft of brilliant sunshine, whereas where we stood was somber and gray. I snapped a photo that still graces my study wall thirty-eight years later.

We arrived at Lamayuru, one of the largest and oldest *gompas* in Ladakh, with a population of around 150 permanent monks. A *gompa* was a compound with both a monastery and a university. We had planned a short side trip here for an initial foray into Buddhist culture. The guide took us to see some of the monks meditating and chanting, and he pointed out several of the well-known fresco paintings on the exterior of the temple. This structure was built as a Bonpo (pre-Buddhist) monastery, but then it was taken over by the Kadampa sect and still later by the Gelugpa, the best known of the Tibetan Buddhist sects and the one headed by the Dalai Lama. Before we left, a monk showed us to a side room and prepared real butter tea for us. He strained the tea through a reed colander into a wooden butter churn and then added a large lump of yak butter and salt. He then churned this mixture until it reached the proper consistency. Tibetan butter tea was not to my liking, but I was finally tasting the real thing!

We arrived in Leh in the early afternoon. We were staying in a Ladakhi guesthouse that was simple but clean. I couldn't wait to go out and see the city. At that time, not many tourists had visited the area. It was still unspoiled by the rapid influx of cash and Western cultural influences that would eventually transform it. We could walk the paths and not be besieged by begging children or people trying to sell us things. The people there practiced a Tibetan custom of sticking out their tongues and saying, "Julay, julay," which meant a thousand and one things, from good morning to hello to namaste to good-bye. They were curious about us travelers but not overly impressed. The pace was slow.

Buddhism was very much present in the everyday lives of the people, in the way they walked around chortens, in their going to temples to pray, and in how they treated each other. Everyone wore Ladakhi *gonchas*—heavy, long-sleeved dress coats—and the married women wore headgear called *perak*, which was made of black lambskin studded with semiprecious turquoise stones and covered the head like a cobra's hood, tapering to a thin tail reaching down the back. They also wore traditional tall hats made from embroidered silk. We only had three short days in Ladakh, and we rushed around to see the famous monasteries of Thikse, Hemis, and Spituk, which were some distance from Leh. When we visited the monasteries, it was only in Hemis that we ran into several other tourists; this was because Hemis was putting on some masked dances. The dances were part of a normal festival that happened every year, and we were just lucky to be in the right place at the right time. We could meditate with the monks or walk around taking photos. Nothing was being performed just for us. The Ladakh trip has remained a singular, unparalleled voyage for me, impossible to duplicate, and leaving an everlasting memory.

It was hard to return to Delhi. We all had places to go and promises to keep. My time in India was rapidly drawing to a close. I was back in the Delhi airport for the final time. The departure lounge looked all too familiar. I heard the loudspeaker call for Kabul. The Air India flight was not full, and I was the only woman on board. Maybe Afghanistan was not such a great choice after all. Now was the time I wished I had a travel companion. Still, the overlanders had given me one great tip: Mustafa Hotel, a dollar a night, near Chicken Street. Let the adventure begin!

POSTSCRIPT

It's been forty years since the days when I worked on smallpox in India. Over the years, I regaled my friends with different vignettes from those days. They said, "Connie, you have got to write a book!" And I said that I would someday, when I retired. I thought it would be fairly easy because Mom saved all my letters since my days in Florence, Italy. When Mom died, I scoured the house, tore up the garage, and could not find my letters anywhere. Yet I had faithfully checked them each time when I came on home leave from my postings abroad. There are no words to describe my feelings about their loss, but all the ranting and raving in the world could not bring them back. Well, did there need to be another smallpox book, anyway? D. A. Henderson already wrote the definitive book on smallpox. I wrote D. A., saying I was thinking of doing a book on my experiences, and he was very encouraging. He said there were only a handful of women in the smallpox program (definitely a male preserve), and I was the only black American woman, so I would have a different perspective. And Dr. Stan Foster scoured his records of Bangladesh to help me find the village where I searched for the smallpox cases. So the die was cast.

When I retired to the Lake Chapala area in Mexico in August 2013, one of my priorities for the first year was to join a beginners' writing group. By this time, a number of friends from my smallpox days had already died. I sorely miss Dr. Mary Lou Clements and Ms. Jane Brown, both of whom worked in the program. My writers' group was very encouraging and made suggestions as I read what I had written each month.

Although I have written scientific articles, doing this memoir was a different type of writing. As I began to write, the memories flooded in, and I realized I would have to choose the stories to tell—there were so many! The events in the memoir all happened. Some names have been forgotten over the years. If a description includes a first and last name, it describes the real person. If there is only a first name provided, then either it was done to protect the innocent, or the name is fictitious.

When I went to medical school in 1968, there were only five women in my freshman class, and we all had to fight to be there. There were also five black students in the class; two of us were female. In 1968, UC San Francisco School of Medicine admitted their first black American *women* students. There was prejudice against women because they were "taking slots away from men," and there was even more prejudice against minority students—blacks, Hispanics, and American Indians. In 2014, nationally, 48 percent of all medical students are females. How times have changed! My perception, even now, however, is that it remains difficult for minority students, particularly black students, to gain admission to medical school.

I never planned on working in international public health, but the smallpox eradication program cast a significant spell on me. I actually returned to India a number of times. Some twenty years after smallpox, I worked in India again as the country director of the Joint United Nations Program on HIV/AIDS (UNAIDS 1996). India had changed over the intervening years. During the smallpox days, there were the very rich and the very poor. Now there was a middle class. I tried to find my Rajasthani smallpox team, but they had long since retired to their ancestral villages. I did find E. P. Pram, my Rajasthani tour guide friend and we reminisced over our exploits back in the day.

I went on to work some thirty-plus years in international public health and infectious disease control in a total of twenty countries in Africa and Asia. The journey has been fun!

AUTHOR BIOGRAPHY

Dr. Cornelia E. Davis, MD, MPH, was raised in the San Francisco Bay Area, and she graduated from Gonzaga University in Spokane. In 1968, she was one of the first black women admitted to the University of California, San Francisco School of Medicine. After finishing her pediatric residency at USC Los Angeles County teaching hospital, a chance opportunity led to the World Health Organization hiring her for their smallpox eradication program in India (1975-1977). *To date, smallpox is the only human disease that has been eradicated.*

Davis returned to the United States in 1977, earned a master of public health degree (MPH) from the Johns Hopkins School of Public Health, and went on to work at the Centers for Disease Control/Atlanta. She battled disease outbreaks in Africa and Asia in twenty countries. She worked in development with UNICEF and the US Agency for International Development.

While working in Ethiopia during the civil war, Connie adopted her daughter Romene. Now semiretired, she lives on the northern shore of Lake Chapala, near Guadalajara, Mexico. She currently writes memoirs – starting with her smallpox days- *Searching for Sitala Mata*. She is thrilled the book won a ***Gold medal in the 2017 Global EBook Awards, Non-Fiction, Inspirational!***

BRING DR. CORNELIA "CONNIE" DAVIS TO YOUR ORGANIZATION

Dr. Davis is available for consulting and speaking to groups and organizations. She is an Author, Consultant, Medical Pioneer, Speaker, and Wayfarer.

Her topics include Inspiration, World Health Issues, Intercountry Adoption, and Traveling to Remote Destinations. At a recent gathering, participants said, "She took us along on a journey to places that most of us will never experience. We were all captivated and inspired by her adventures. We loved her book." And so will your audiences.

Her Topics include:

One Person Can Make a Difference
Eradicating Everyday Diseases that Kill
Trekking One Step at a Time
Discovering the Love of My Life 8996 Miles Away

Contact information below

Email: CorneliaEDavisMD@gmail.com
Author website: www.CorneliaEDavisMD.com

Follow her:

FB: www.Facebook.com/CorneliaEDavisMD
Twitter: www.Twitter.com/CEDavisMD

Author Dr. Connie Davis

Dear Reader, before you go could you please place a review on Amazon about the book? There are many readers just like you, who want to know if they would like it.

www.amazon.com/dp/0999303406

If you are using a Kindle simply swipe to the next page!